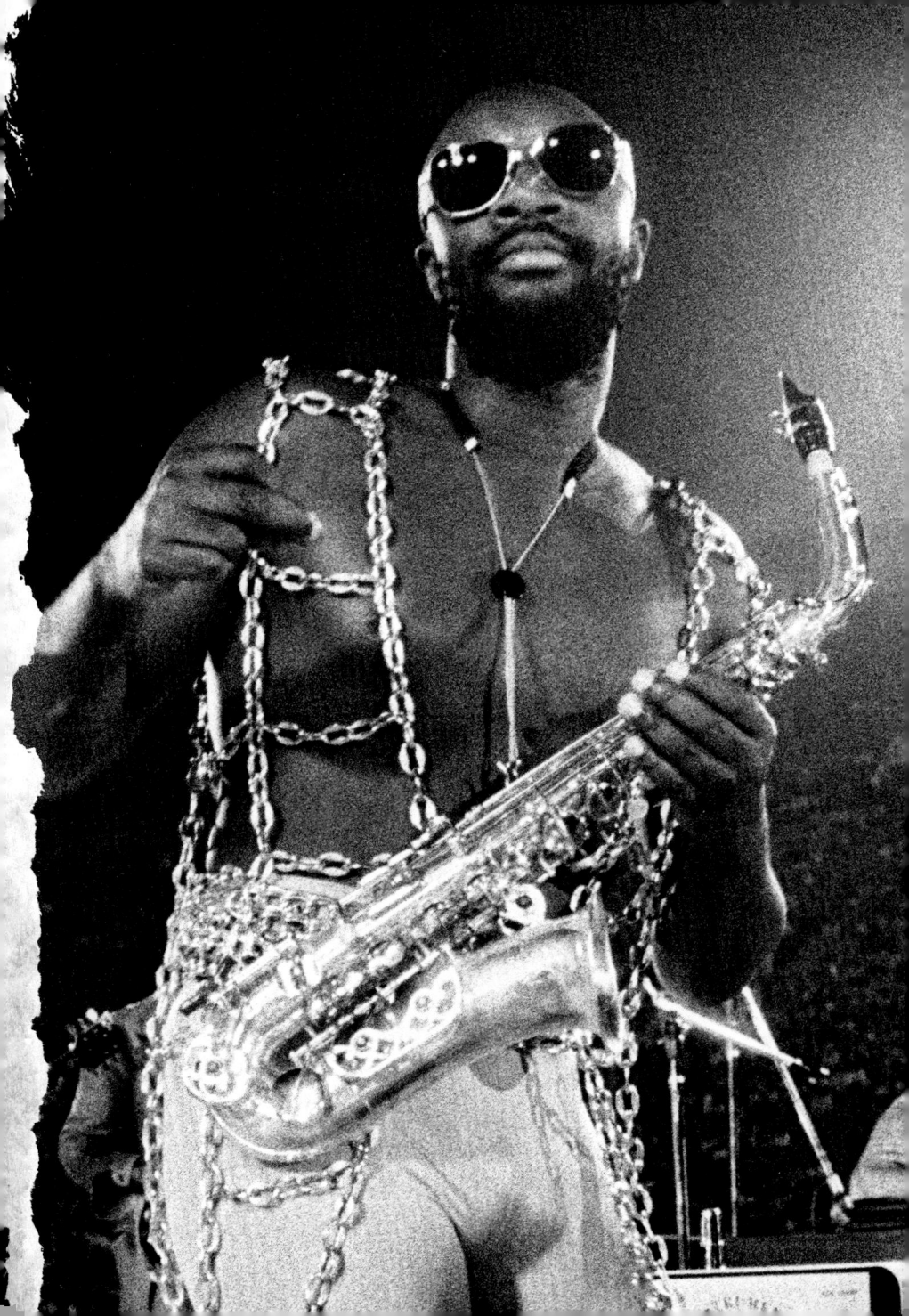

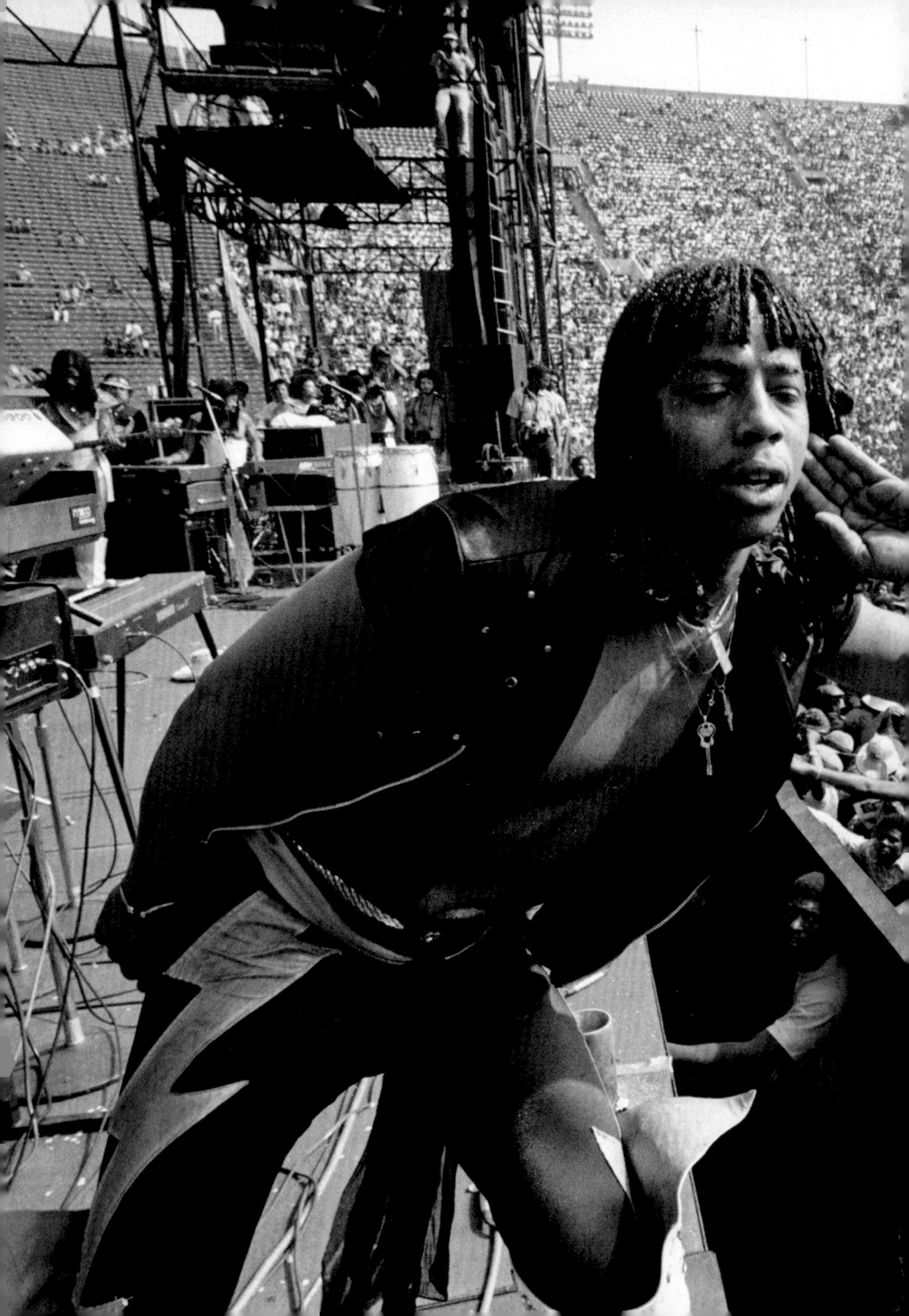

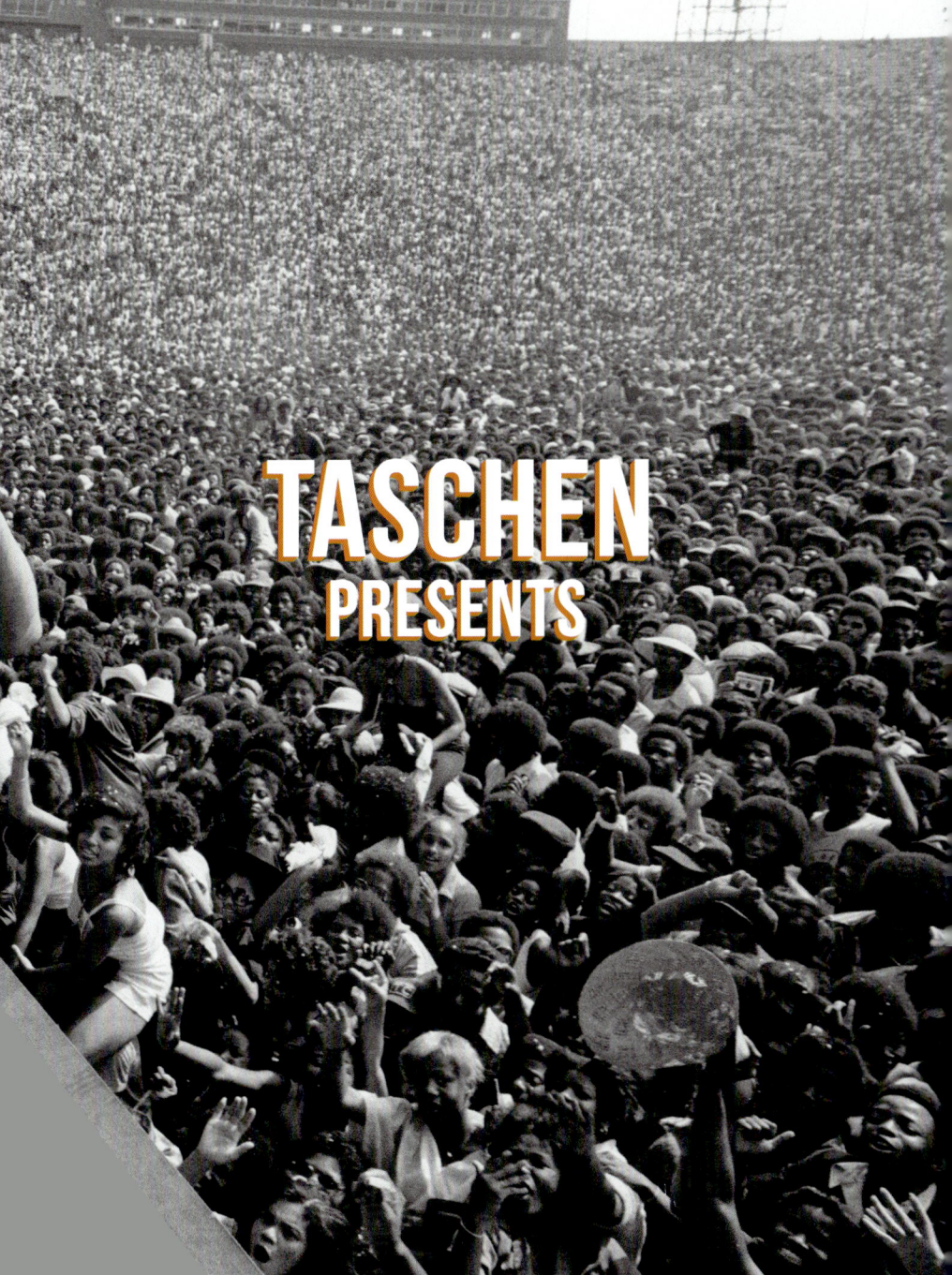

SOUL
R&B
FUNK

PHOTOGRAPHS BY
BRUCE W. TALAMON

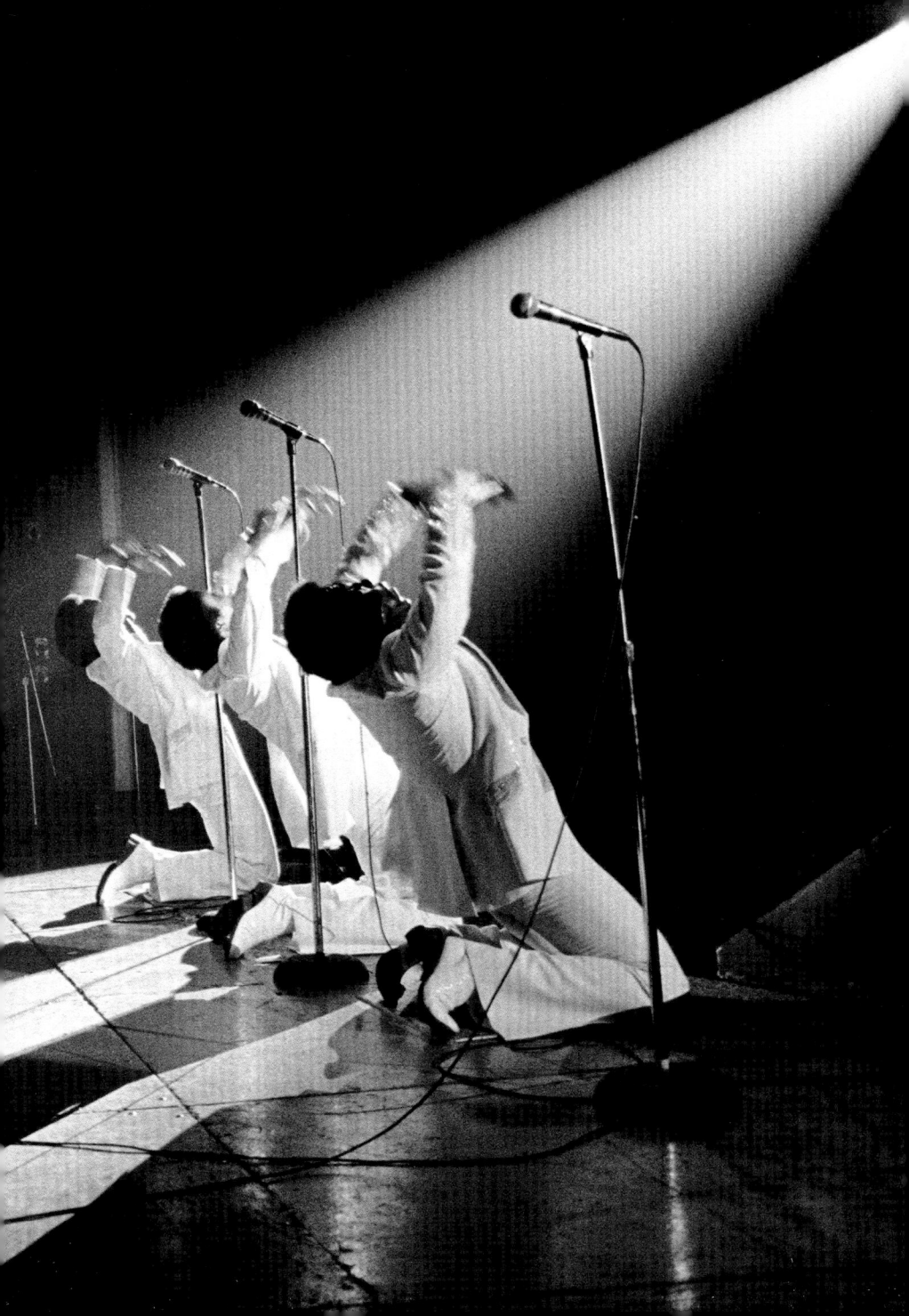

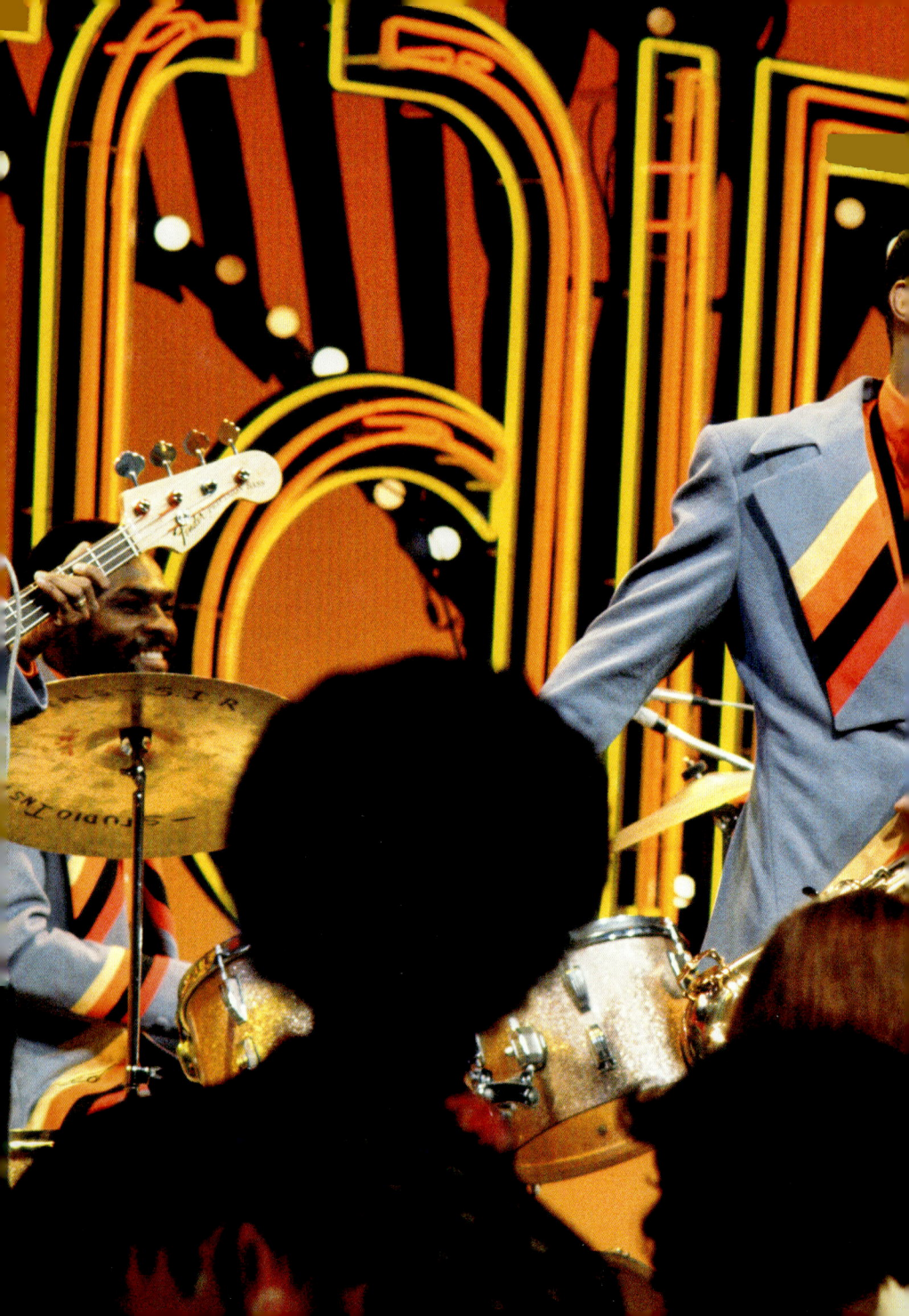

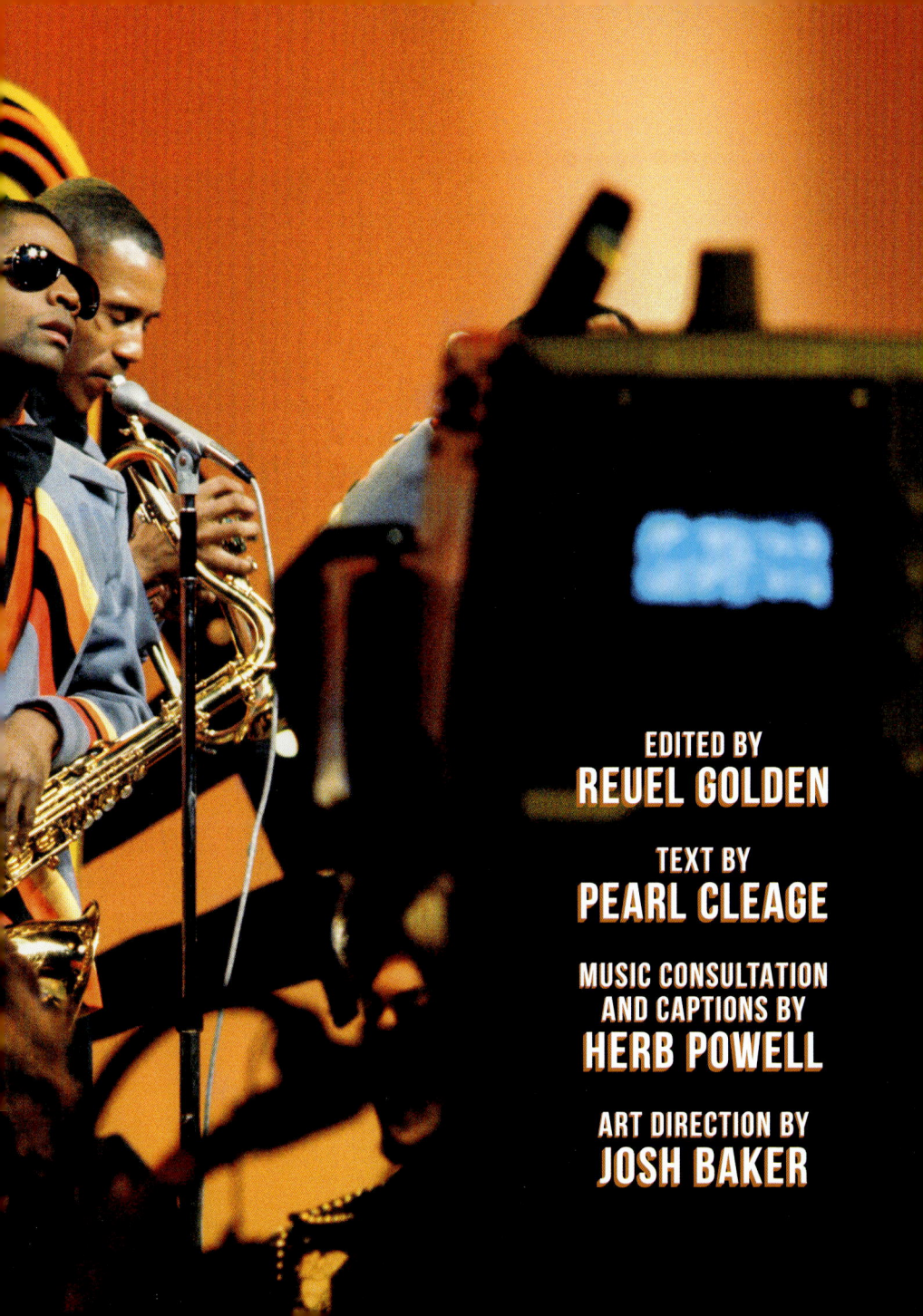

EDITED BY
REUEL GOLDEN

TEXT BY
PEARL CLEAGE

MUSIC CONSULTATION
AND CAPTIONS BY
HERB POWELL

ART DIRECTION BY
JOSH BAKER

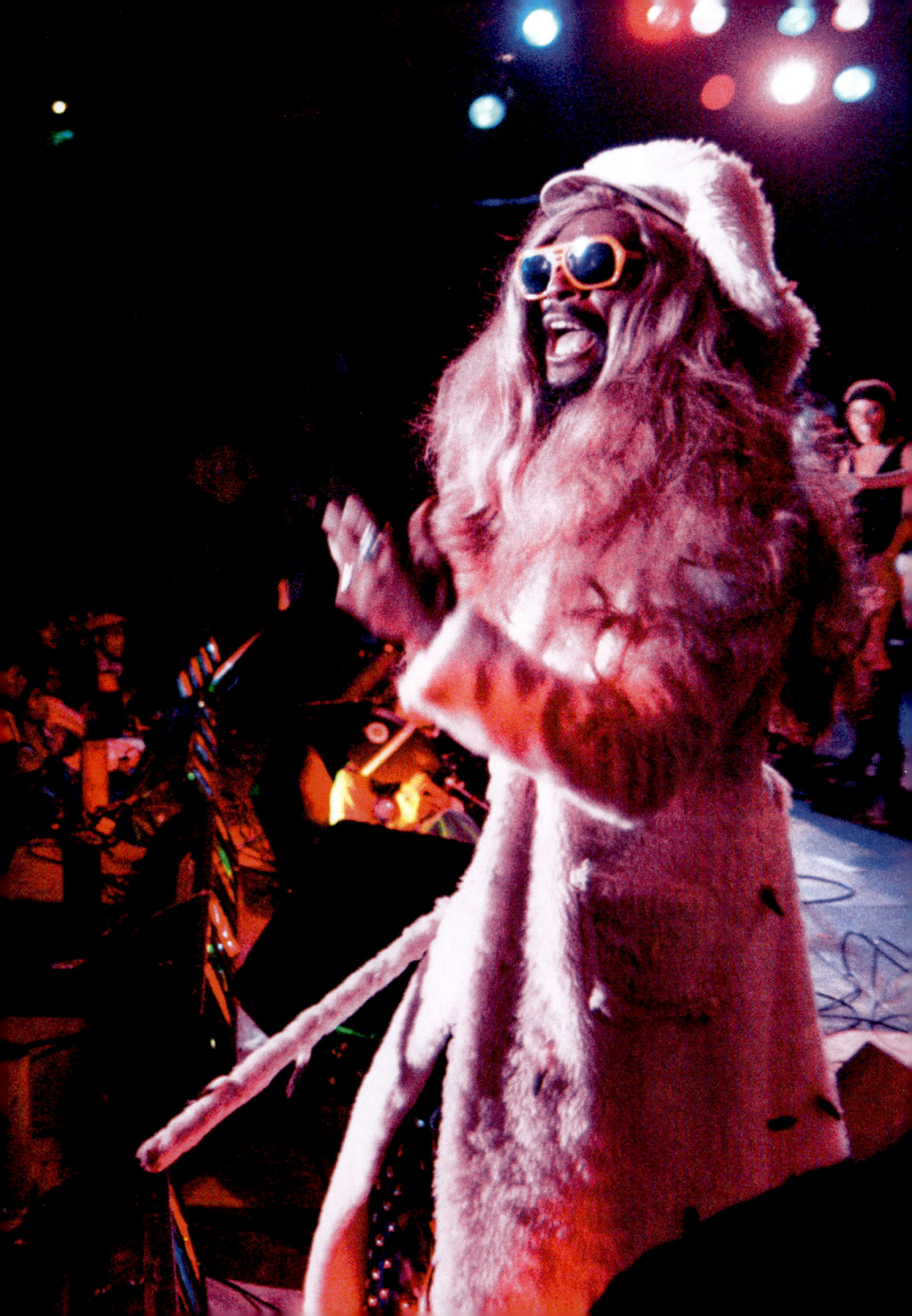

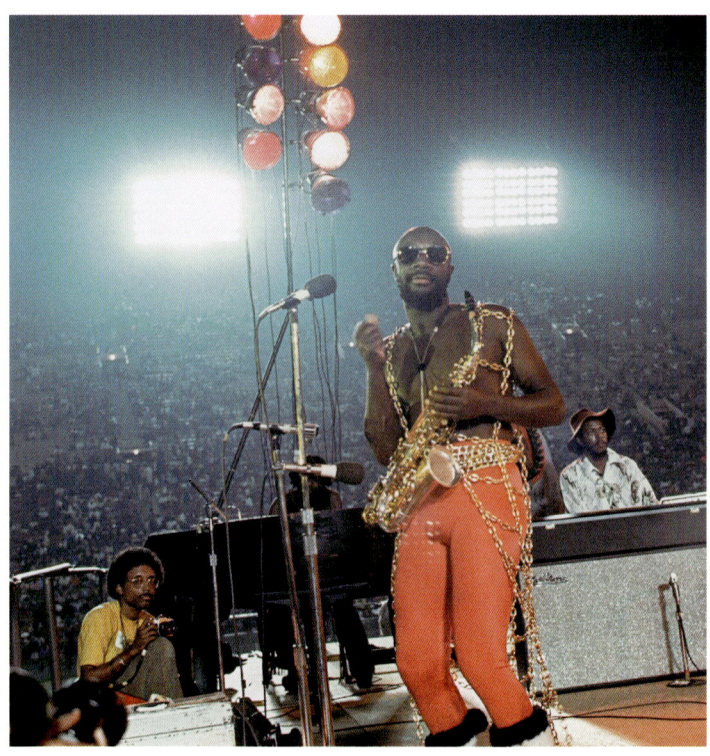

ISSAAC HAYES AND BRUCE TALAMON
Wattstax, Los Angeles Coliseum, 1972.
*"This photograph was taken by Howard L. Bingham.
He was my friend for 44 years."* —Bruce Talamon

Taking a photograph of a singer onstage is the easy part. The hard part is gaining their trust. This is a book about R&B, funk, and soul music, as seen through the lens of a young African American photographer at the start of his career. From 1972 to 1982, I was documenting the rehearsals and sound checks, the recording sessions and costume fittings, the TV shows, life on tour, and, of course, the wild photo sessions and memorable performances. I was there when they exhaled. From the smoke-filled clubs on the Crenshaw strip in Los Angeles to the largest arenas around the world, my cameras recorded the frenzy and beauty of the music. My cameras had a love affair with Chaka Khan. I will gladly acknowledge that I was seduced. I was seduced when I photographed Labelle's Sarah Dash. And again when Shirley Brewer sang Stevie's lyrics on "Ordinary Pain."

James Brown; Al Green; Aretha; Labelle; L.T.D.; Marvin; the Isley Brothers; Stevie; Earth, Wind & Fire; The Jackson 5;

P-Funk…all the usual suspects. It was a visual period in R&B music that lasted way past the midnight hour. This is what I saw.

I've always thought of my photographs as documents that went beyond screaming into a microphone. My body of work has been about the whole unvarnished process, as opposed to just that portion that publicity machines and record companies want you to see. I chased that fleeting visual record for 10 glorious years.

I have always loved the problem-solving. For me, the process became the adventure. The first thing you learn photographing R&B is that you have to gain the artist's trust. And you have to be quick. What I learned during those years prepared me for the adventures to come when I left music to work in the movie business. The same skills that helped me choreograph intimate portraits or capture action prepared me for the movies.

One day you're trying to melt into the wall as Denzel Washington and Don Cheadle rehearse for Carl Franklin, and the next you're hanging out the door of a Bell Jet Ranger helicopter for a chase scene with the director John Badham, or shooting a poster on a little movie for Julia Roberts and Tom Hanks.

However, I always remembered my foundation from R&B. Because you learn something fast: You have to be prepared. When Steven Spielberg turns to you and asks, "Did you get the shot?" — trust me, there is only one answer.

I knew how to stage people, but Jim Britt, the staff photographer for Motown, showed me how to light them. Then there was Jim Marshall, the slightly unhinged photographer who shot the Rolling Stones on tour and Janis and Jimi at Monterey and Woodstock. He defined rock 'n' roll photography and then shot iconic jazz images of Miles and Coltrane. He introduced me to a 28mm and a Leica. He was an artist with an extremely discerning eye. I can always tell the people who were his true friends by the way they reference Jim.

There were a number of African American photographers who guided me during those formative years when I was figuring out what being a photographer actually meant. There were late-night dinners and easy conversations. These men were there at the beginning: Howard L. Bingham, Win Muldrow, Lester Sloan, Ted Williams, Tony Gleaton, Joe Flowers, Bobby Holland, and Vince Frye.

If you were smart, you would listen. You learned technical and social skills that you mentally tucked away. Back then if we could get just five minutes… it's crazy what we could do with two Norman strobe lights, a nine-foot backdrop, gaffer's tape, and a little bit of charm.

The instincts that I developed can be traced directly back to all those photographers. My successes as a photographer, including this book, are a tribute to them. But there is one photographer in particular whom I must single out: Howard L. Bingham. If I had never met Howard, if he had never called me (after I chickened out and didn't call him), and offered his guidance and friendship, I would not be a photographer today. I would have gone to law school. I would not have done this work, and I would not have had great adventures. My life would be totally different. Because of Howard, I did have adventures. And I did the work. He was my friend.

You and me, Bingham. Always.

— **Bruce W. Talamon**, Los Angeles

CAN I GET AN AMEN?

BRUCE W. TALAMON
IN CONVERSATION WITH
PEARL CLEAGE

So there we are, me and my true love, riding through Georgia, headed home from a gig in Albany, smoking a joint and laughing about the fact that all black writers have to hit the road in February in honor of African American History Month, when the voice of George Clinton comes blasting out of the satellite radio. We stop to shout our approval because when Parliament sings "I just wanna testify," attention must be paid right there in the mile between Possum Trot Road and Prosperity Creek. In the middle of all those south Georgia cotton fields so close to the road that you can almost see the ghosts of your ancestors looking up as you speed by.

That's what it's like to look at Bruce Talamon's photographs of the artists he calls "R&B royalty." The amazing photographs in this book represent a visual record from 1972 to 1982, when you could stand so close to the stage that you'd be drenched by the end of the night, so that Al Green might hand you a red rose, or Ronald Isley might actually invite you up on the stage to dance.

A time when the idea of getting old wasn't even a cloud on the bright blue horizon.

These photographs make you remember when there was no separation between what you imagined and what you would actually do if the opportunity presented itself. When the possibility of ascending to the heavens in the Mothership with George and Bootsy was not entirely out of the question.

Bruce captures the rituals of the tribe. Rick James in full strut before a stadium full of screaming funk fans. Gil Scott-Heron taking a quiet moment before stepping out to call the Spirits in. Chaka Khan supine on a roadie's crate, throwing back her beautiful head and parting those amazing lips in a smile that could have melted the camera. He has a photographer's cool eye, but a beating human pulse that cannot help but quicken when Sarah Dash flutters the giant wings for which Labelle was famous, turning the full force of her clearly cosmic energies in his direction.

There has never been a false separation between sex and love in R&B. They are complementary, equally necessary in the fullness

AL GREEN
***Soul Train*, Los Angeles, 1974.**
Roses for the ladies. Al Green's personal touch during live performances only added to his sensual persona.

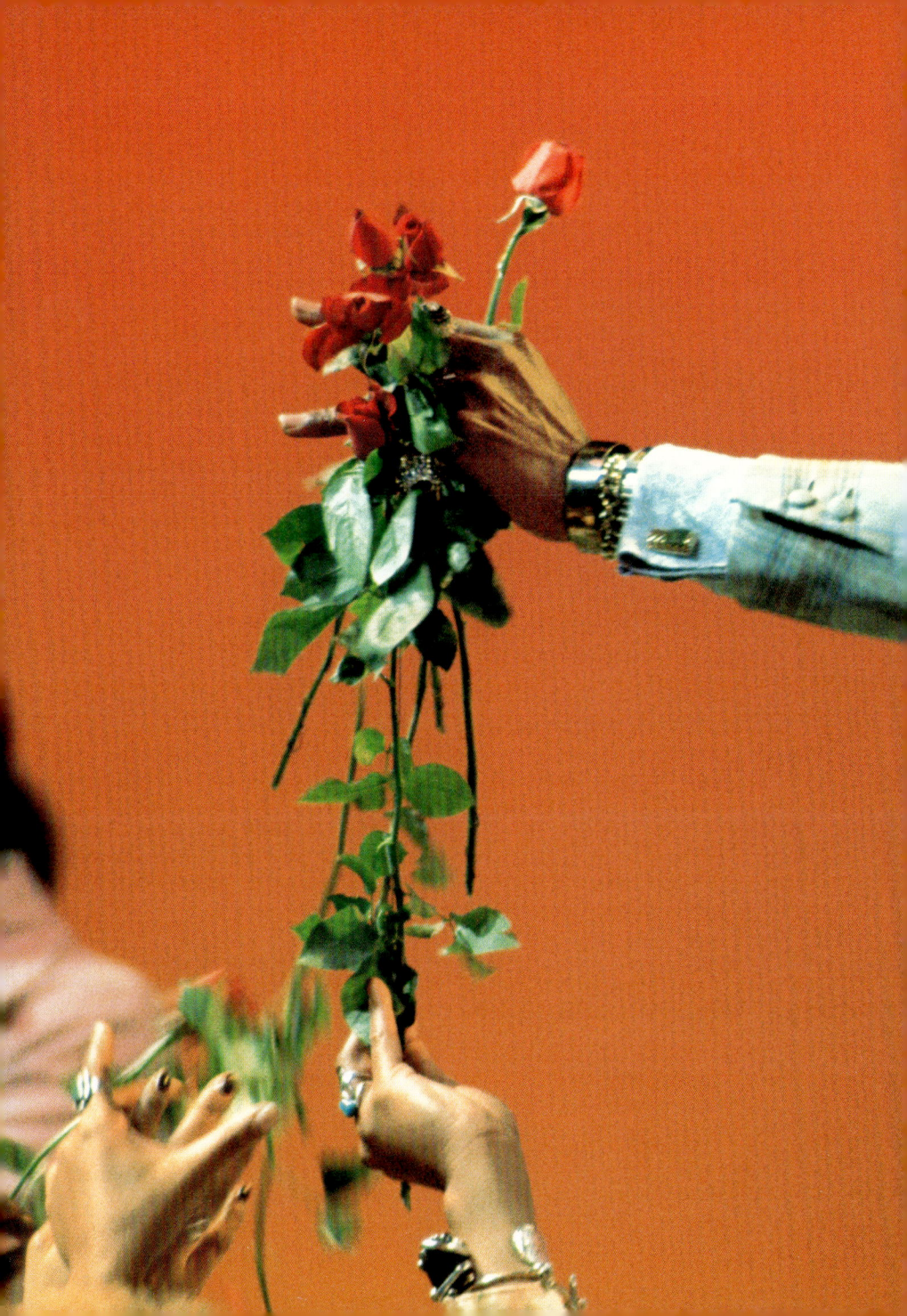

of life. The sweet confluence of sweat and music, passion and desire, was part of the gift these artists were offering, and the audience could not have been more eager to receive it.

The first time I saw these photographs I knew what a treasure I was holding in my hands. As an undergraduate student, Bruce planned to be a lawyer. But the world is full of lawyers, and I am forever grateful that he made the different and sometimes difficult choice to pick up a camera and never put it down.

I met Bruce Talamon in 1979 when we worked together on a Hollywood movie that shall remain nameless. The experience was awful in almost every respect, but the friendship first forged when Bruce busted me attacking a hallway vending machine in the motel where the company was housed has become a lifelong conversation. The machine had taken my last quarters. Bruce invited me to join him for Chinese food, offering an alternative to the violence I surely intended to visit on that machine until it rendered up Cheetos or died for the crime of withholding them. At dinner we talked about all things Marley and R&B music. By the time the fortune cookies arrived, we realized that we would be friends for life.

Asking a photographer to tell you how he got the shot is like asking actors how they managed to make you cry. They can't do it. Bruce is a photo griot, a witness. He is a Zelig, able to change his appearance or attitude so as to be almost invisible. He has a fierce confidence and a supplicant's humility.

If you are already a believer, these photographs will renew your faith. If you are new to the congregation, sit back and let Brother Talamon introduce you to the choir. Can I get an amen?

—Pearl Cleage, Atlanta, 2018

Pearl Cleage: Let's talk about the pictures.
Bruce Talamon: Forty-two years. That's a lot of memories. It has made me think about the work.

Why?
Because now I know that the work will stand. One day you realize you have a body of work and maybe it was good. I've always had this sensibility about documenting and storytelling visually, but when I figured out the gift—the power of a camera—a whole world opened up. I knew I wanted to be a photographer, and I became one. Along the way I had some generous teachers. But I never stopped to think how that was going to happen. I was lucky that I ran into people like Howard Bingham and Regina Jones. They not only offered guidance, they gave me opportunities.

Any other photographers in your family?
None. After I graduated from college I announced that I was going to be a

VARIOUS ARTISTS
(Pages 15, 16, 19, 20)
This collection of covers and spreads exemplifies how *SOUL Newspaper* was the curator, bible, and photo album for the greatest generation of R&B artists.

THE SPINNERS AND THOM BELL
Los Angeles, 1976. (Opposite, bottom right)
Thom Bell produced the biggest hits of The Delfonics, The Stylistics, and The Spinners. Here, he works out an arrangement of the group's hits for an appearance on the *Dinah!* show.

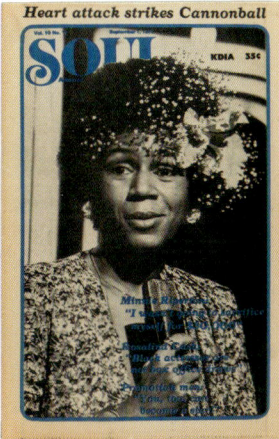

Heart attack strikes Cannonball

SOUL
Vol. 19 No. Vol. 19 No. 50¢
KDIA 35¢

Minnie Riperton:
"I can't tell you
how much healthier
my life is now."

Emotion on
Black activism:
Are the new
young artists
selling out?

Promotion men:
Can you hear
these drums too?

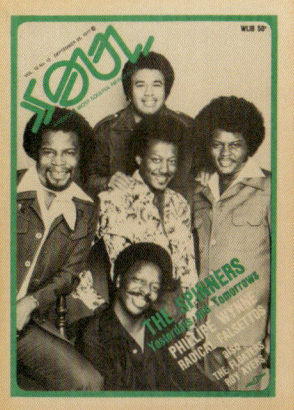

WLIB 50¢

SOUL

THE SPINNERS
Yesterday's...and Tomorrows

PHILIPPE WYNN:
RADICAL FALSETTO

THE SPINNERS
ROY ROBERTS

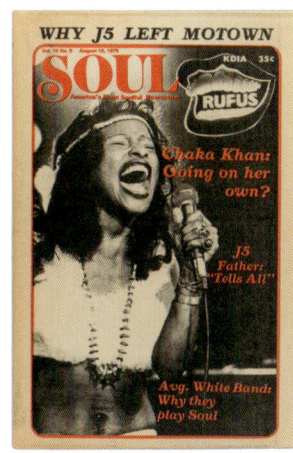

WHY J5 LEFT MOTOWN

SOUL
America's Most Soulful Newspaper
Vol. 10, No. 9 August 18, 1975
KDIA 35¢

RUFUS

Chaka Khan:
Going on her
own?

J5
Father
"Tells All"

Avg. White Band:
Why they
play Soul

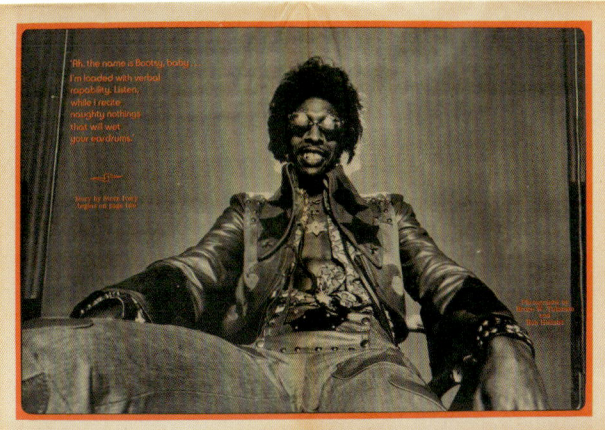

Ah, the name is Bootsy, baby...
I'm loaded with verbal
capability. Listen,
while I recite
naughty nothings
that will wet
your eardrums.

—Bootsy

Story by Vince Frey
Begins on page five.

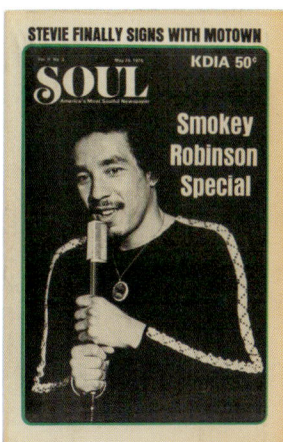

STEVIE FINALLY SIGNS WITH MOTOWN

SOUL
America's Most Soulful Newspaper
Vol. 9 No. 2 May 26, 1975
KDIA 50¢

Smokey
Robinson
Special

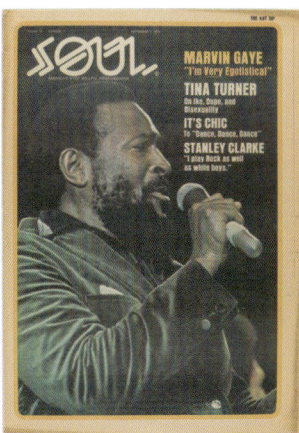

SOUL

MARVIN GAYE
"I'm Very Egotistical"

TINA TURNER
On Ike, Dope, and
Bisexuality

IT'S CHIC
To "Dance, Dance, Dance"

STANLEY CLARKE
"I play Rock as well
as white boys."

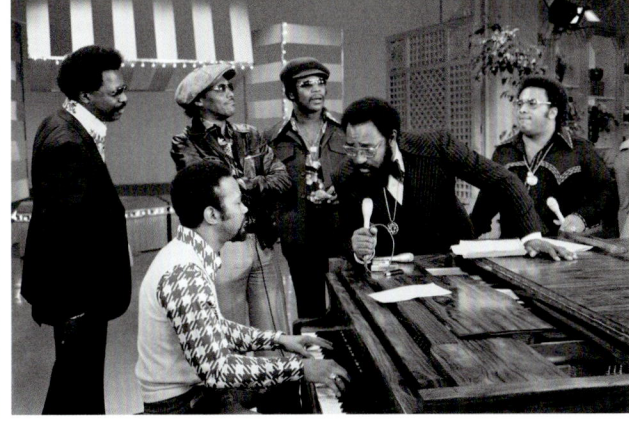

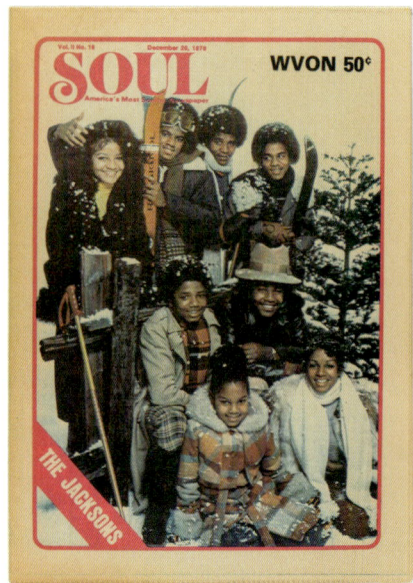

do the work. And I used those skills learned from my parents and school. I just used them in a nontraditional job and have been fortunate that it has paid off. I've had a great photographic life. I've been able to do the work professionally for 40-plus years, done the work well, and had a great time. But I had opportunity. I know too many talented African American photographers who never got that traction, who never got a foot in the door.

Now, folks get uncomfortable when you bring up race. But I find myself addressing that because it is a fact. And, unfortunately, sometimes people confuse their good fortune with how fabulous they are, and forget about others who came before them or opened the door. But at a certain point in your career, you can't wait for someone else to do it. I want this work to show that yes, I was there, and I took some fabulous photographs.

photographer. That did not go over well with James Talamon Jr. Once, I overheard him describing my work to a friend. It was not a charitable description. He wasn't the only one. A couple of my classmates are still scratching their heads. But back to my father…I understood. He was afraid for me. This was a black man trying to figure out how to warn his son about the dangers of the world.

Did your father ever forgive you for not going to law school?
Before he died, my father got to see my work in a museum in Los Angeles. I had the lead print, 10 feet by 20 feet, a young man flying his pigeons off a roof in Harlem at sunrise. I think that's when he understood that I was a professional, doing something that I loved, and I would be OK.

Did you encounter those dangers he was worried about?
Let me be clear. I picked a nontraditional job. I had no point of reference, and was in uncharted territory. Yes, I did encounter those dangers. But as I look back, I realize that my parents did their job perfectly. They protected me, and made me understand that there were no limits. They instilled confidence. I went off to college with a goal. And then I picked up a camera. But I still had to

When did you start photographing musicians?
Nineteen seventy-one. I was on an exchange program, and bought my first camera when I was in Berlin. When we arrived in Copenhagen, we heard that Miles Davis was coming to play Tivoli Gardens. Well, we had to see Miles. So I took my camera.

We were in the cheap seats, and I walked down closer to the stage. Finally, one usher stopped me, and I talked my way out of getting thrown out. So now I was sitting at the feet of Miles.

The professional photographer sitting next to me had a camera with a loud motor drive, and after a while, Miles emptied his spit valve on him because he said the noise of his motor drive was messing up the vibe. After the guy left, Miles looked at me and said, "You can stay, young brother."

That was my first concert picture. I learned a valuable lesson: Stay out of the way, and don't mess up the vibe.

So how did you go from Miles in Copenhagen to Isaac Hayes in chains at Wattstax?
One weekend I was visiting my parents and a childhood friend stopped by. He worked for the Watts Festival, and they needed a photographer. I did not get the job. Later I found out they hired someone named Howard Bingham. I checked around and found out that he was Muhammad Ali's photographer.

My friend did secure a backstage pass for me, and on the day of the concert I worked my way up onto this platform, which was full of unaccredited photographers. Security people started checking credentials. Just before I was kicked out, the photographer next to me said, "He's with me." His name was Ted Williams, and if it wasn't for him that would have been the end of this story.

Later, I managed to not only get on the stage, but as I crawled between the cases I ended up three feet away from Isaac Hayes. That shot of Isaac Hayes at Wattstax in 1972 is the first R&B photograph I ever shot. It never entered my mind that somebody would remove me because I didn't have the proper credentials. At that moment, I knew this was what I wanted to do for the rest of my life. I was home.

Is that when you met Howard Bingham?
Yes. After the show, I introduced myself. But, here's where it gets weird. We traded cards…but I didn't call him.

Why not?
Because I knew I wasn't ready. A week later, my phone rings. It's Howard saying, "I thought you were going to call me?" Every photographer in town wanted to be his assistant, but he calls me. Howard and I were friends for 44 years. I was never able to get a straight answer out of him as to why he decided to follow up and call. I owe my photographic career to Howard L. Bingham. I showed him my work, and then two things happened that changed my life: Howard introduced me to his lab, then he took me to *SOUL Newspaper* to meet Regina Jones.

What was SOUL Newspaper?
Ken Jones and his wife, Regina, started *SOUL* in 1966, the year after the Watts rebellion in Los Angeles. At that time, it was the only black-owned paper exclusively devoted to R&B and soul music. Ken knew that black kids bought records, and had a hunch that they would buy a newspaper filled with interviews and stories about the musicians creating that music. And they were national. *SOUL* partnered with radio stations all over the country—WVON Chicago, WWRL New York, WJLB Detroit. Philly, Memphis, Atlanta, Dallas. Everywhere. The affiliation with the radio stations gave *SOUL* on-air time, where a DJ talked about *SOUL* to an enthusiastic listening audience. The radio stations got their call letters on the cover of *SOUL* and advertising space. Eventually they went bi-weekly, with an average of 24 pages per issue. Their largest-selling issue of *SOUL* was Michael Jackson, August 10, 1970.

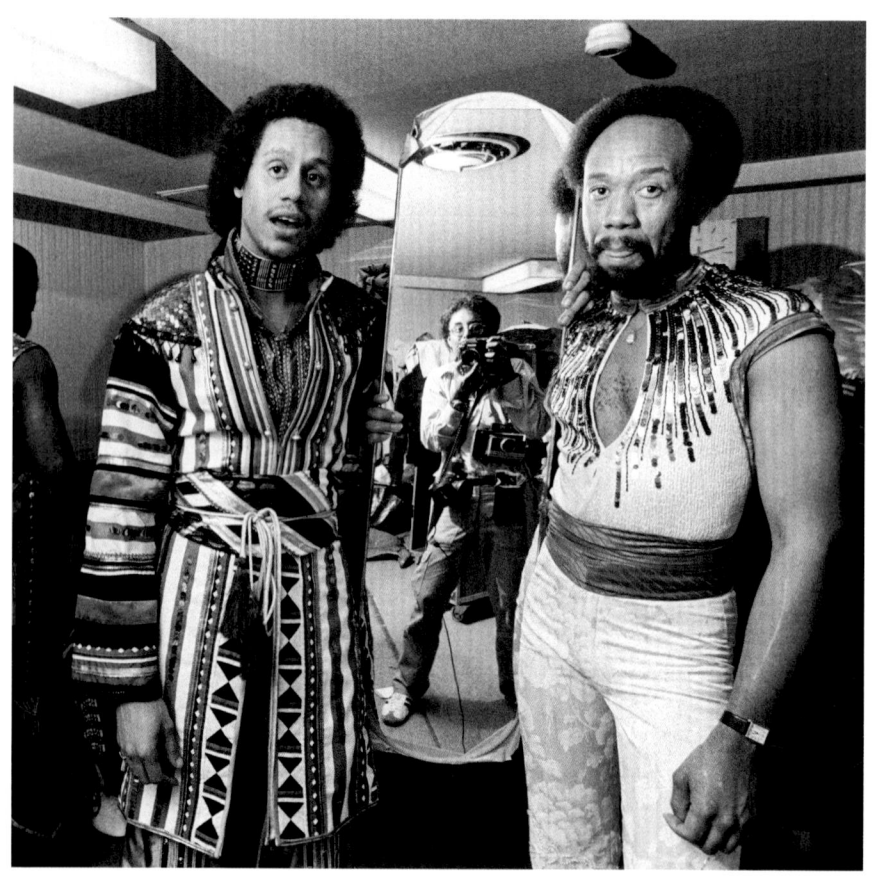

EARTH, WIND & FIRE
Amsterdam, 1979.

Why is Regina so important to you?
Regina gave me confidence and a place to do the work. She validated a group of young black writers and photographers who went on to have successful careers in the entertainment industry and as journalists. Here's one example: She gave a young man named Leonard Pitts Jr. his first gig. Leonard went on to win a Pulitzer Prize with the *Miami Herald* in 2004. I showed up at Regina's

door in 1972, and she took a chance on me. My first assignment was Billy Paul at the Crenshaw Palace nightclub in South L.A. I went on to be a contract photographer for *Time* magazine in 1984 and have had a successful career working in movies. But after all our adventures, I suspect we had the most fun on that Stevie Wonder cover we shot at Roscoe's Chicken & Waffles at two in the morning in 1977 for *SOUL*!

Did Regina send you to Soul Train?

Yes, she did. And when you talk about *Soul Train*, the conversation must begin with the man who single-handedly put black music on American television every Saturday afternoon for 35 years: Don Cornelius. He called it "the hippest trip in America." The music! The dancers! The clothes! The hair!

In December 1972, James Brown makes his first appearance on *Soul Train*. For me, there was something subversive about being there at that moment to make a visual record of those two men, equally powerful and at the height of their careers. James Brown had been watching the directors interact with Don. Finally, during the break, James turned to Don and asked him, point blank, "Who you with on this?" "What do you mean, James?" (I was close and could hear the conversation.) "Who you with?" "James, it's just me. This is my thing. This is my show."

It wasn't until I was putting this book together that I realized that I might have captured an important little historical footnote in black music. Don knew what James meant. James Brown was asking if Don was being assisted by backers who were primarily not of the colored persuasion. And the answer was, "James, it's just me."

I made my first big money from James Brown's manager — a crisp $100 bill for 10 photos of Mr. Brown. I have a framed copy of that $100 bill.

How much of your backstage work was composed?

Let me tell you about P-Funk, L.A. Sports Arena, 1977. I was hired to shoot a publicity portrait before the concert. It was supposed to work like this: They walk from the dressing room, we shoot the photo. They then proceed to the stage. We did not factor in

the 20,000 rabid fans stomping their feet, screaming at the top of their lungs in anticipation while we were wrestling George and the Funk Mob onto my 13-foot backdrop. And understand, you don't just line 'em up and shoot. You have to stage them. And you gotta do it now! Meanwhile, the band is bouncing off the walls ready to rock. But they got into it. I held them for three rolls. And I knew I had it. It was the best publicity session I ever did. It was…delicious.

Probably the best thing I could tell young photographers would be to pay attention. It's all around you. Observe the details. That's as important as the performance. The great photographers have this intuitive quality to their work. That's why they consistently come back with the great shots.

You have to get the artist to trust you. The great photographer Bob Willoughby once told me, "If they ask how long, never say you

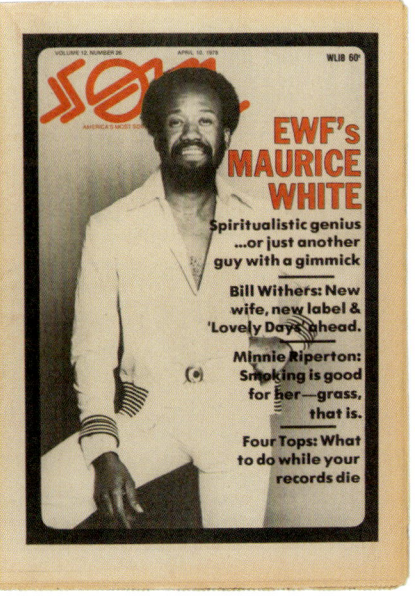

need a half hour. Tell them 10 minutes. They will give you a half hour."

When did you start working with the record companies?

Nineteen seventy-four. Thelma Houston, the Troubadour. Bob Jones from Motown was my first record-company client. I was so clueless. I said $35 for the evening. He smiled and said, "How about $50 plus expenses? And bring a flash." Eventually, I got more.

In addition to the live performances and backstage shots, you did some amazing portrait work.

I was good, but the guys who got me there were Bobby Holland and Jim Britt. Bobby was instrumental in convincing Regina to buy a basic lighting package. And Jim Britt was the staff photographer at Motown. Jim taught me not to fear studio lighting.

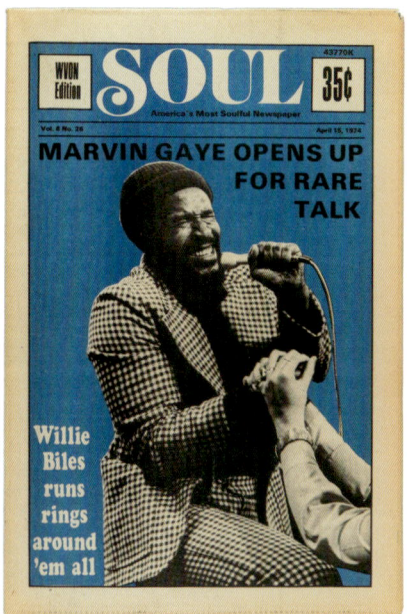

The turning point was the 1977 Donna Summer cover. Casablanca Records wanted to give us a publicity photo that someone else had shot. Regina basically told the guy, "If you want to reach my audience, you must let my writers and photographers have access." They agreed: 20 minutes.

The shoot was for 3 P.M. We were ready at 12:30 when Donna walked in. She looked at our setup and said, "You brothers are serious." And Bobby shot back, "Yes, we are, sister." She stayed for four hours. Six months later, when *Ebony* magazine asked her to sit for a cover-photo session, Donna Summer said, "I work with Bruce Talamon." And that was my first national magazine cover.

I have to ask you about one of your most well-known photographs, Maurice White at the Great Pyramids.

March 21, 1979, Egypt. We had been in Europe and were taking a break before going on to Japan. Maurice wanted to take some pictures at the pyramids, so I suggested a sunrise shot. But when I told him we needed to be in place at 4:30 A.M. to catch the sun breaking from behind the pyramids, he suggested we shoot at noon. So much for the sunrise. I wanted Maurice with all three pyramids rising up behind him. Again, that takes staging. You have to pick the proper angle for the pyramids to line up for the shot. Using an 85mm telephoto lens to compress the image in the camera, I was able to create the illusion.

The ironic thing is that this photograph has taken on a life of its own since Maurice White's death. It's all over social media.

It was the end of the photo session, and he was walking away holding my white camera-strobe umbrella as a shield from the sun. That's when I saw it. But now the wind was howling and blowing sand I yelled at

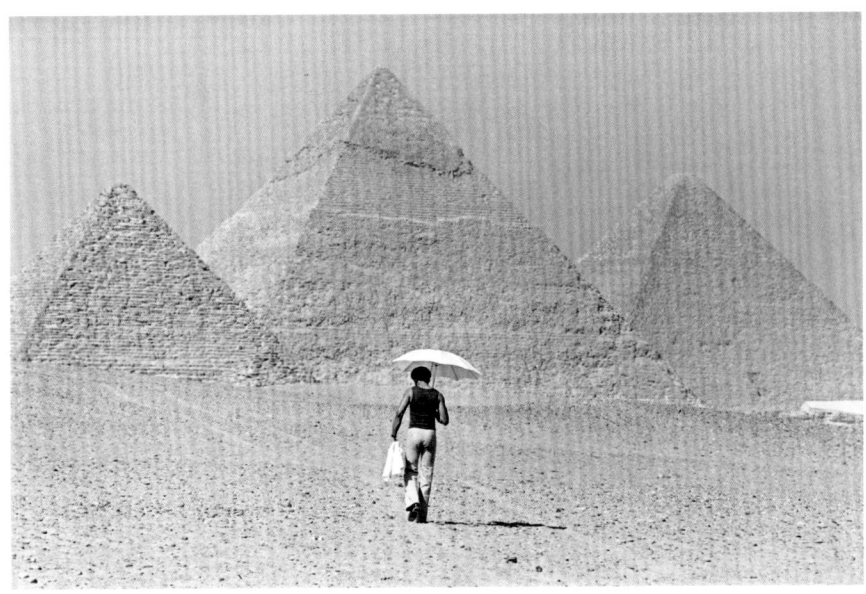

EARTH, WIND & FIRE
El Giza, Egypt, 1979.

him to turn around and walk toward the pyramids. He hesitated, and then walked back. I followed him in my viewfinder, composing the shot, and then everything came together. I shot one roll.

It was one of his favorite photographs.

When did you first photograph Earth, Wind & Fire?

May 1977. One of the biggest bands in the world, coming to our little studio. I was dealing directly with Monte White, Maurice's brother and road manager. I asked what kind of food they preferred. He suggested a mostly vegetarian menu, maybe some chicken or fish, and lots of fruit. Then he said, "Maurice likes kefir."

I had sense enough not to blurt out, "What's kefir?" On the day of the shoot,

the band was on time, they ate the food, and Maurice drank kefir. Again, the key was the staging. Nine guys. Broad lighting so they can move. Black and white, and Kodachrome, Maurice in the center, and build from that. And remember it doesn't matter who they are. For a brief moment they defer to you. You have to be decisive and quick.

A few months later, I received another call from Monte, who told me that Maurice was impressed with the way I handled myself at the session and he wanted me to come on their 1979 Tour of the World: Europe, Egypt, and Japan. And that's the way it started.

What other memorable photo sessions come to mind?

Stevie, Bootsy, George. Chaka Khan at the Roxy ... but let's talk about the Jacksons

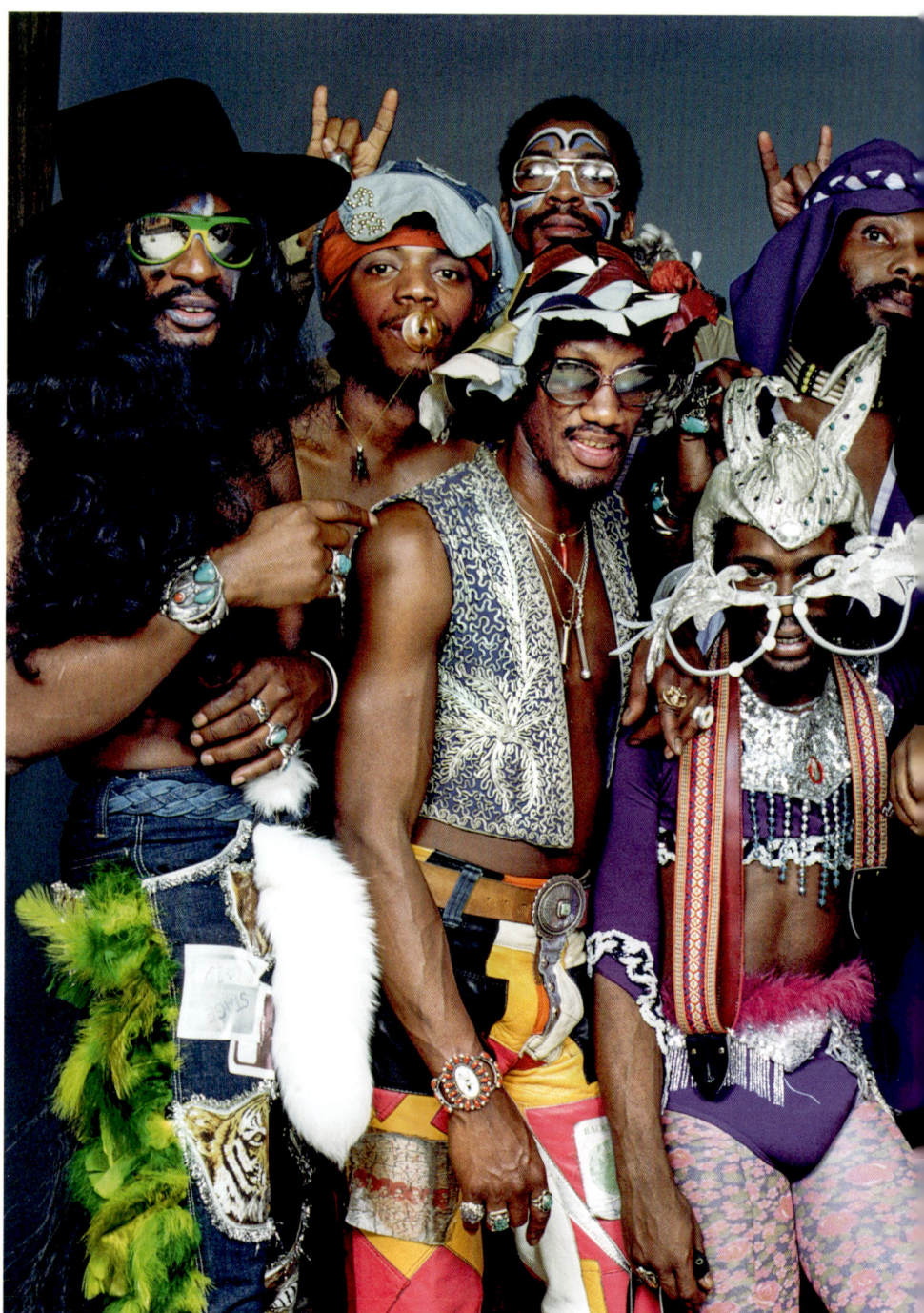

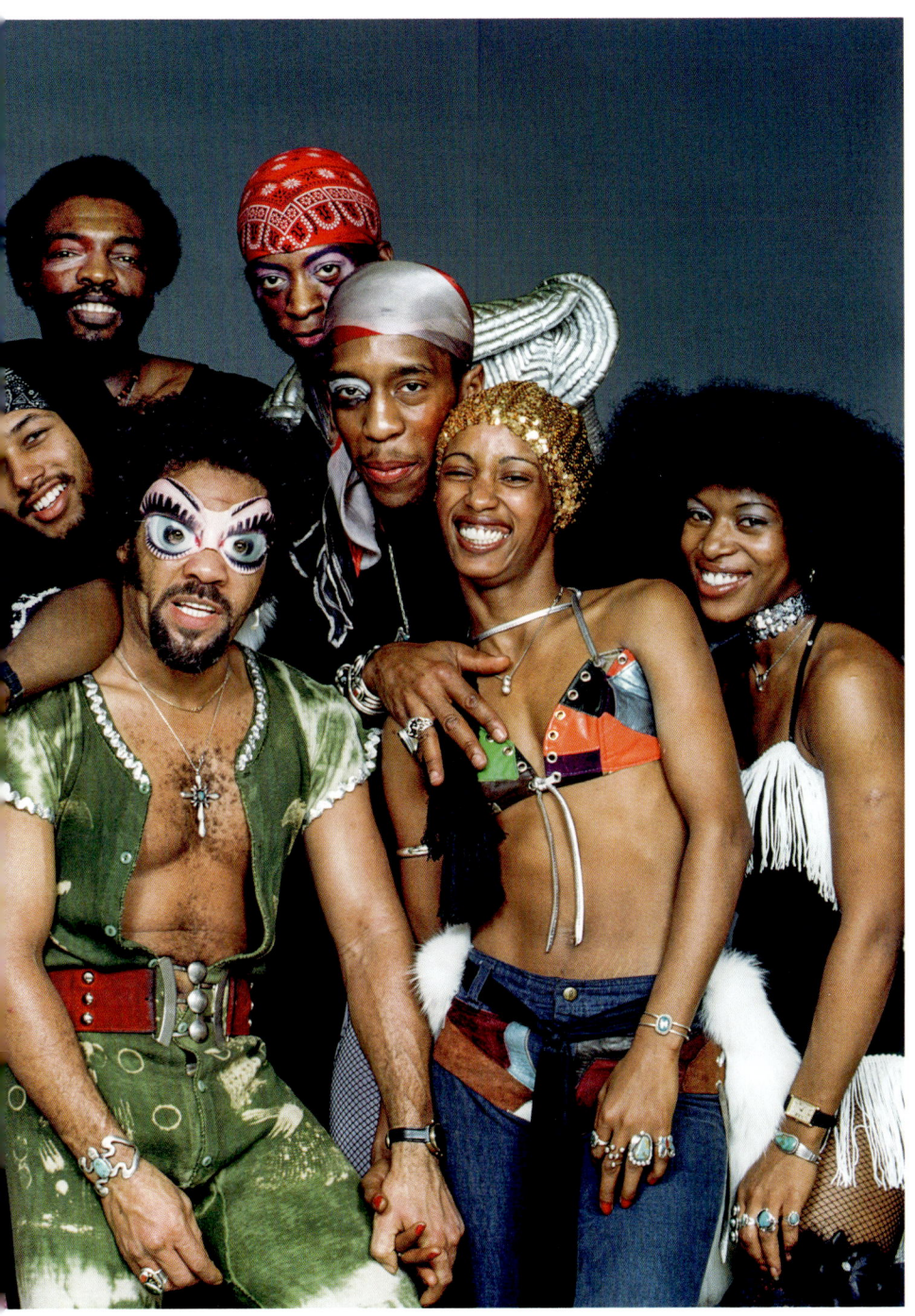

shoot, December 1976. The moment Michael stepped onto the white seamless, he started to dance. It was as if someone had wound him up. The music was blasting and you could feel the excitement. And then his brothers started their routine. Trying to keep them on that seamless backdrop? All of that went out the window. Truly in that instant I had to make a decision: Be perfect, or hold on and try to keep them in focus? Thirty-eight years later we don't care about the damn backdrop. Look at the joy on their faces. They were with a new record company, making new music. They were free.

What's the biggest difference in the music business now?
Access is gone. Publicists used to let you shoot. They didn't snatch the Jack Daniel's out of the artist's hand or dare to take the spliff out of Bob Marley's mouth.

Now someone's at the door saying, "Wait until they change out of those wet clothes and wipe the sweat off." There was a spontaneity at concerts. Someone could come in unannounced and sit in, and you could photograph the whole time. But now they say you can only shoot the first song and you've got 15 seconds. Fifteen seconds…

That time will never come again. The kind of access we had is gone. I had the best seat in the house every time I picked up the camera.

How would you like people to respond to these photographs?
These photographs are a celebration of the music, an aesthetic, a style that's gone. But for that moment, it was magical. I would like to think that maybe I caught a little bit of that magic and was able to leave a record of what these musicians did and how good they were.

I want people to be amazed by the photographs. I want them to remember Melvin Franklin and Otis Williams backstage with Stevie. To remember a young Teddy Pendergrass in a powder-blue tuxedo. Or being able to jump on the stage and dance with the Isley Brothers. I want people to look at these pictures and remember how badass James Brown, Michael Jackson, B. B. King, Natalie Cole, and Maurice White were, and what they looked like when they were being badass. And I want them to be seduced by Chaka Khan like I was. I want them to think about where they were when they first heard "Love and Happiness." I want people to remember it all. And Smile.

PARLIAMENT-FUNKADELIC
Los Angeles Sports Arena, 1977. (Pages 22–23)
Another shot from this same session became the most recognized photo of the band.
L to R: George Clinton, Garry Shider, Calvin Simon, Bernie Worrell, Grady Thomas, Cordell "Boogie" Mosson, Michael Hampton, Raymond Davis, Clarence "Fuzzy" Haskins, Glenn Goins, Jerome Brailey, Debbie Wright, and Jeanette Washington.

DONNA SUMMER
SOUL Newspaper cover-photo session, Los Angeles, 1977. (Opposite)

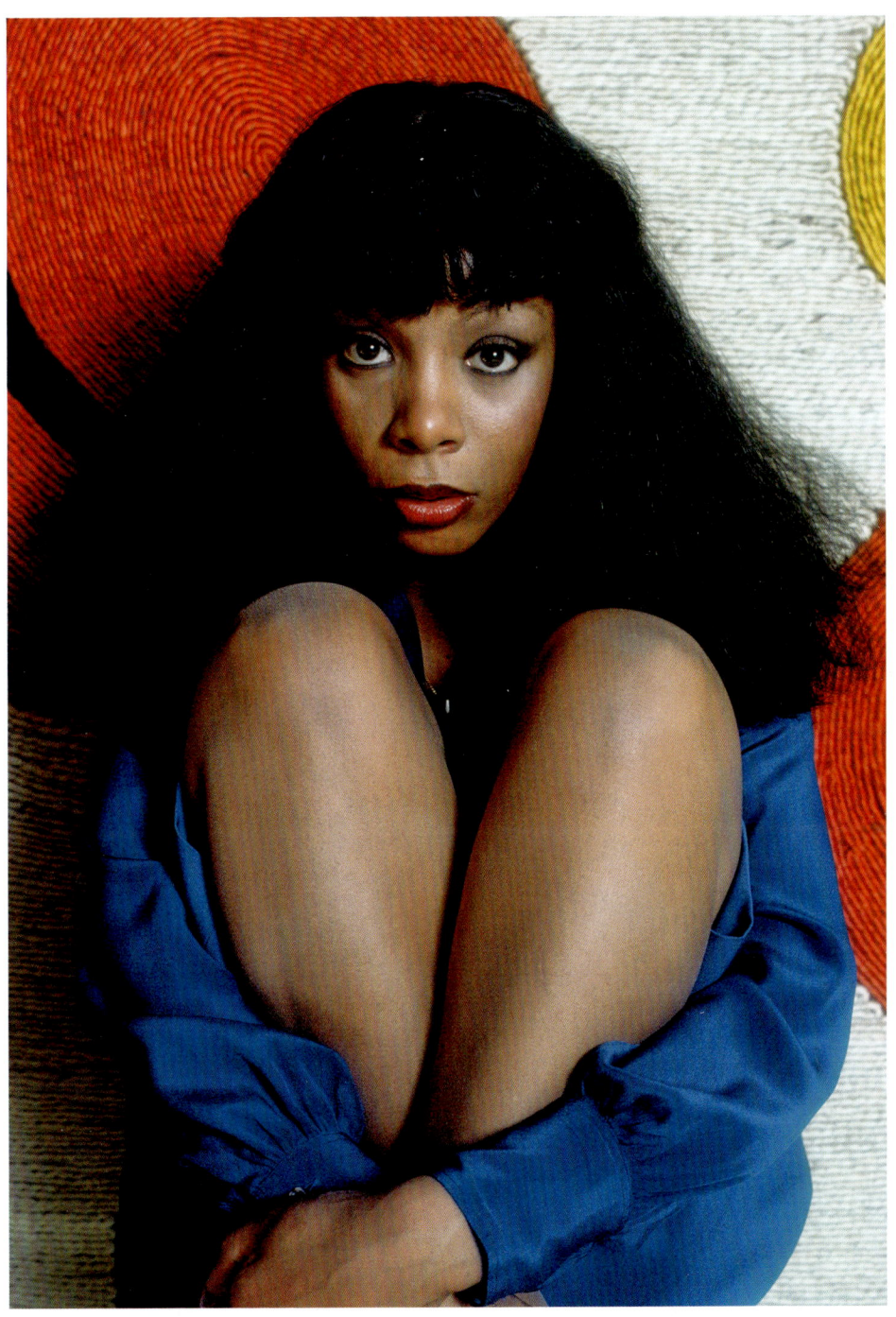

LET'S GET IT ON

MARVIN GAYE
AL GREEN
EDDIE KENDRICKS
BILLY PAUL
TEDDY PENDERGRASS
SMOKEY ROBINSON
DAVID RUFFIN
BARRY WHITE
CHARLES WRIGHT

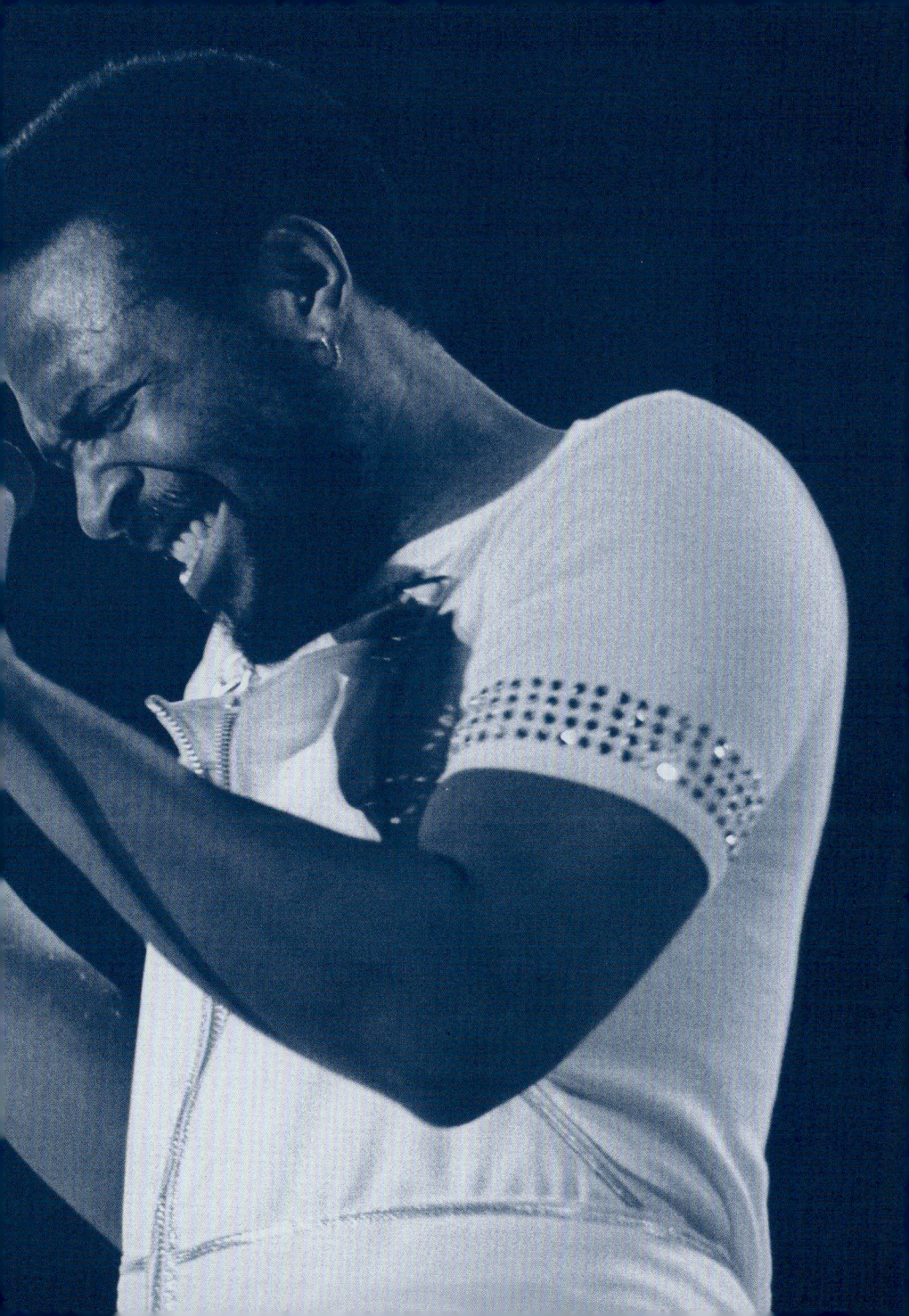

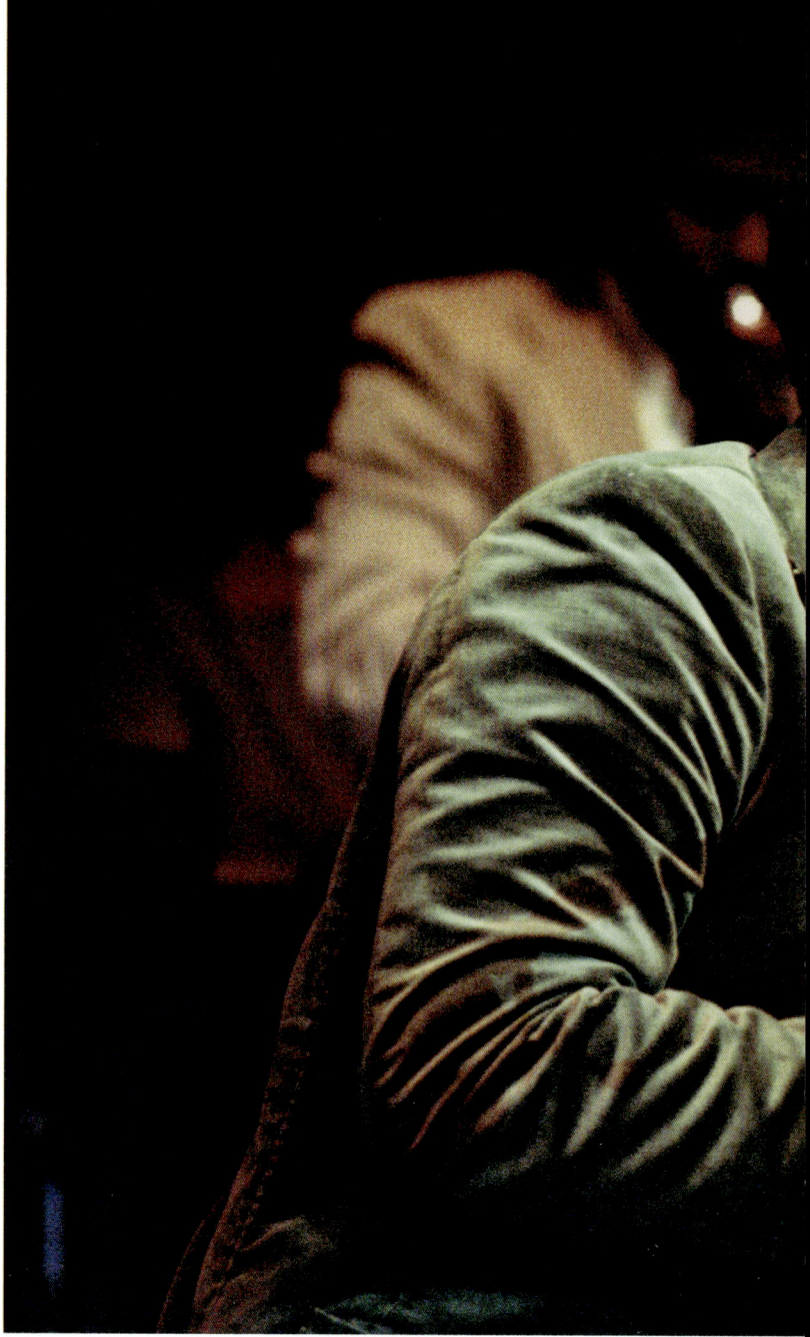

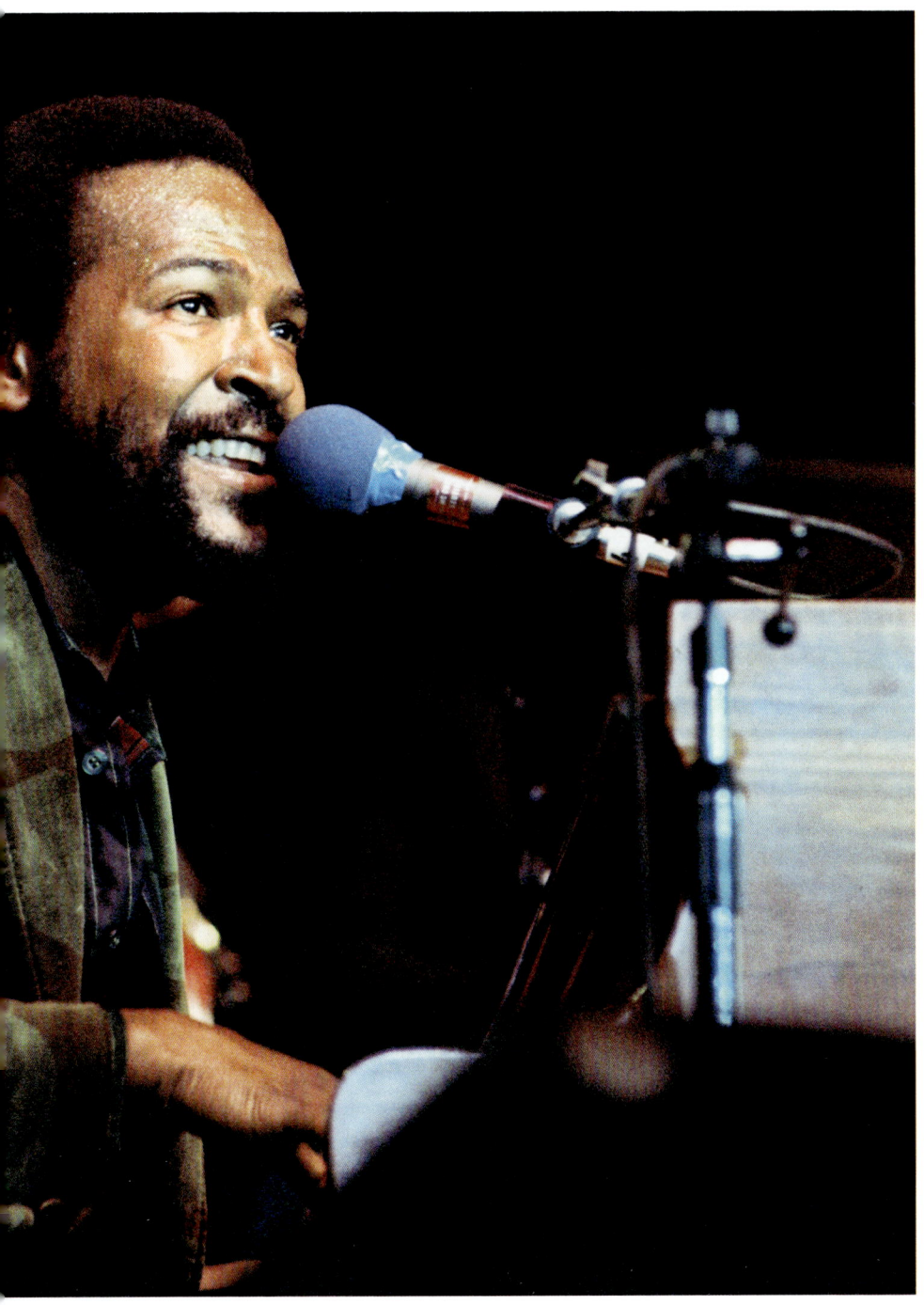

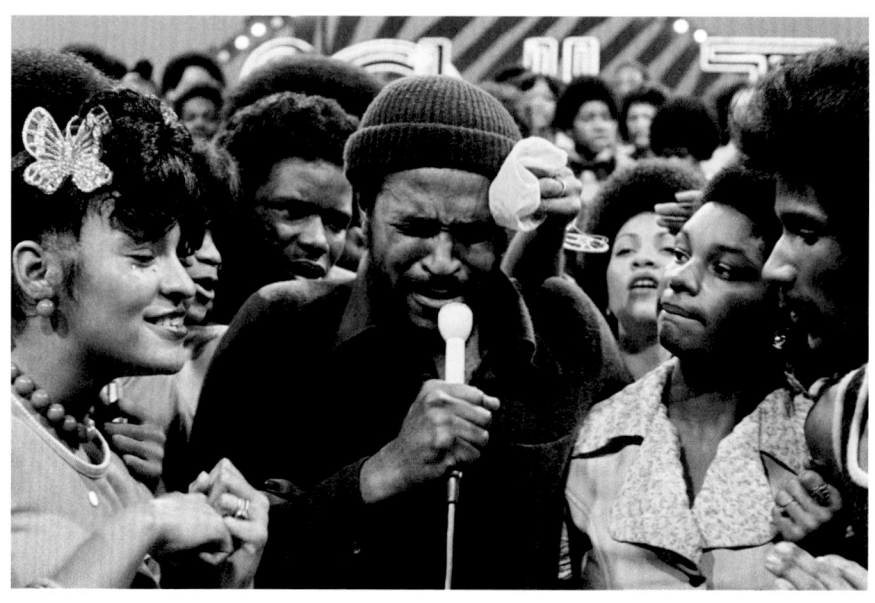

MARVIN GAYE
The Forum, Inglewood, California, 1974. (Pages 26–27)

San Diego Stadium, California, 1977. (Pages 28–29)

Soul Train, Los Angeles, 1974. (Above)
Decades after his tragic death, Gaye remains one of the most talented and lasting figures in music. L to R: Freddie Maxi, Dwayne Hargrave, Marvin, unidentified dancer, and Tyrone Proctor. Years later, it is still a mystery who held the white handkerchief as he sang "Let's Get It On."

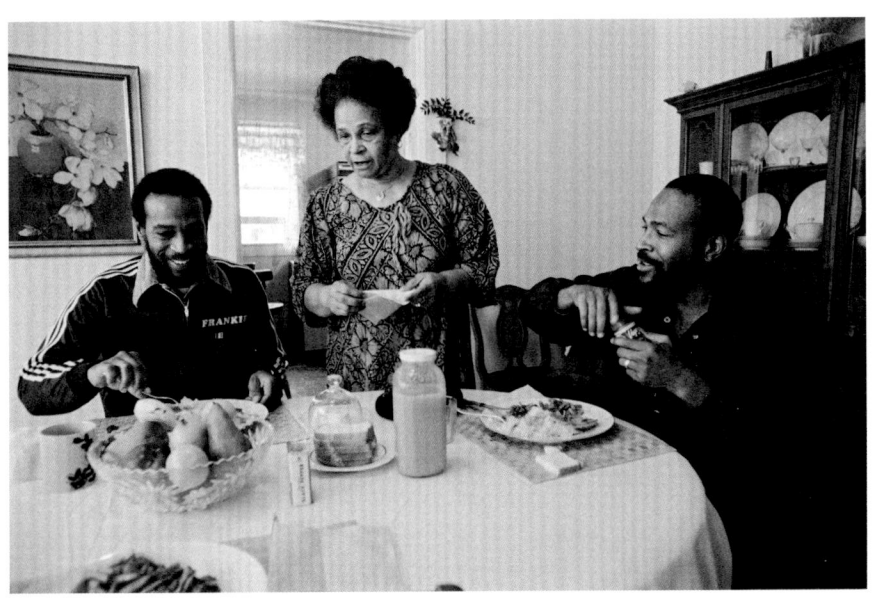

MARVIN GAYE

2101 South Gramercy Place, Los Angeles, 1978. (Above)
"Just after Thanksgiving, I had been photographing Marvin and his brother, Frankie, running at the beach. We ended up at their mother's house for leftovers. She wouldn't let me just take pictures — she set a place for me. I looked at her table... just like my mother's — with the green beans, mashed potatoes, turkey, and white bread. We ate well that day." — Bruce Talamon

Los Angeles, 1978. (Pages 32–33)
In his Rolls-Royce.

Topanga Canyon, Los Angeles, 1978. (Pages 34–35)

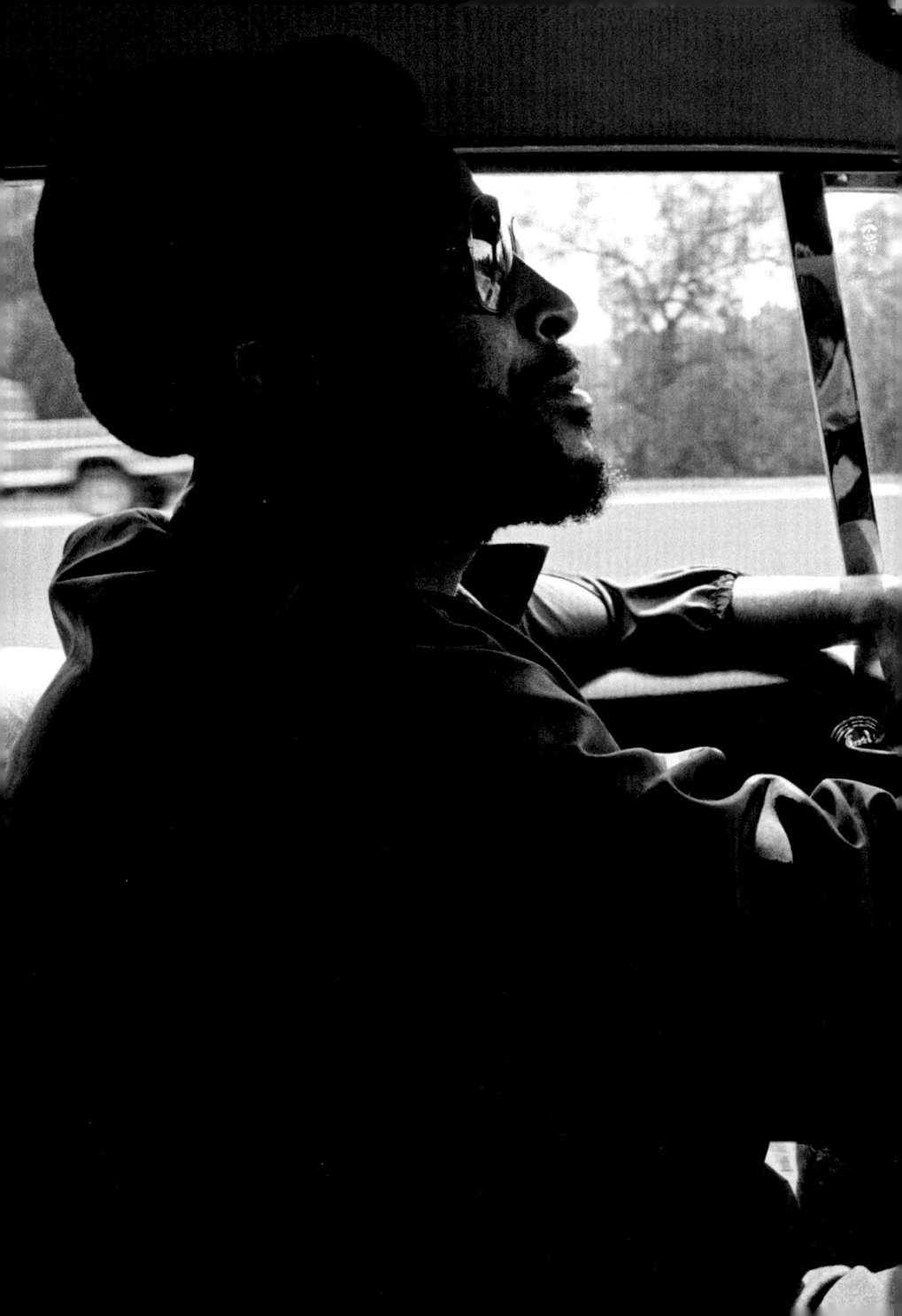

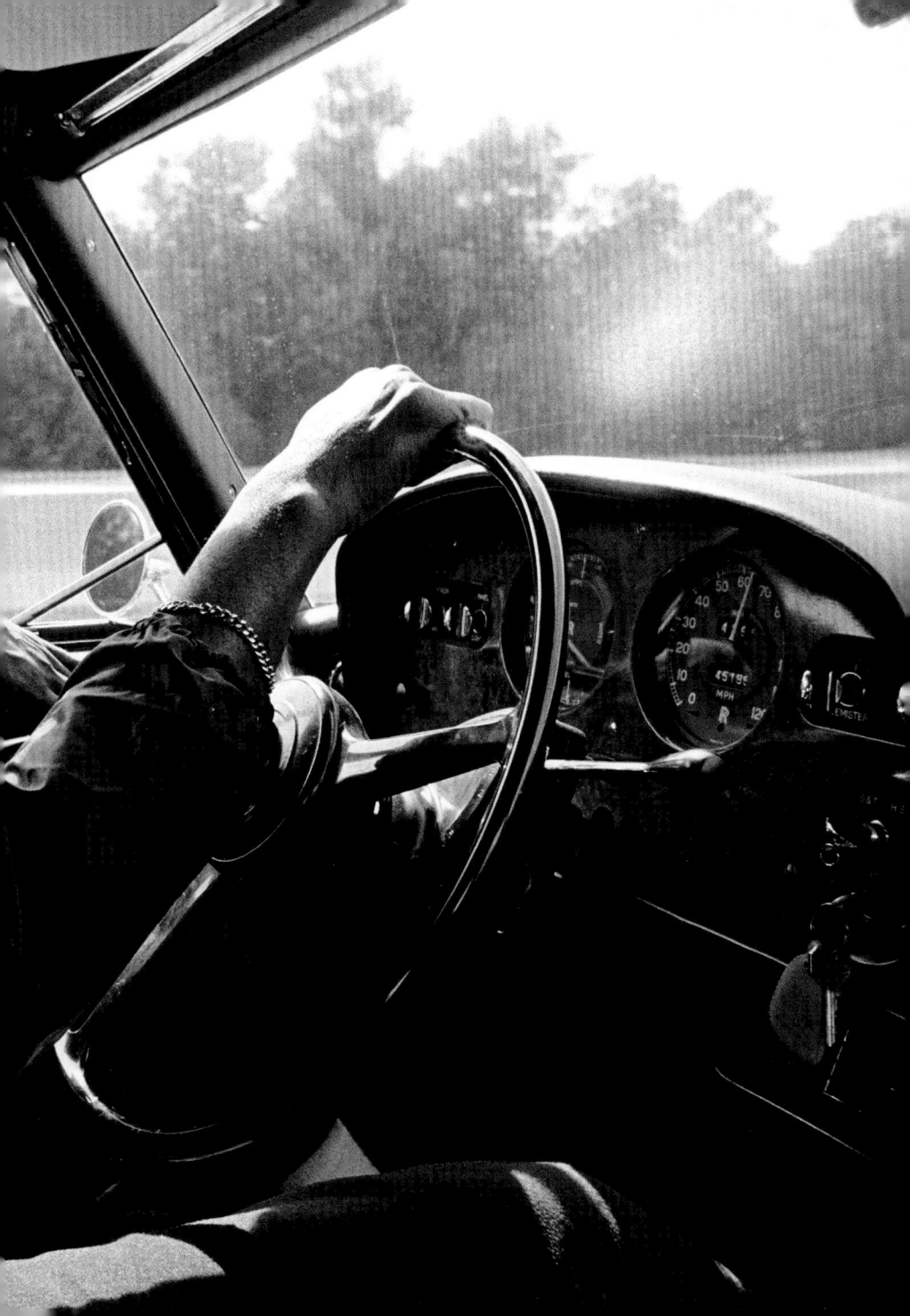

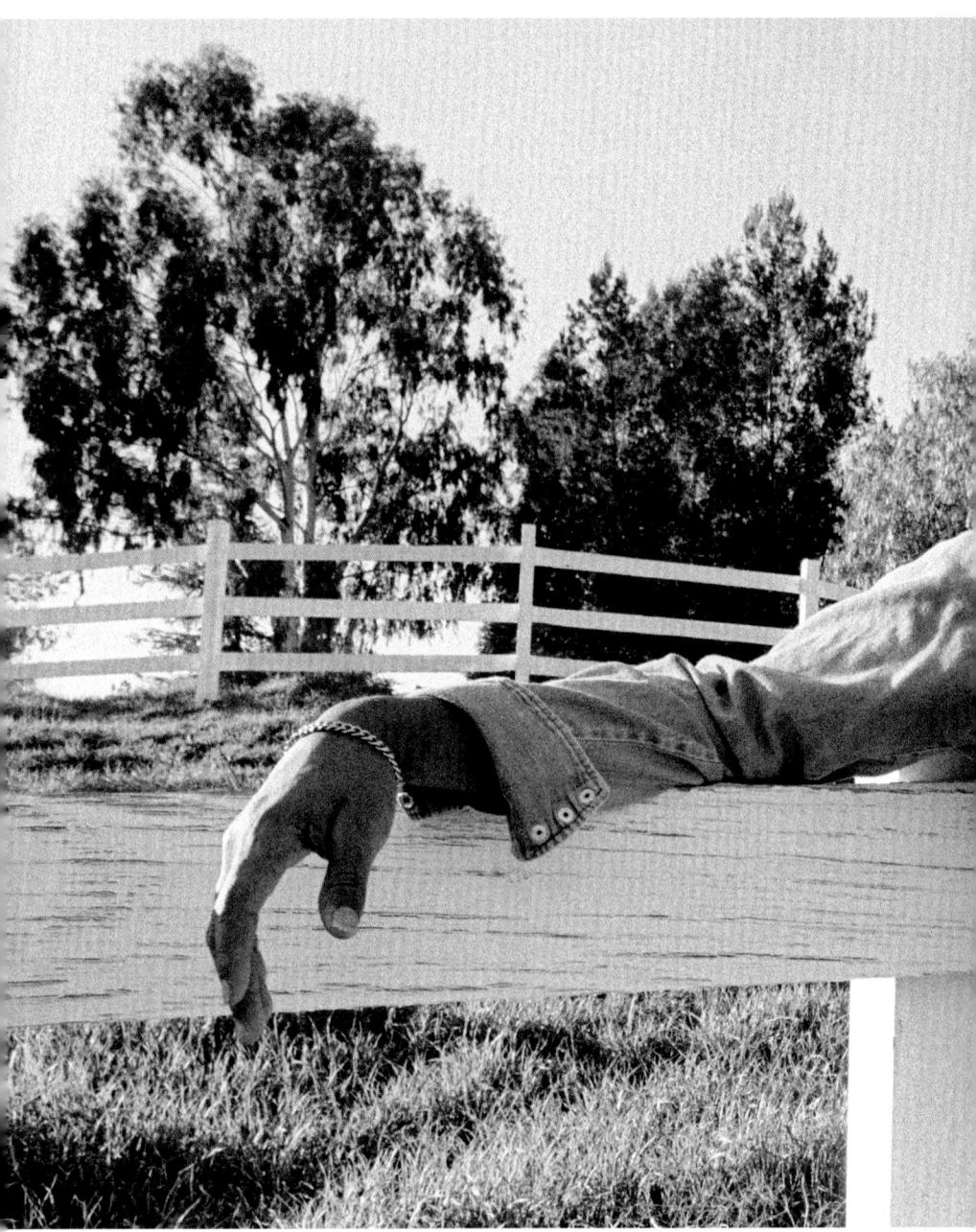

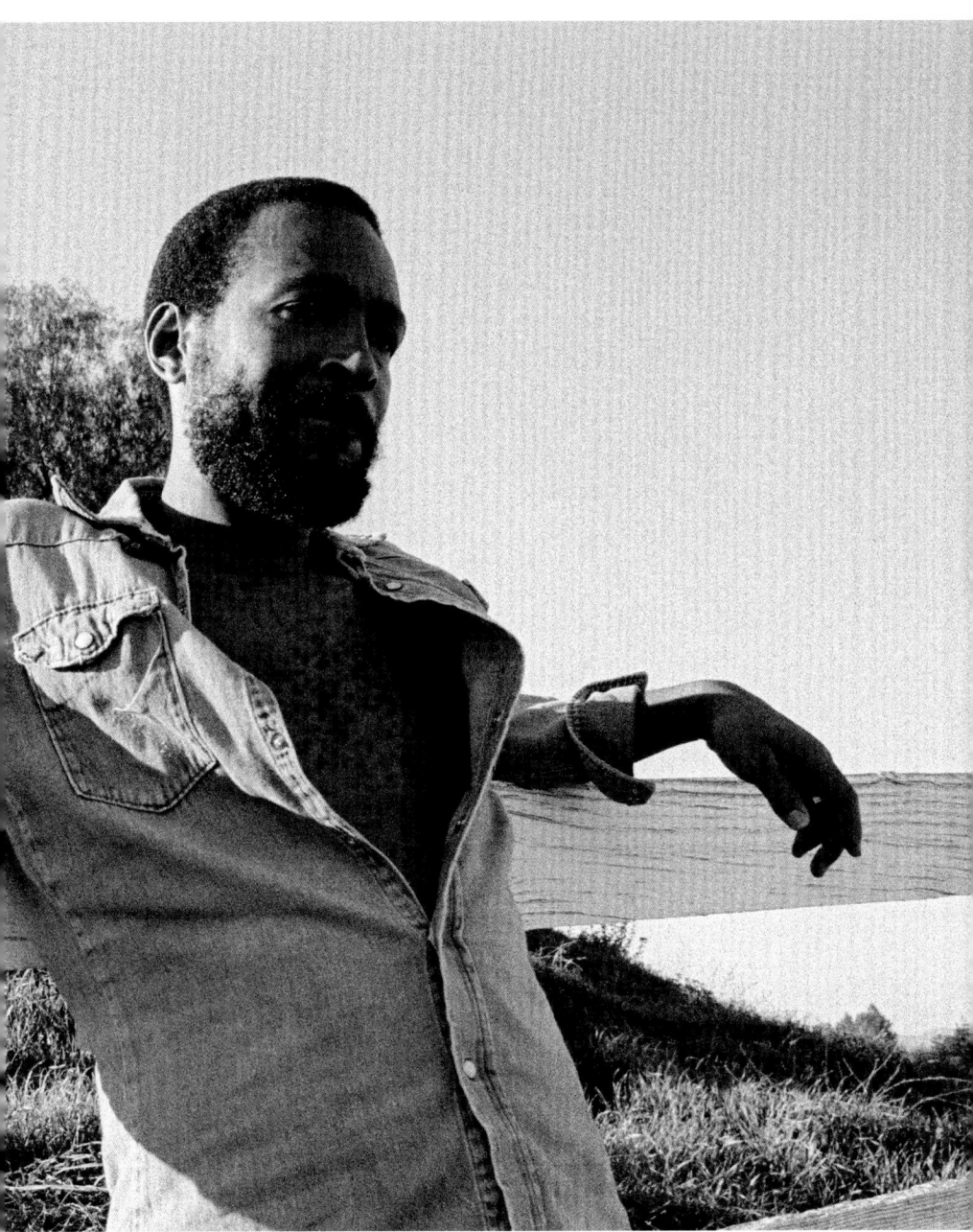

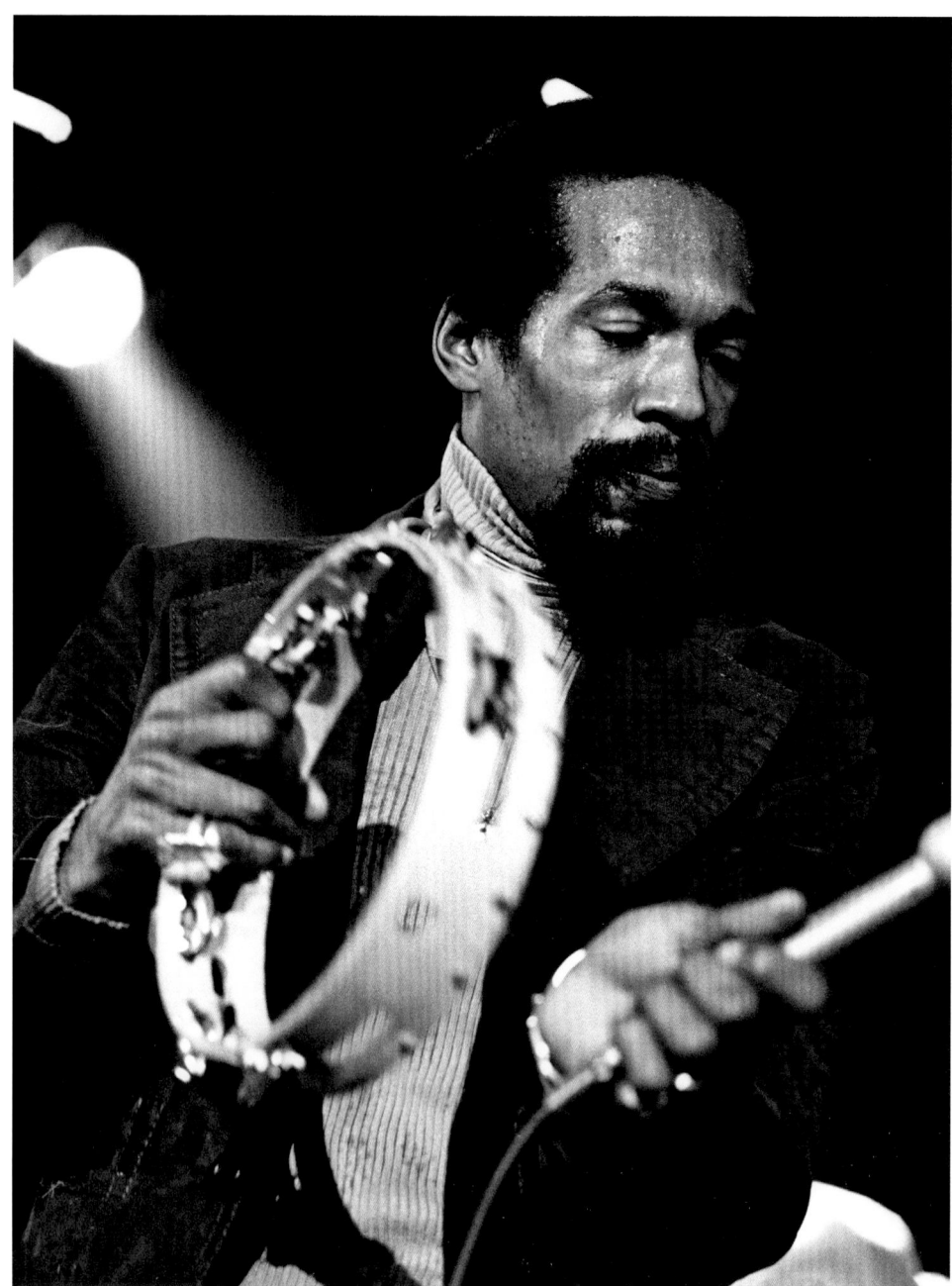

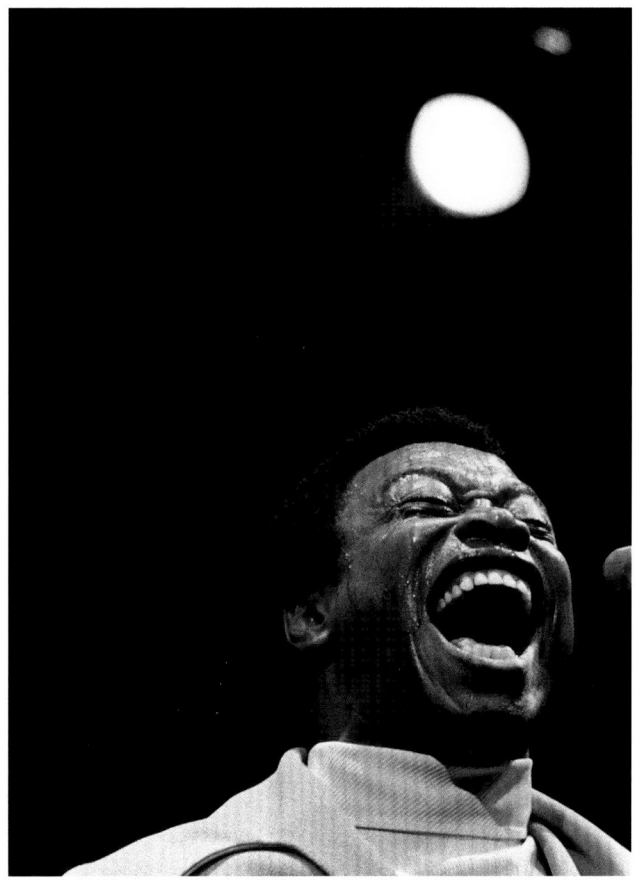

EDDIE KENDRICKS
The Roxy, West Hollywood, California, 1973. (Opposite)
Possessing one of the great falsetto voices in soul, Kendricks would
score a number-one hit only two years after leaving The Temptations,
with 1973's "Keep on Truckin'."

CHARLES WRIGHT & THE WATTS 103RD STREET RHYTHM BAND
The Roxy, West Hollywood, California, 1974. (Above)
The band's initial exposure came from opening for Bill Cosby.
Wright's global anthem "Express Yourself" is one of the pioneering
songs that linked 1960s soul and 1970s funk.

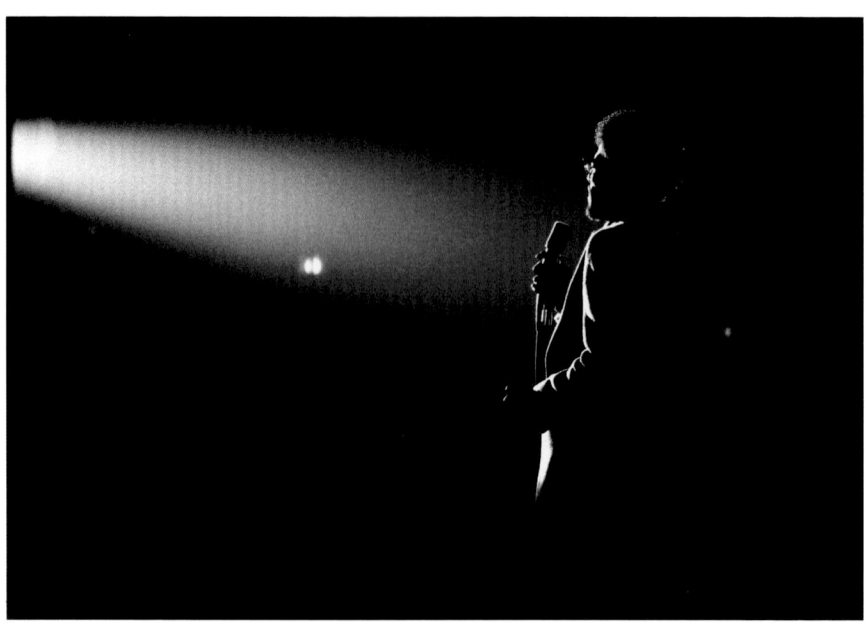

DAVID RUFFIN
The Total Experience nightclub, Los Angeles, 1974. (Above)
Ruffin's heartsick and raspy voice can be heard on The Temptations' early hits "Ain't Too Proud to Beg" and "My Girl." He would exhibit that distinctive tenor voice even more with his 1975 solo hit, "Walk Away from Love."

BILLY PAUL
***Soul Train*, Los Angeles, 1973. (Opposite)**
Paul's 1972 number-one pop and R&B hit, "Me and Mrs. Jones," was so massive that people thought he was an overnight sensation. The dapper Philadelphia native had been in the music business since the 1950s.

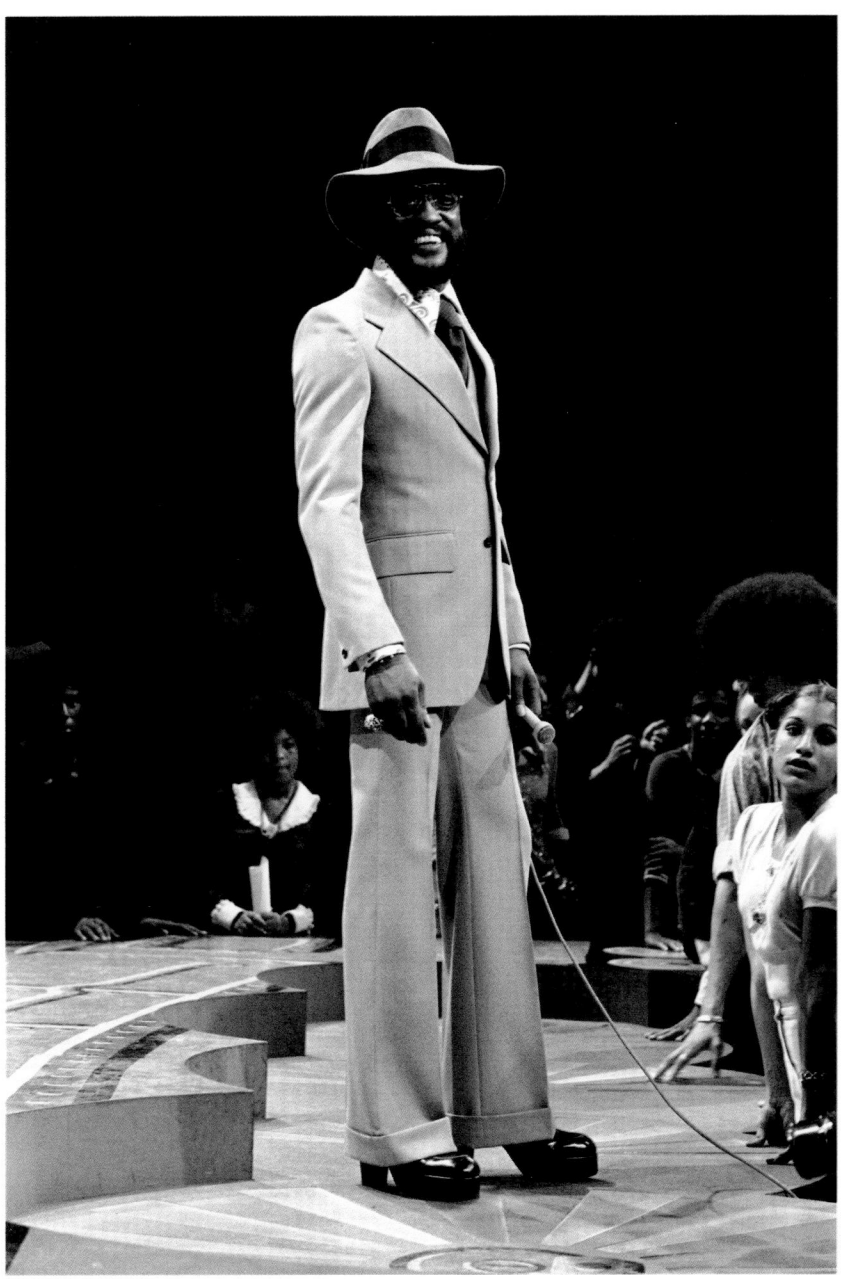

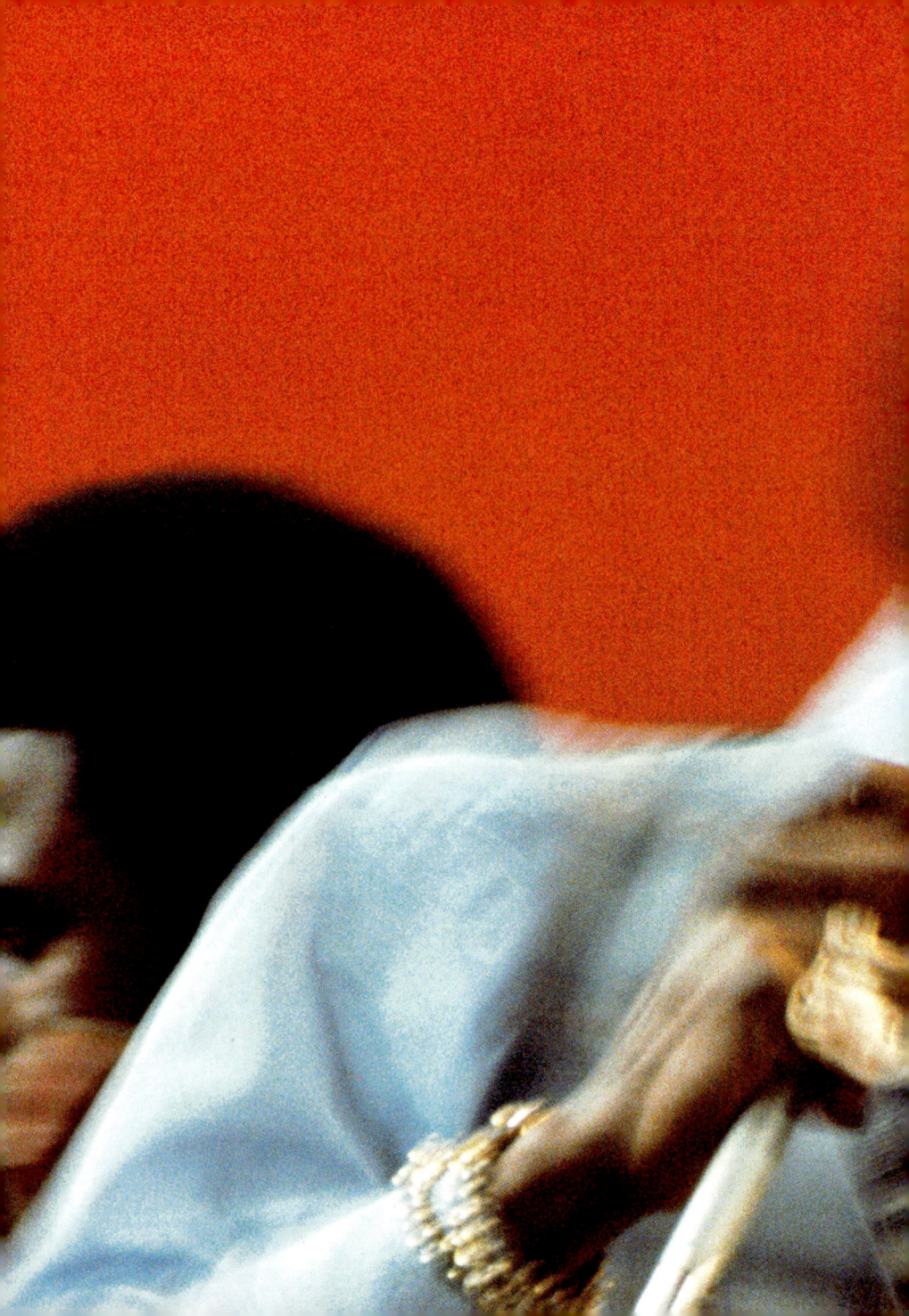

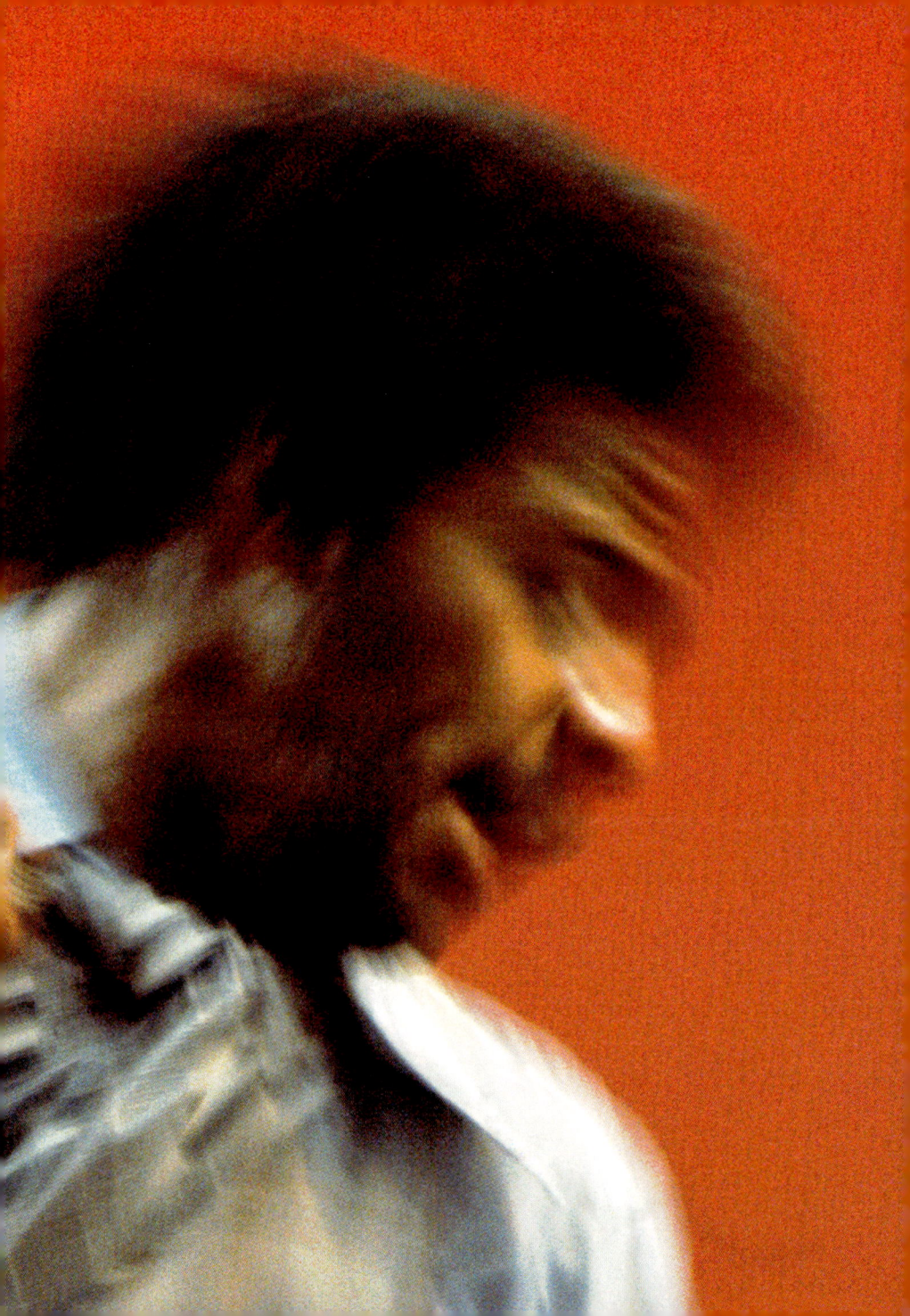

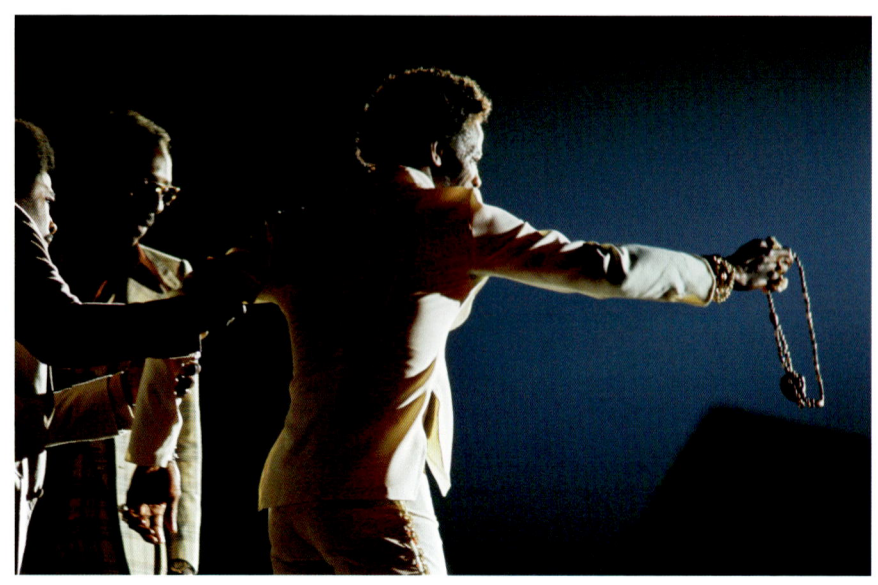

AL GREEN
Soul Train, Los Angeles, 1974. (Pages 40–41)
One of the all-time great soul singers, Green appeared on *Soul Train* 10 times.
He often gave performances that felt sanctified—almost like a tent church revival.
Host Don Cornelius would call Green "soul music's messiah."

Los Angeles, 1977. (Above)
"Sometimes Al would hand out beads and necklaces at the end
of his show. His security is holding on to him because the women
would try to pull him into the crowd." — Bruce Talamon

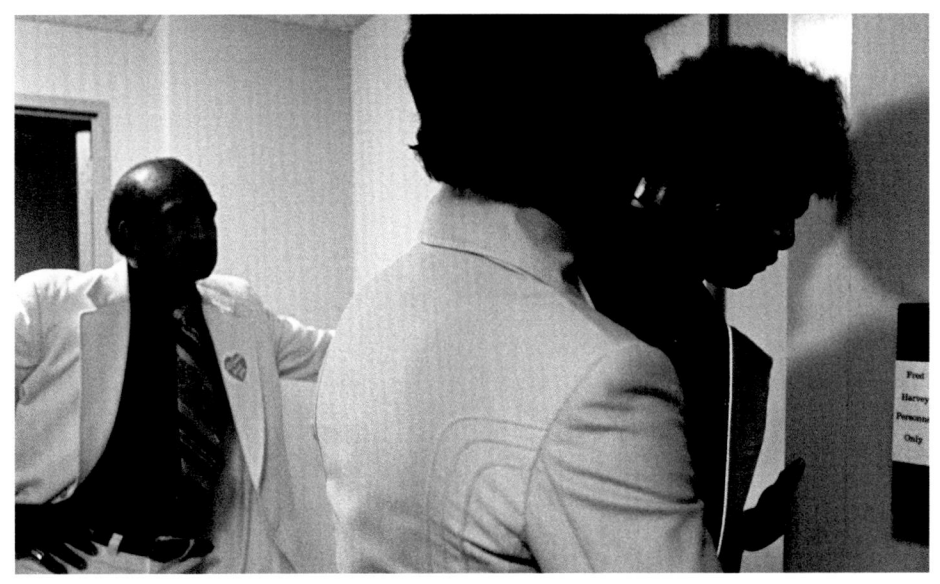

AL GREEN
Dorothy Chandler Pavilion, Los Angeles, 1978.
"After the encore we rushed back to Al's dressing room, and just as we reached the door, he collapsed. That moment would be gone in an instant. Leica M4 with a 28mm lens, a quick move to the right to compose the shot in my viewfinder. Wide-open aperture, slow shutter speed. Hold steady — focus on the eyes." — Bruce Talamon

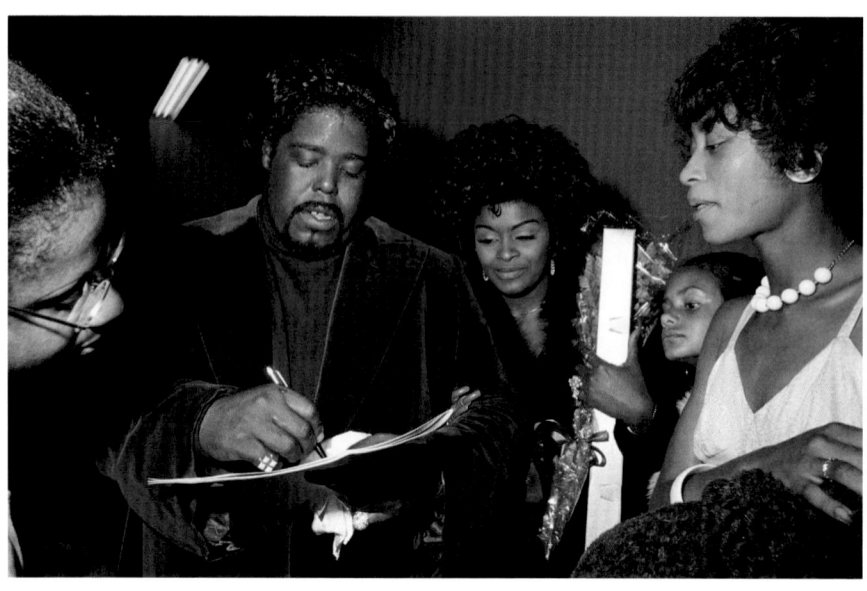

BARRY WHITE
Los Angeles Sports Arena, 1974. (Above)

***Soul Train*, Los Angeles, 1973. (Opposite)**
The Maestro: When White created The Love Unlimited Orchestra,
his music became the cornerstone of the lush R&B and disco sound.
His silky baritone / bass voice was synonymous with everything romantic.
Throughout his life, he only grew in popularity as a cult-like figure
while quietly becoming one of the best-selling artists of all time.

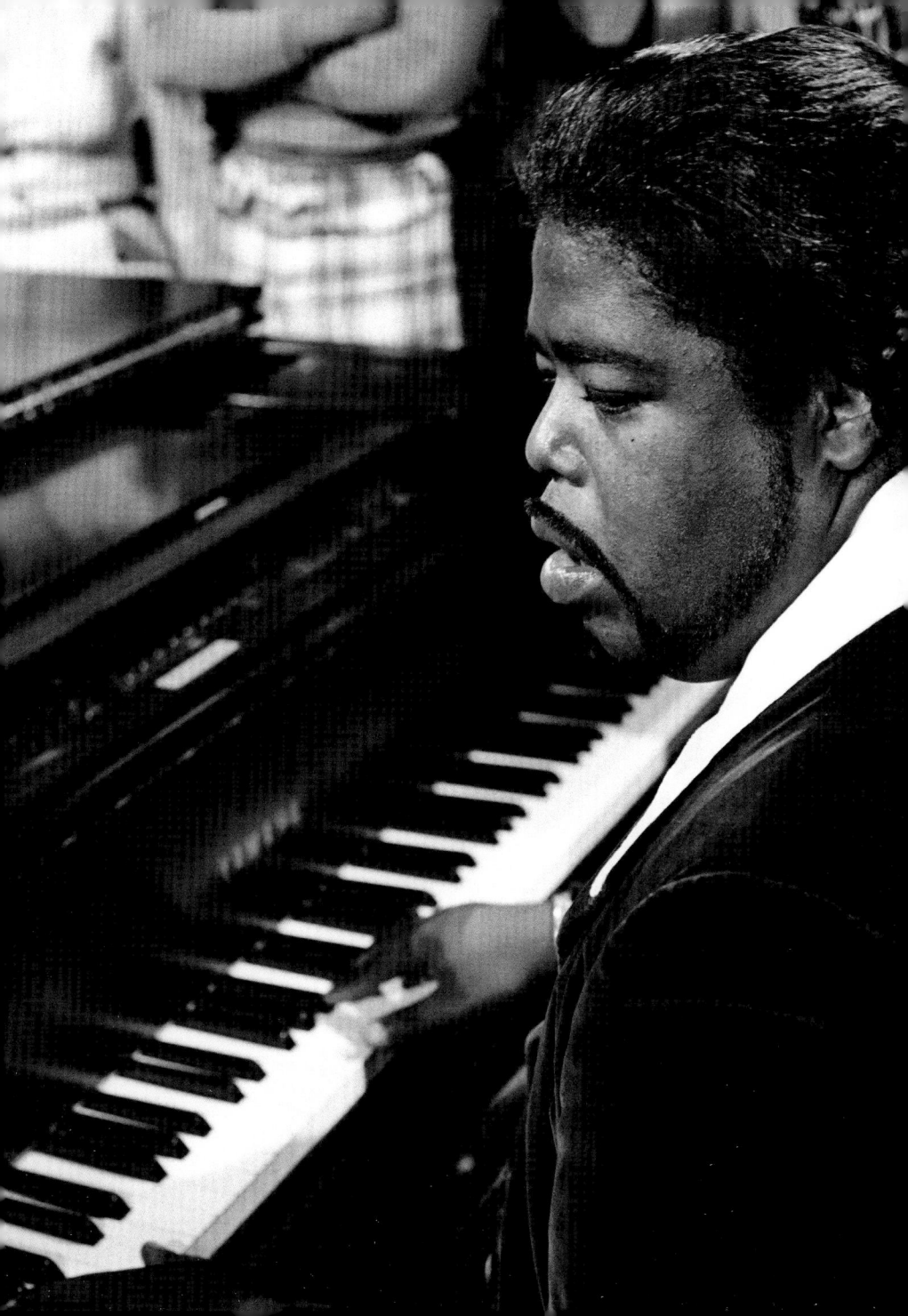

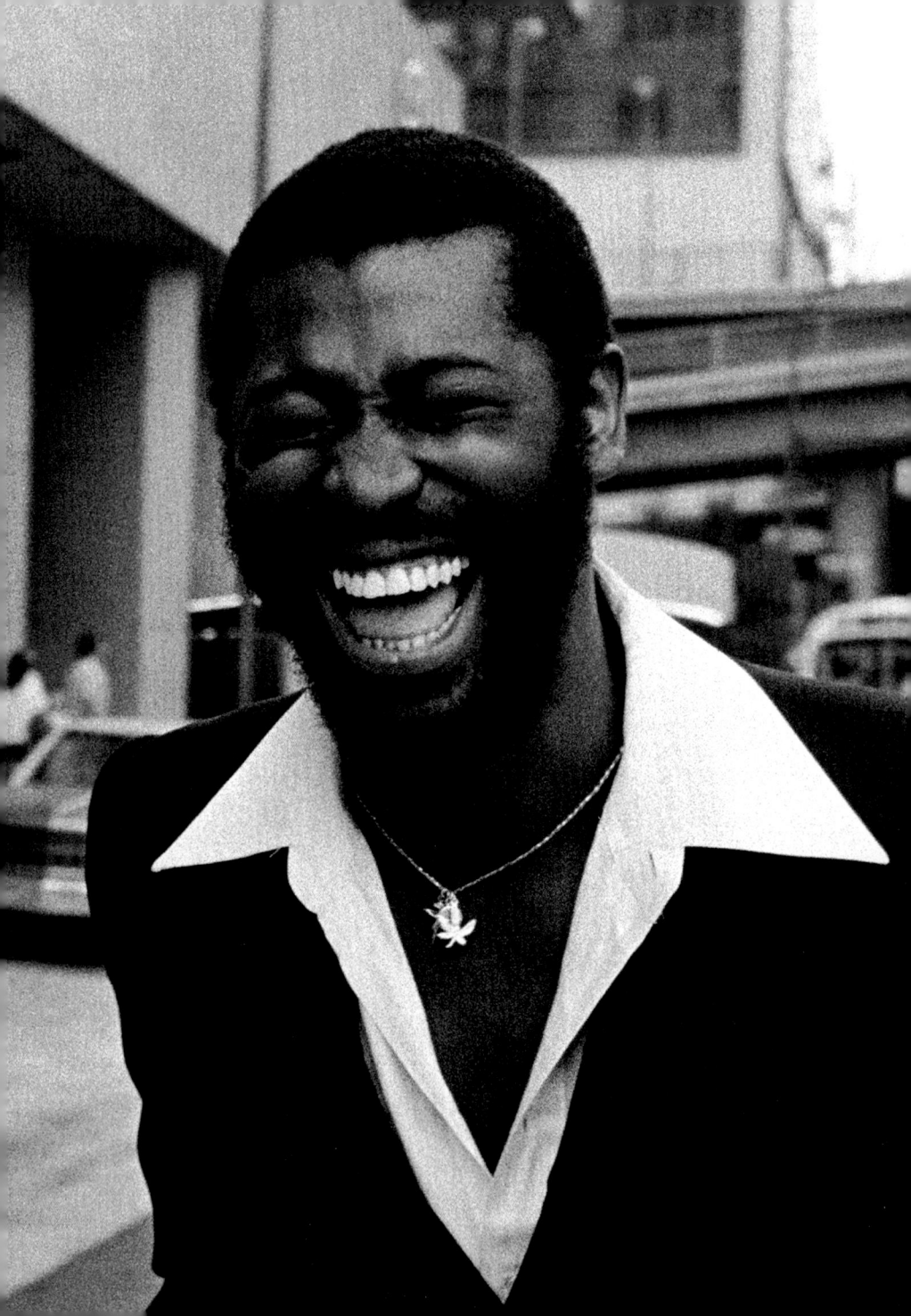

TEDDY PENDERGRASS
Los Angeles, 1977.
After spending three years as the lead singer of Harold Melvin & The Blue
Notes, Pendergrass launched a solo career that would soon make him
the most popular male R&B singer in the world. With hits like "Close the
Door," "Turn Off the Lights," and "Love TKO," Pendergrass' success would
convince him to introduce the concept of concerts "for women only."

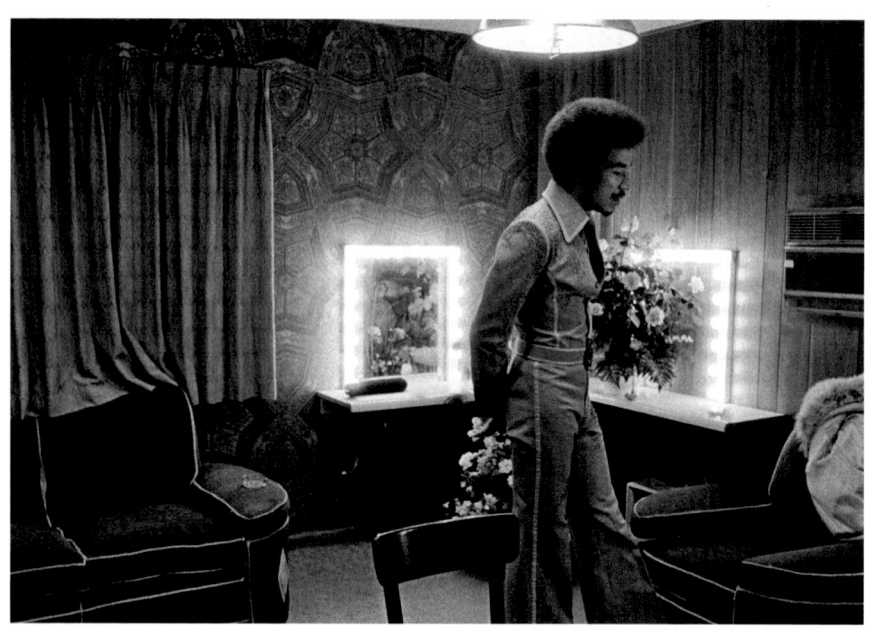

SMOKEY ROBINSON
The Roxy, West Hollywood, California, 1975. (Above & opposite)
As a songwriter and member of The Miracles, Robinson wrote songs that
are synonymous with the 1960s: "Ain't That Peculiar," "My Girl," "The Tears
of a Clown," "My Guy," and many others. After leaving The Miracles, he
would work as a Motown executive and continue to record solo, culminating
with his "Just to See Her" and "One Heartbeat" in 1987.

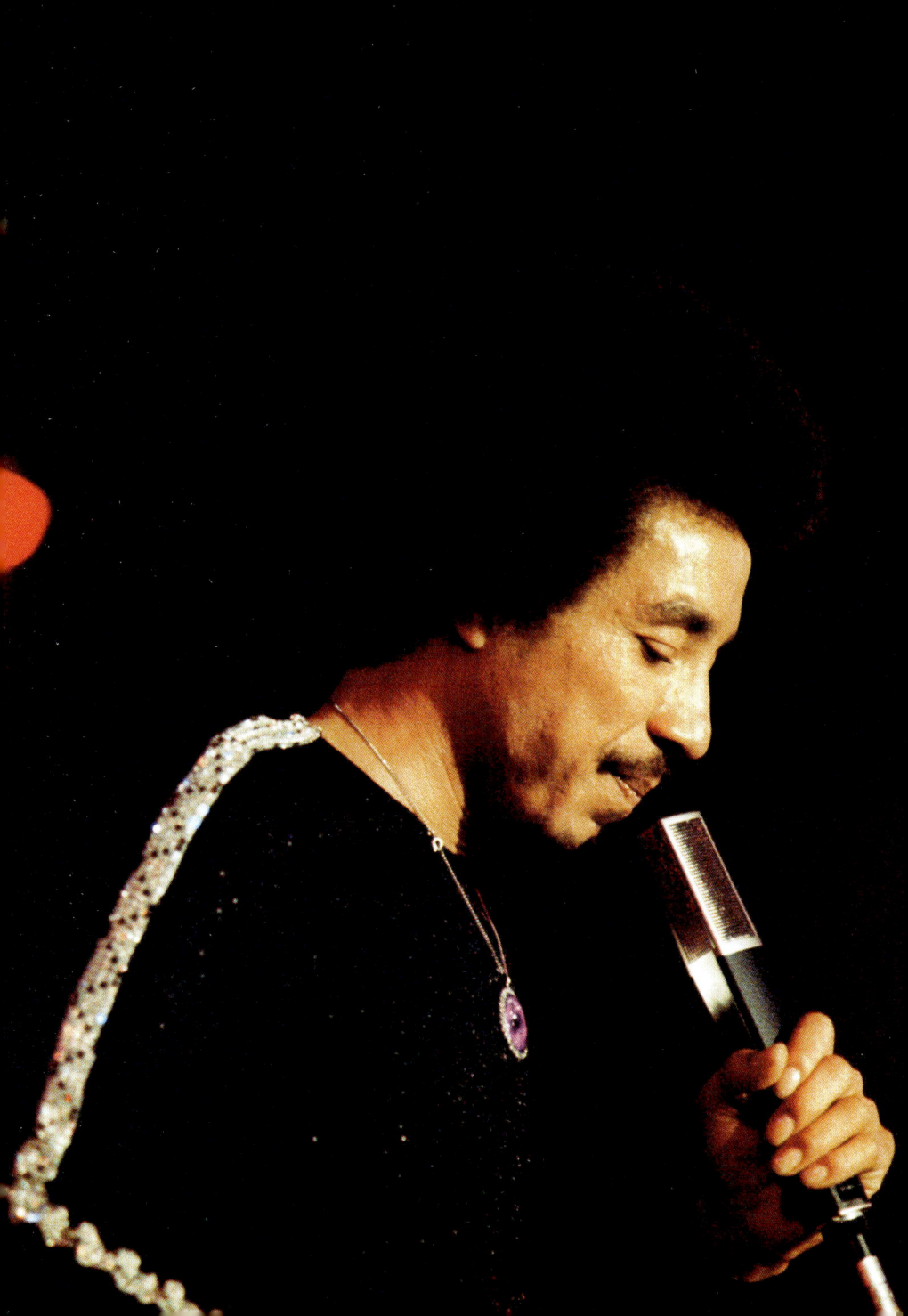

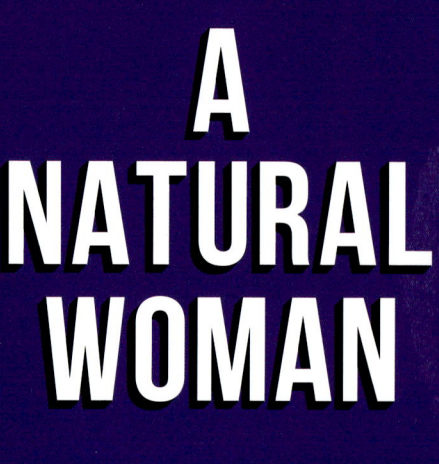

A
NATURAL
WOMAN

ARETHA FRANKLIN
GLADYS KNIGHT & THE PIPS
LABELLE
MINNIE RIPERTON
DIANA ROSS
DONNA SUMMER
DENIECE WILLIAMS

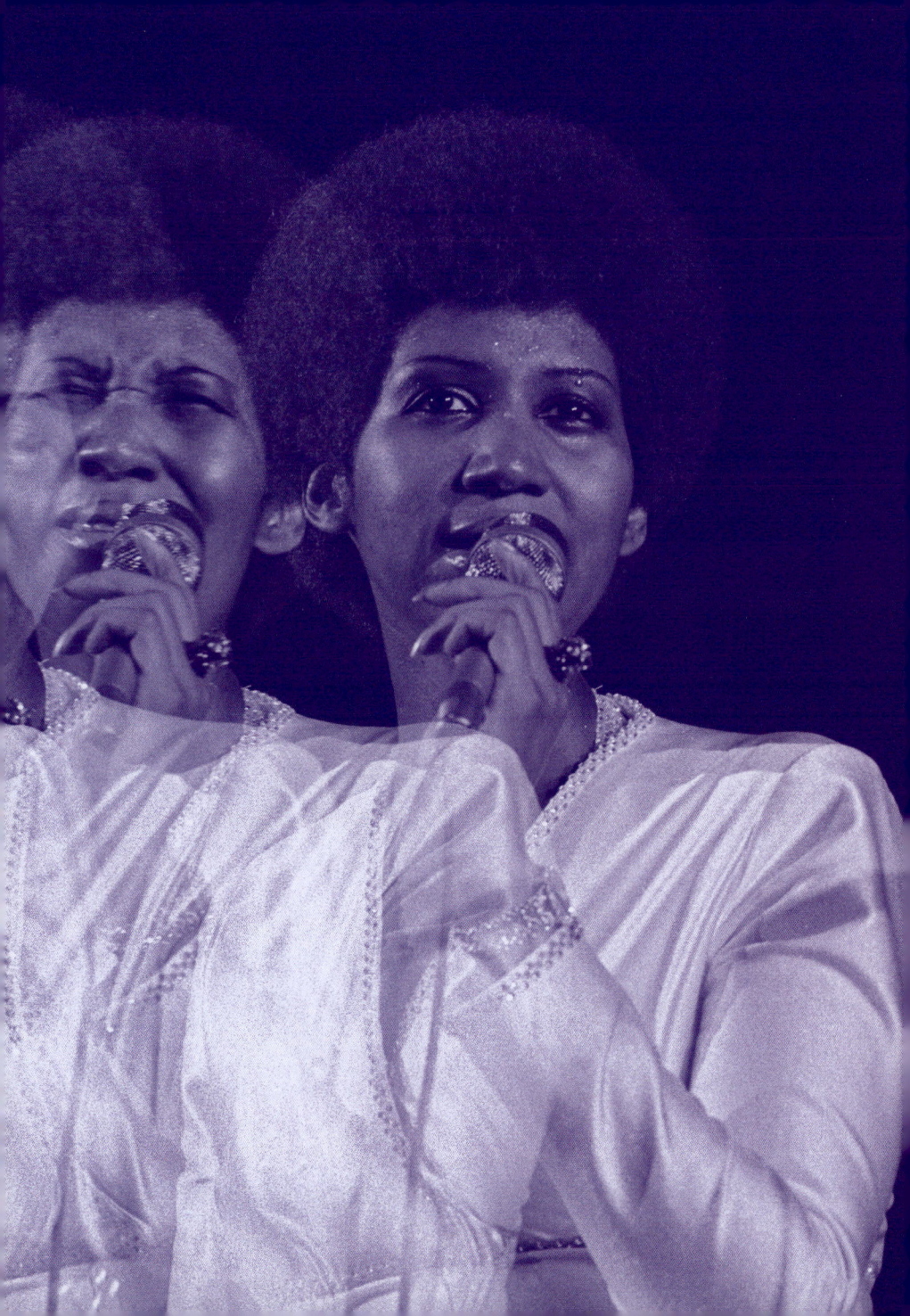

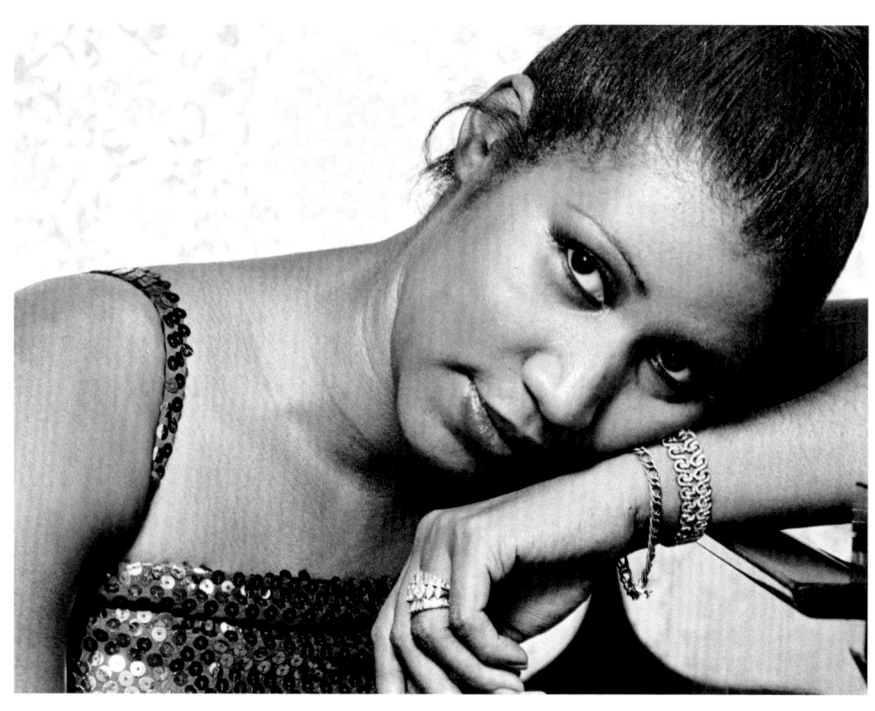

ARETHA FRANKLIN
Hollywood Bowl, Hollywood, California, 1974. (Pages 50–51)

Portrait session at Franklin's home, Los Angeles, 1977. (Above)

**ABC Television Center, *The Muhammad Ali Variety Special*,
Hollywood, California, 1975. (Opposite)**
There is only one Queen of Soul. With her sanctified voice, she represents
the best of the black church. With her success and survival skills, she
represents the best of what it means to be a star. There is no greater icon.

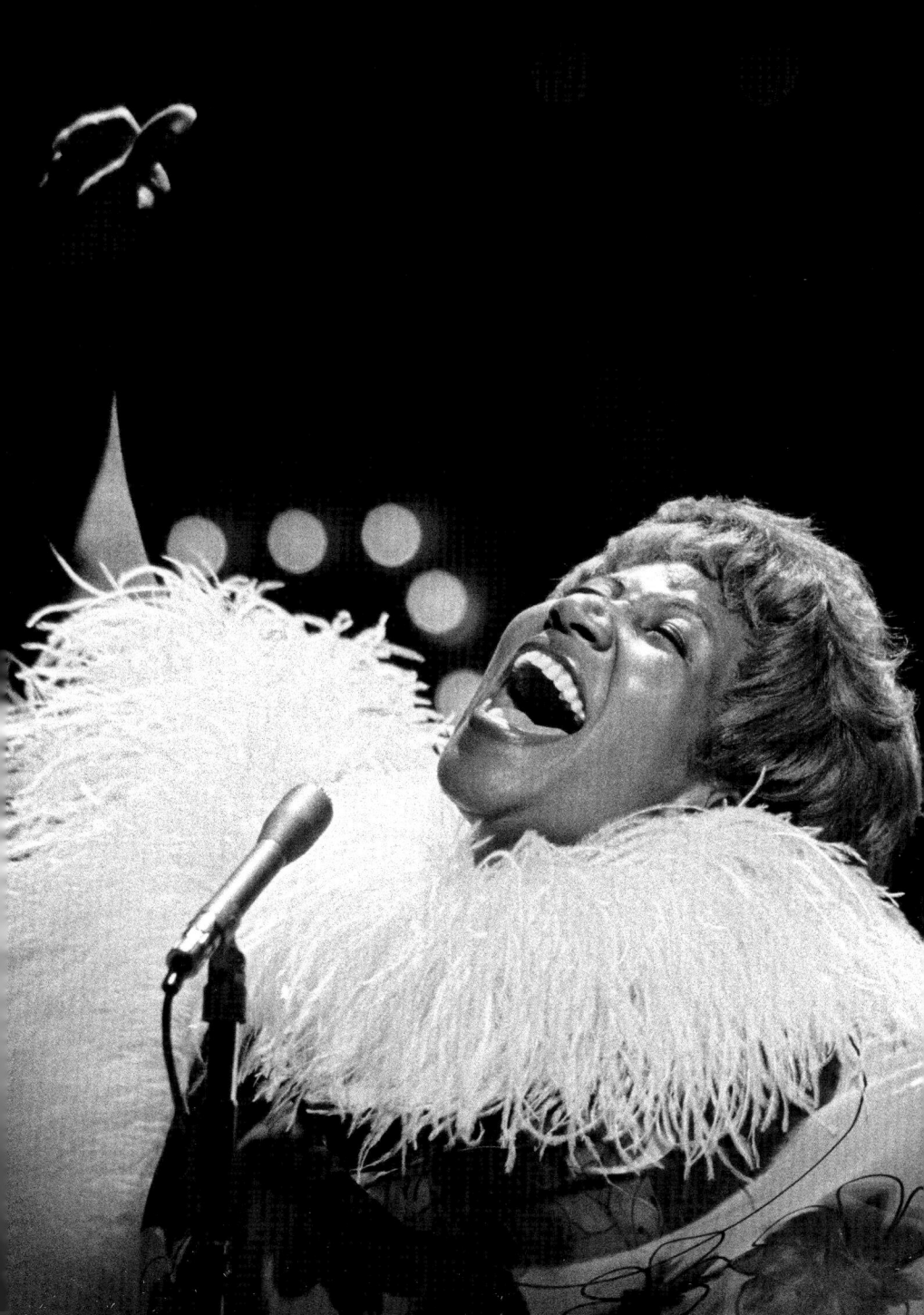

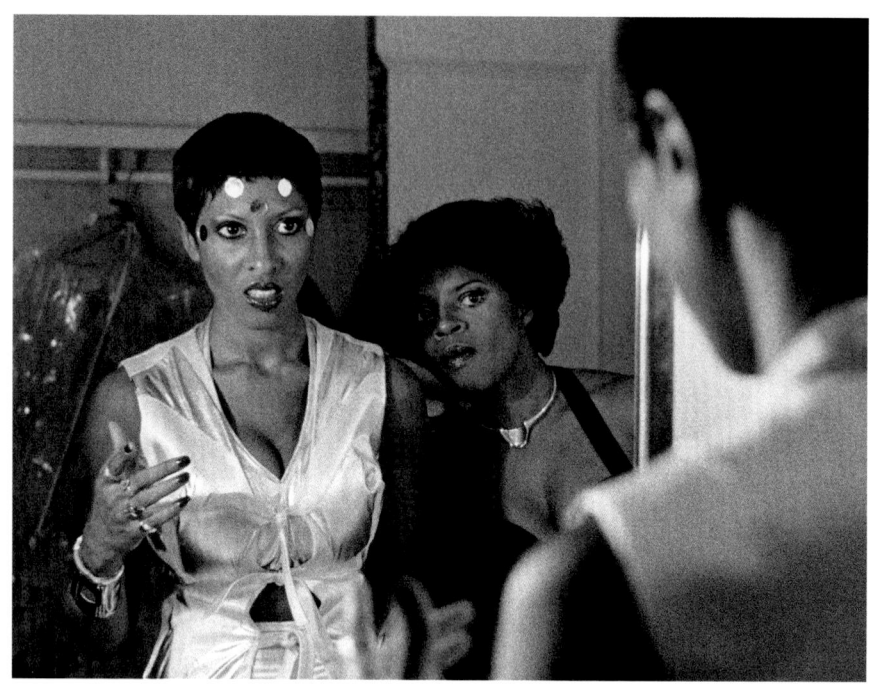

LABELLE
Paramount Theatre, Oakland, California, 1975. (Above)
Nona Hendryx and Sarah Dash perfecting the look.

Paramount Theatre, Oakland, California, 1975. (Opposite)
With their raw edge and exotic wardrobe, the group's performance
style was inherently theatrical.

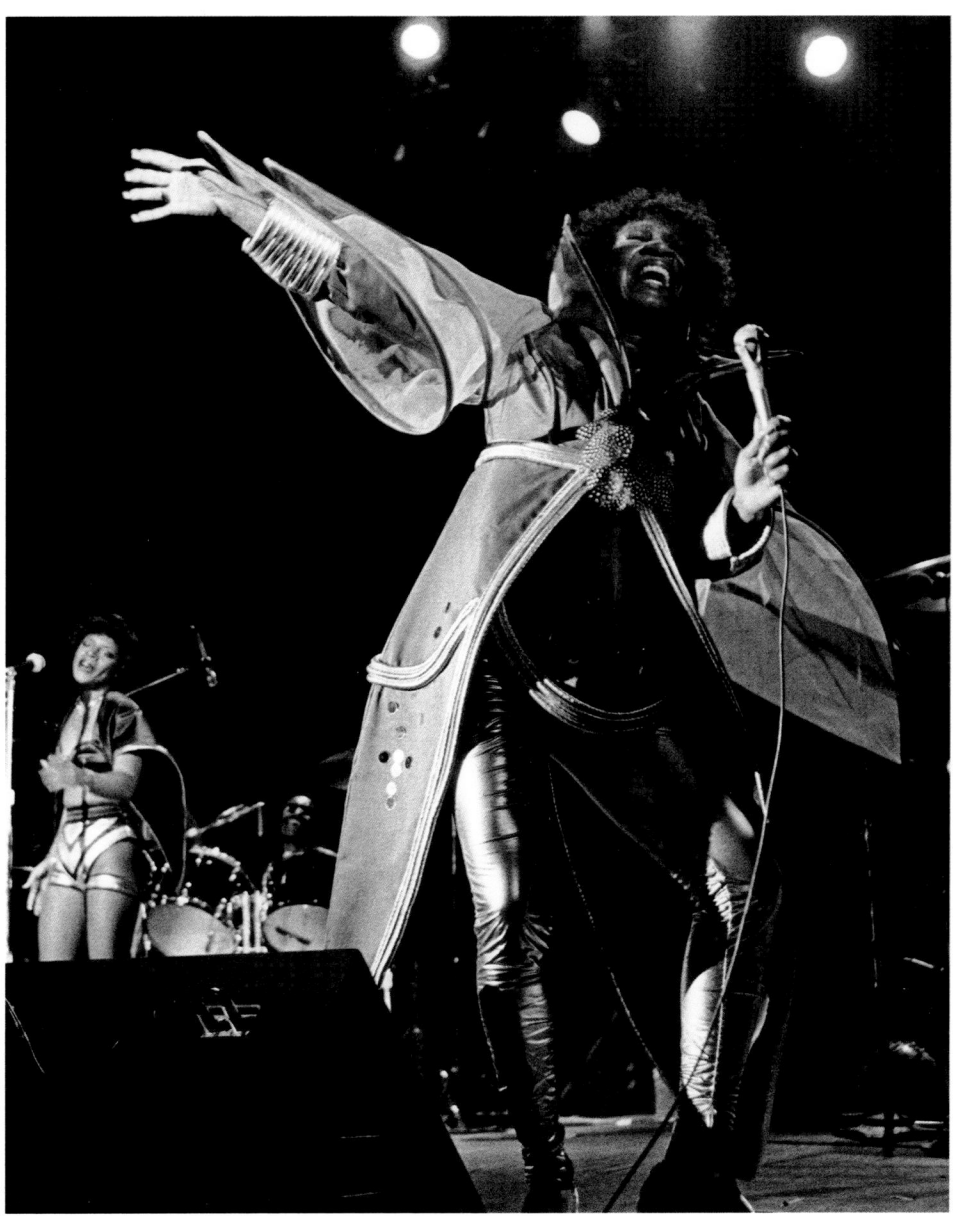

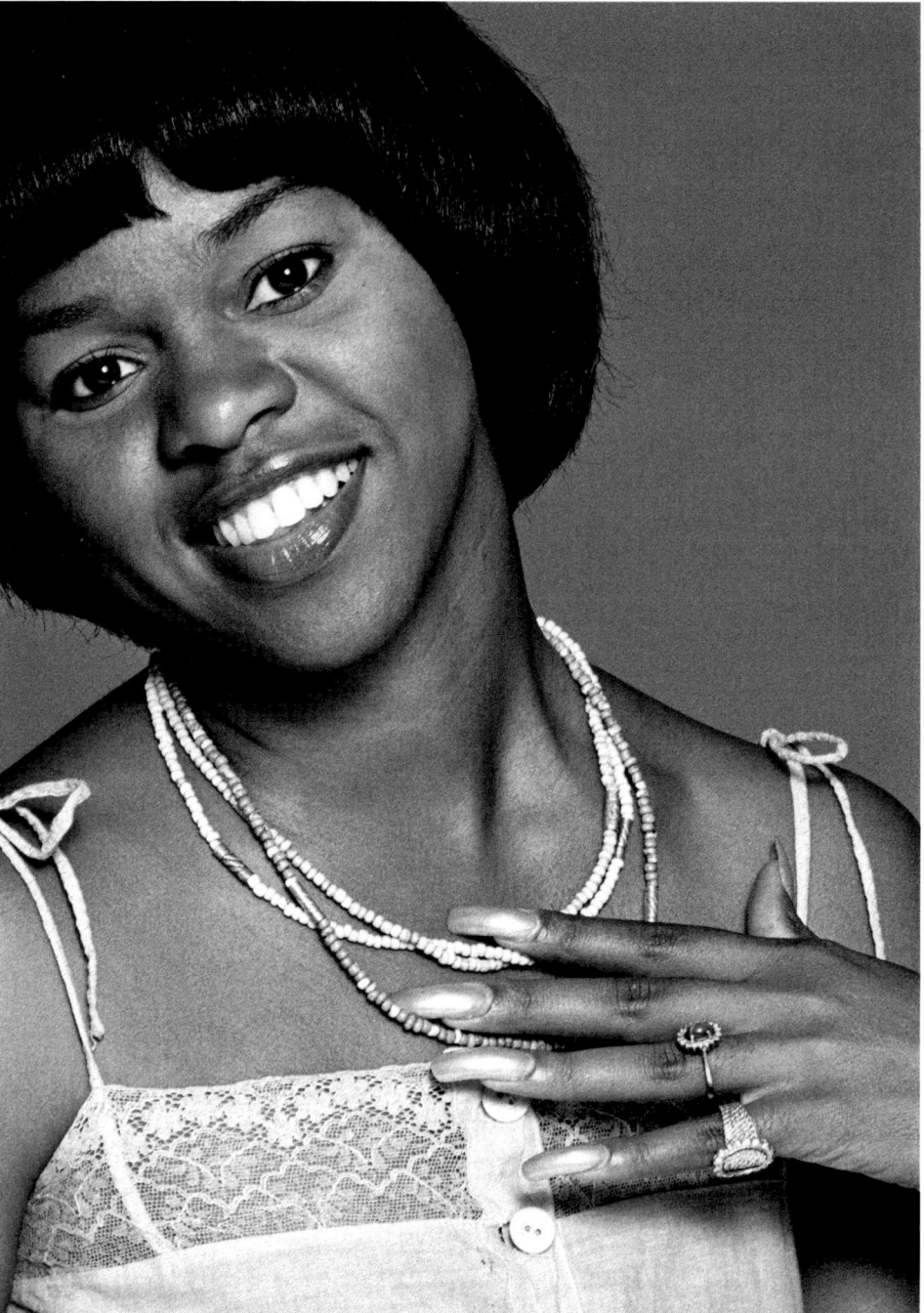

DENIECE WILLIAMS
The Complex Recording Studio, Los Angeles, 1977. (Opposite)
With an angelic four-octave voice, Williams had a career
that earned major success in R&B, pop, and gospel.
*"Maurice White called me to shoot a series of portraits of Deniece Williams
for her album release. We shot this publicity session at The Complex in
Los Angeles, which was the recording studio and soundstage that Maurice
used as his base of operation for his label, ARC Records." —*Bruce Talamon

GLADYS KNIGHT & THE PIPS
Las Vegas, 1977. (Above)
A family-based group consisting of Knight and her brother Merald "Bubba"
Knight, and cousins William Guest and Edward Patten, the act was one of the
most venerable of the 1970s. Between Gladys' distinctive voice and The Pips'
skillfully choreographed steps, they would be adored for over 30 years.

MINNIE RIPERTON

***Soul Train*, Los Angeles, 1974.**

Riperton's signature song, "Lovin' You," perfectly showcased her five-octave vocal range and her eternal sweetness. Taken from us too soon, she was one of the first celebrities to become a spokesperson for breast cancer.

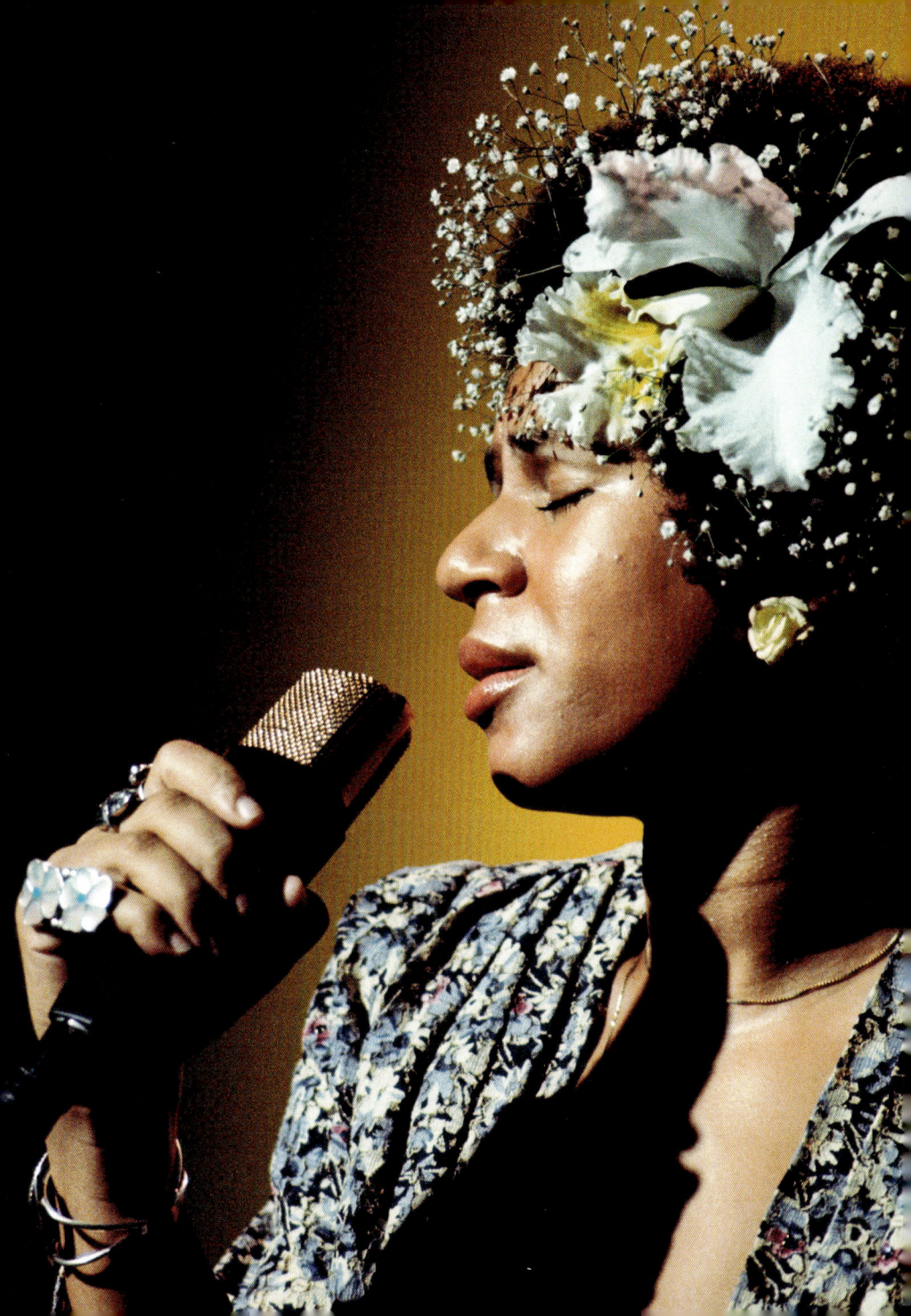

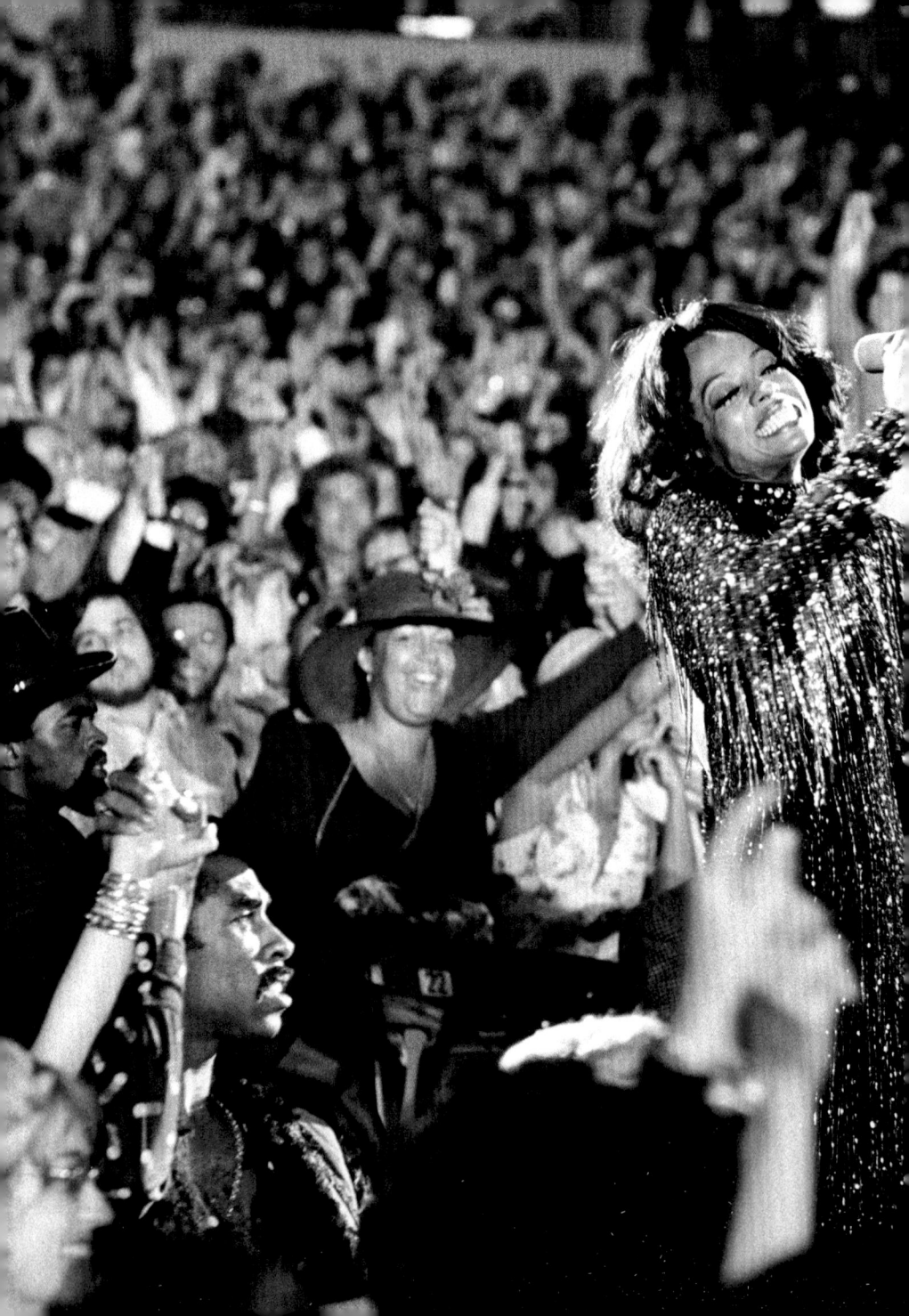

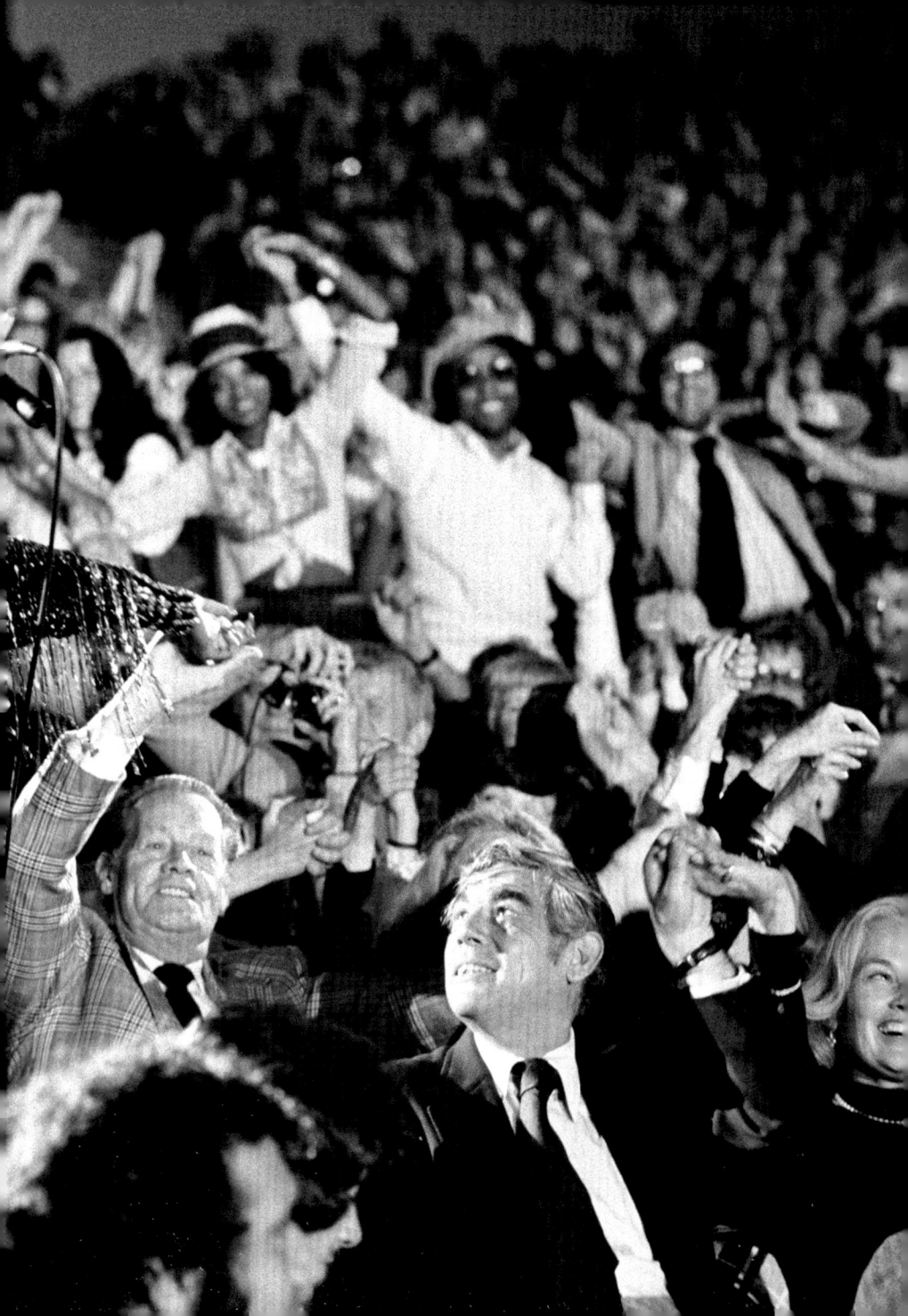

DIANA ROSS

Universal Amphitheatre, Los Angeles, 1974. (Pages 60–61)
Singing "Reach Out and Touch (Somebody's Hand)," Diana is surrounded by her fans.

Los Angeles, 1976. (Opposite)
Singer. Actress. Fashion icon. Legend. The first lady of Motown. Ross and The Supremes would have 12 number-one singles and become the most successful vocal group of all time. A successful solo career would follow for Ross. A Rock & Roll Hall of Fame inductee, Academy Awa Medal of Freedom honoree, and the recipient of several lifetime-achievement awards, Ross is an American treasure.

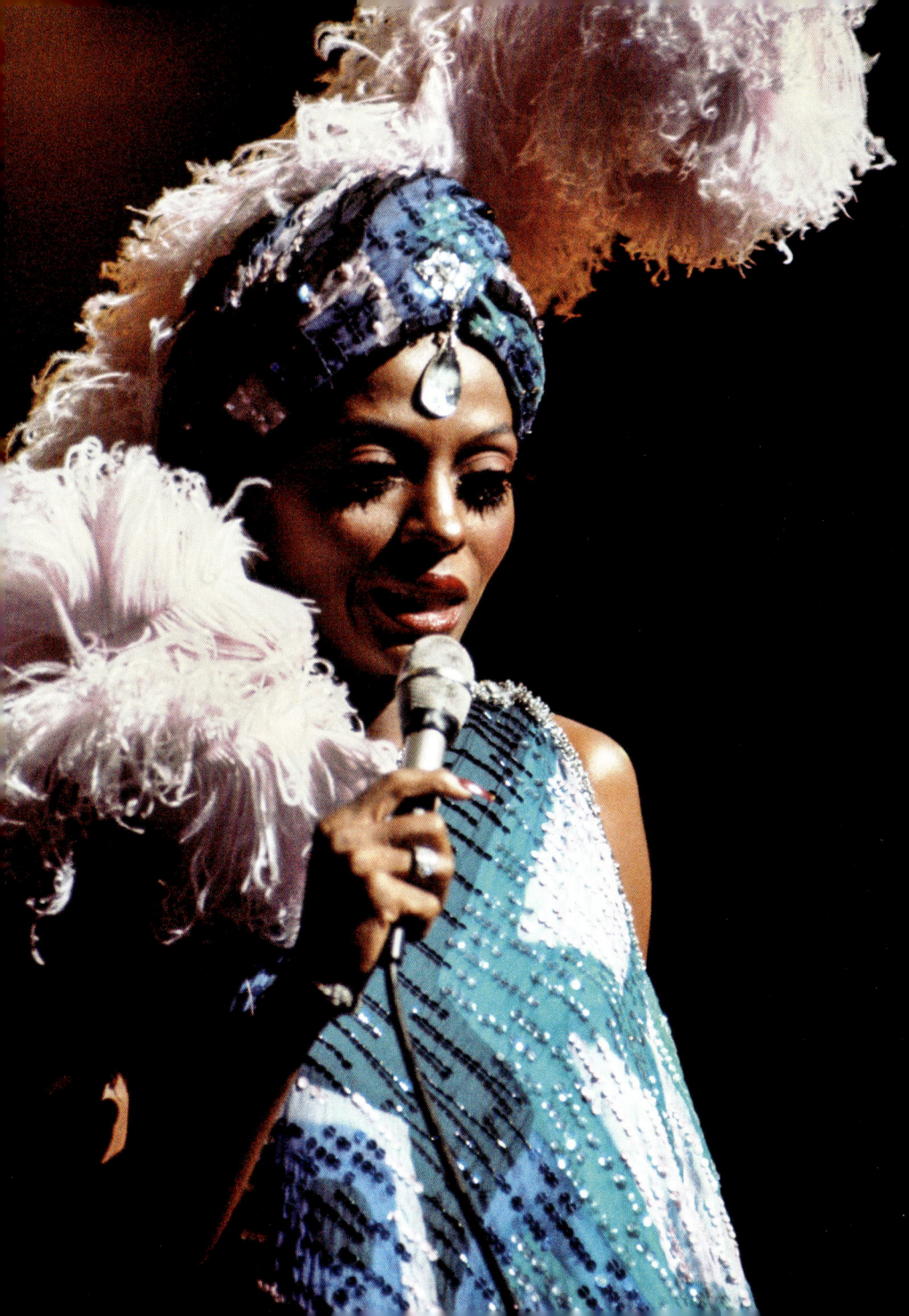

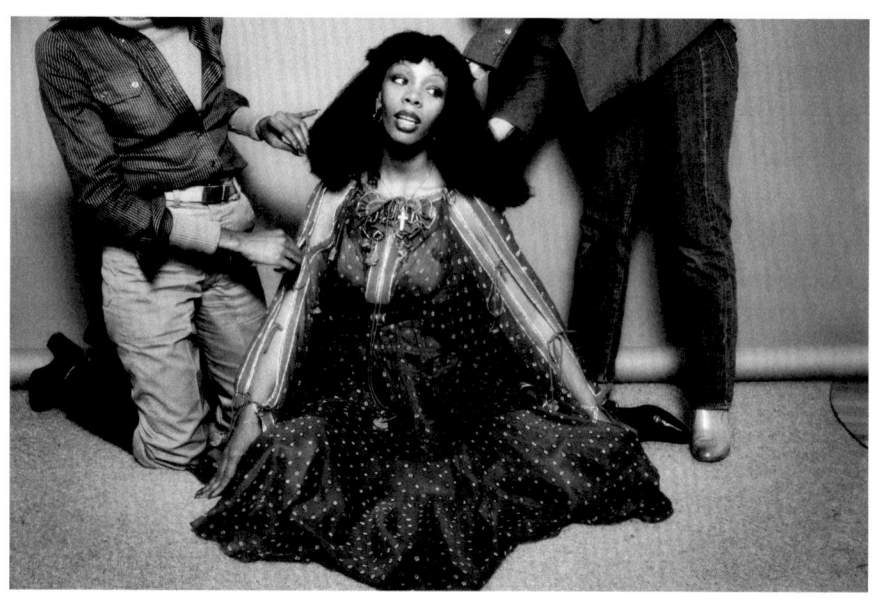

DONNA SUMMER

SOUL Newspaper cover-photo session, Los Angeles, 1977. (Above)
*"Donna Summer's assistants Nellie Prestwood (left) and Pat Naderhoff (right)
adjust her dress before the shoot. When Donna saw that we were serious,
she gave it up, treating us like we were from Vogue or Rolling Stone.
We had fun on that day."* —Bruce Talamon

SOUL Newspaper cover-photo session, Los Angeles, 1977. (Opposite)
The undisputed Queen of Disco, Summer scored a run of hits, including
"Love to Love You Baby," "Last Dance," "Heaven Knows," "Hot Stuff,"
"Bad Girls," and "On the Radio." Recognized for a sensuous yet strong voice,
the five-time Grammy Award winner would have a postdisco era smash with
"She Works Hard for the Money" in 1983.

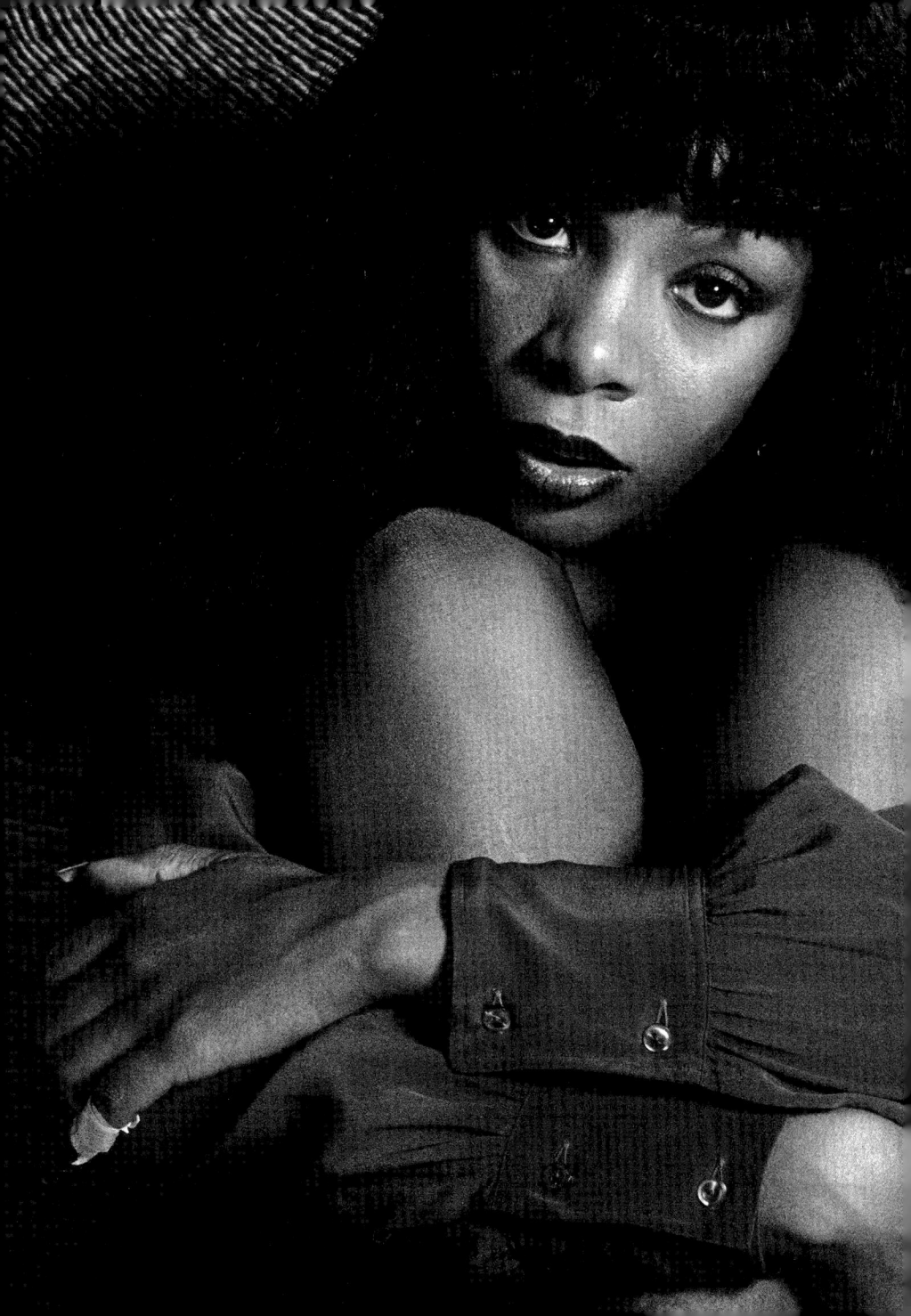

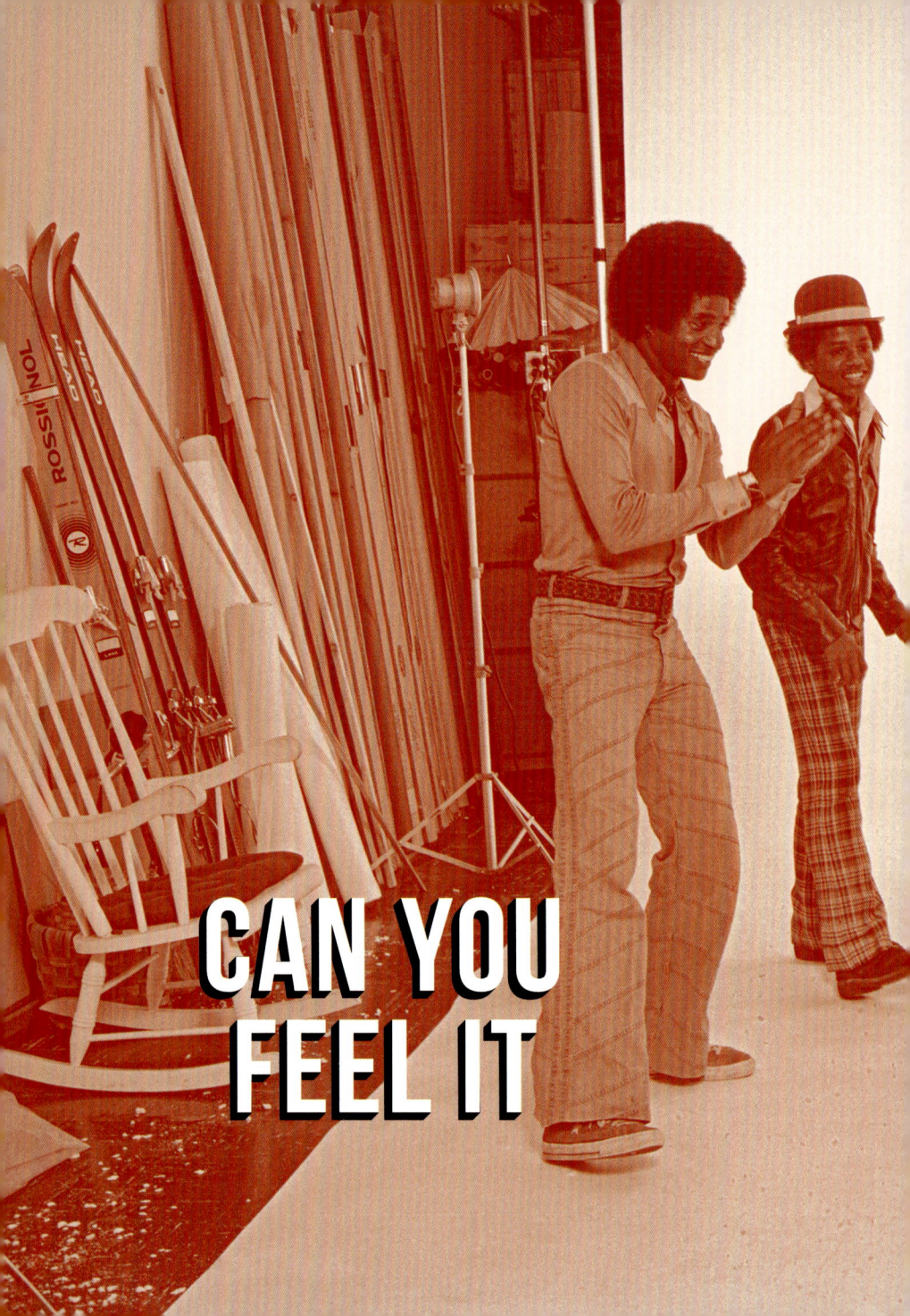

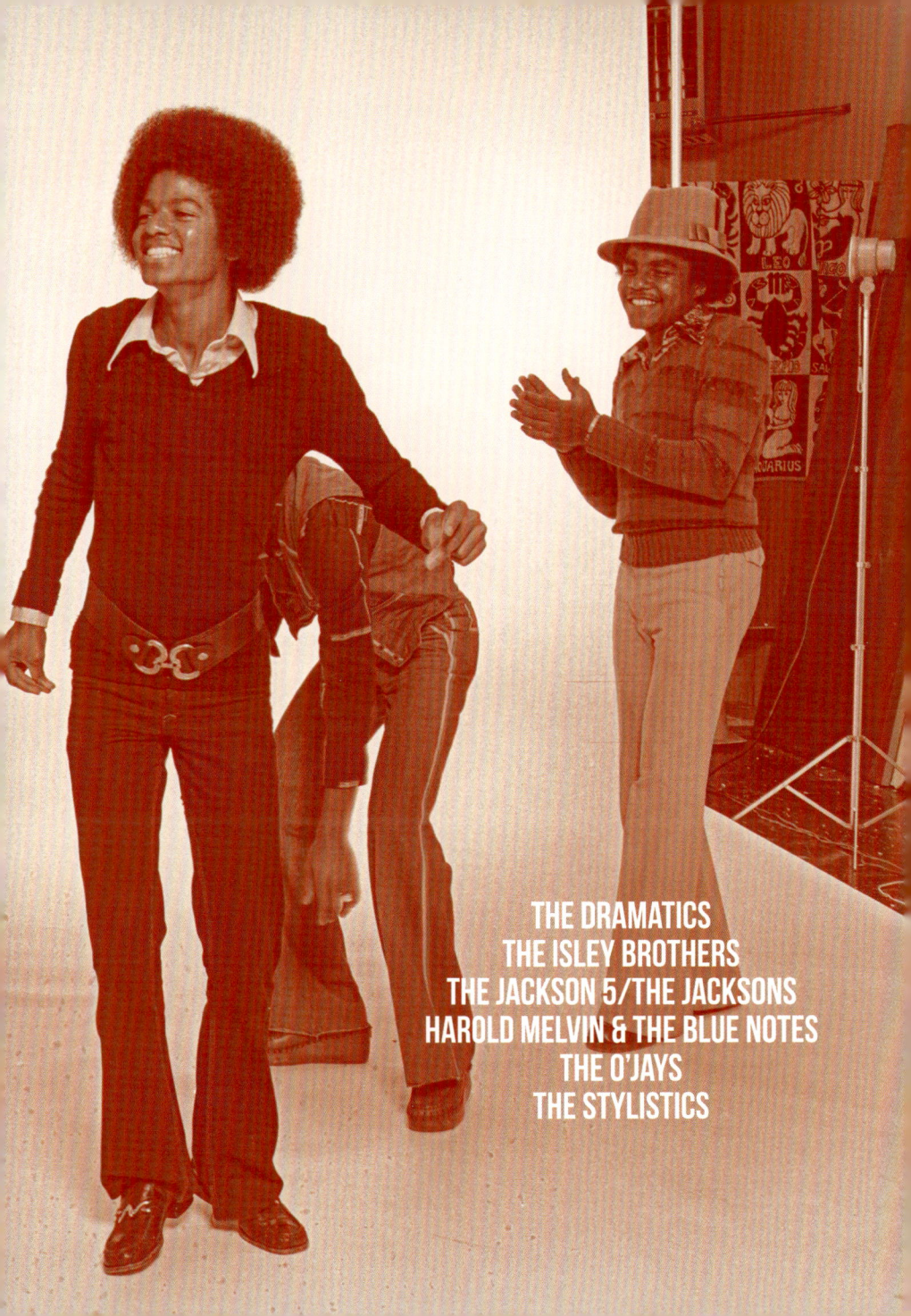

THE DRAMATICS
THE ISLEY BROTHERS
THE JACKSON 5/THE JACKSONS
HAROLD MELVIN & THE BLUE NOTES
THE O'JAYS
THE STYLISTICS

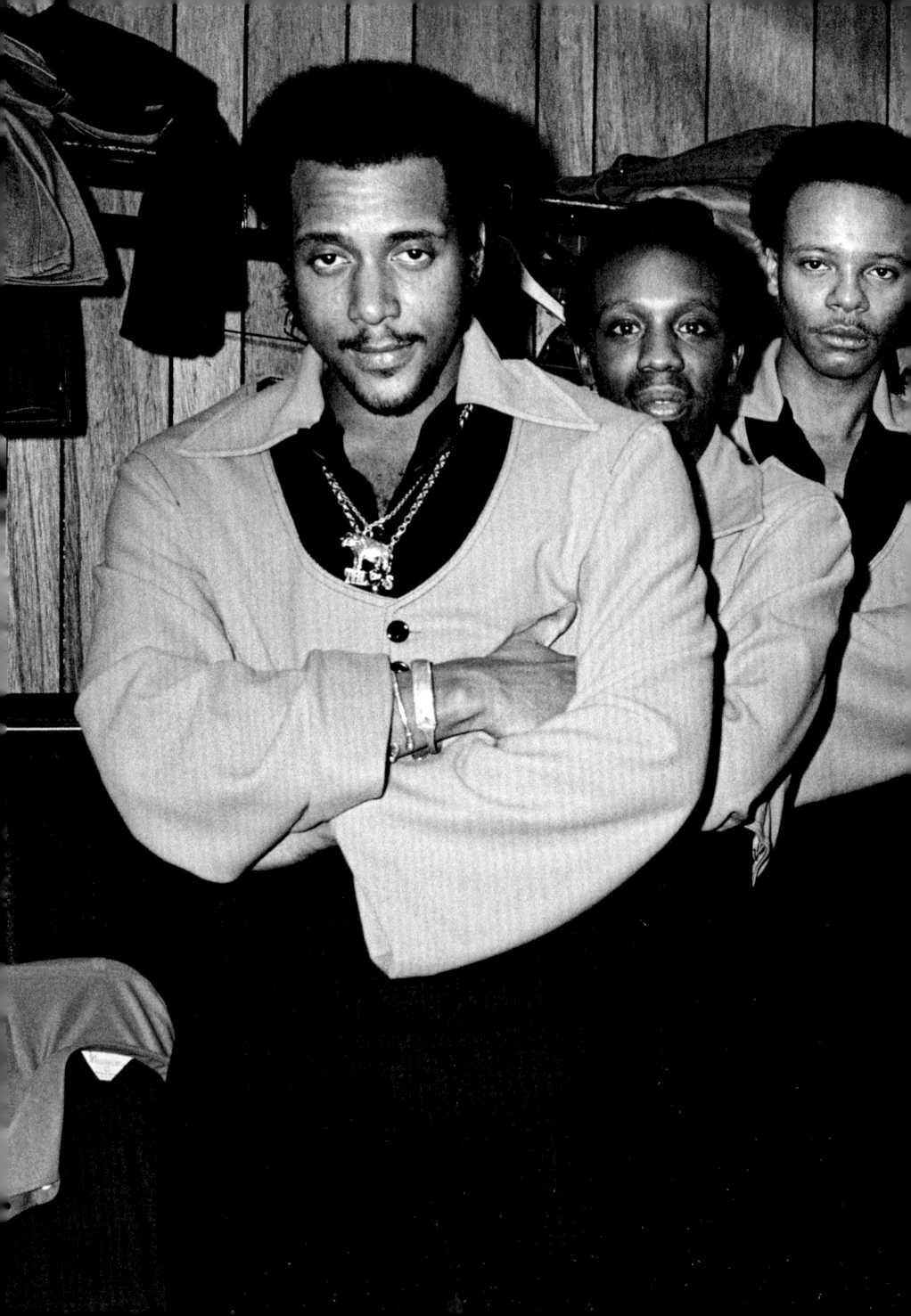

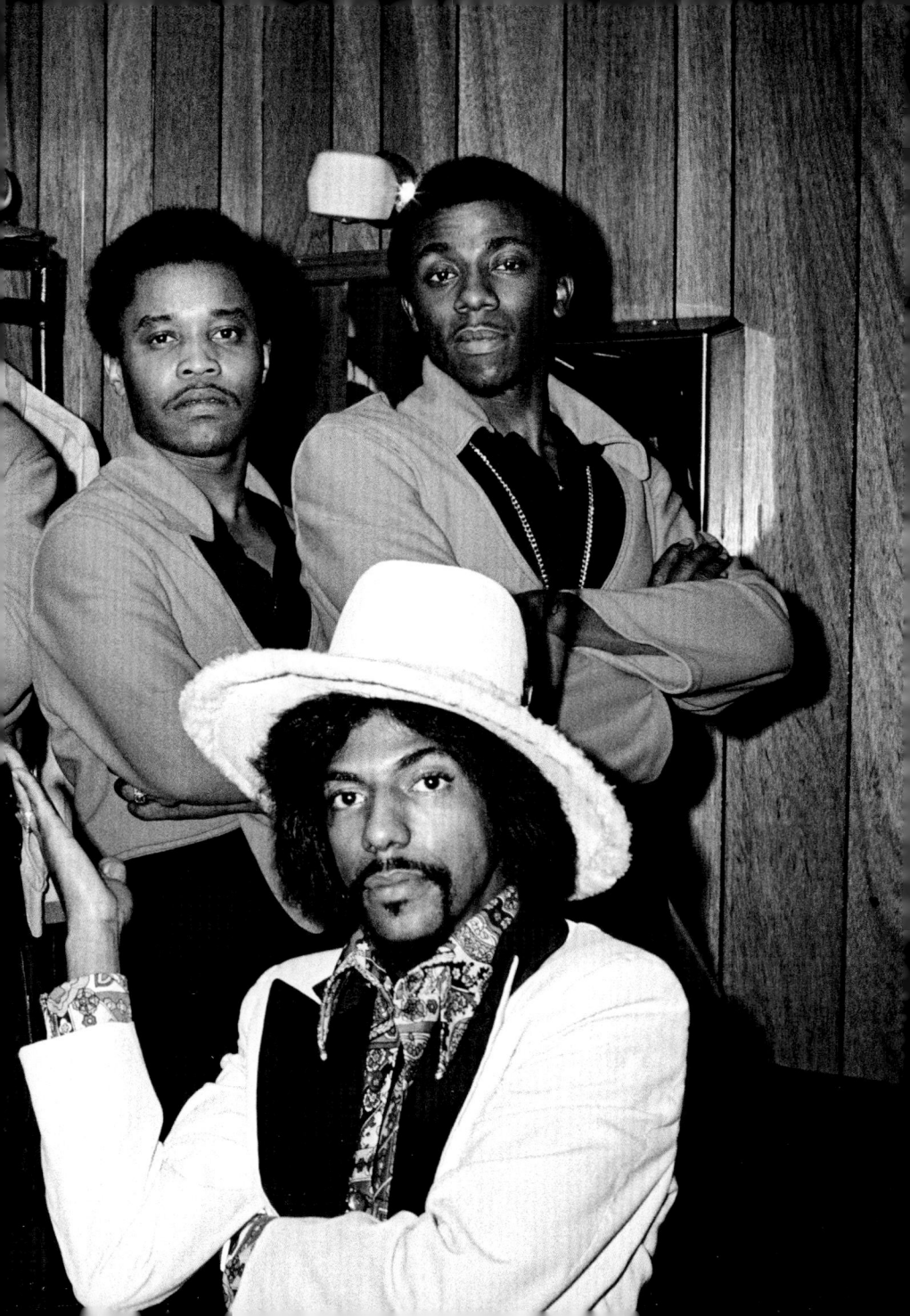

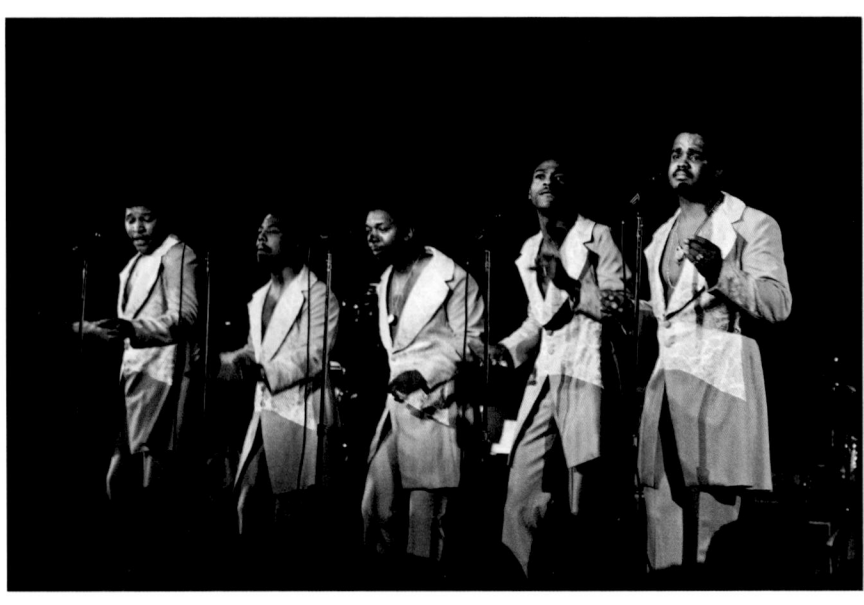

THE JACKSONS
Los Angeles, October 1976. (Pages 66–67)
Taken just after they were signed to Epic Records, the defining characteristic of this photograph is the look on Michael's face. He is free. With the creative restrictions of Motown in his rearview mirror, this is the beginning of a new era for The Jacksons, and especially Michael.

THE DRAMATICS
The Hollywood Palladium, California, 1974. (Pages 68–69)
Who was the man in white? Original member L.J. Reynolds: "That's Champagne, from Detroit! He was with us for 10 or 12 years. He would get the crowd 'in the mood' before we came on. Dancin', spinning around. Best valet and emcee we ever had. Ever!" *"In R&B, there was always somebody who had that role — the guy in the polyester suit with the pressed hair, thick and thin silk socks, and 'gators. That guy who warmed up the crowd. L.J. didn't remember his real name. But for now, we know it's Champagne."* — Bruce Talamon

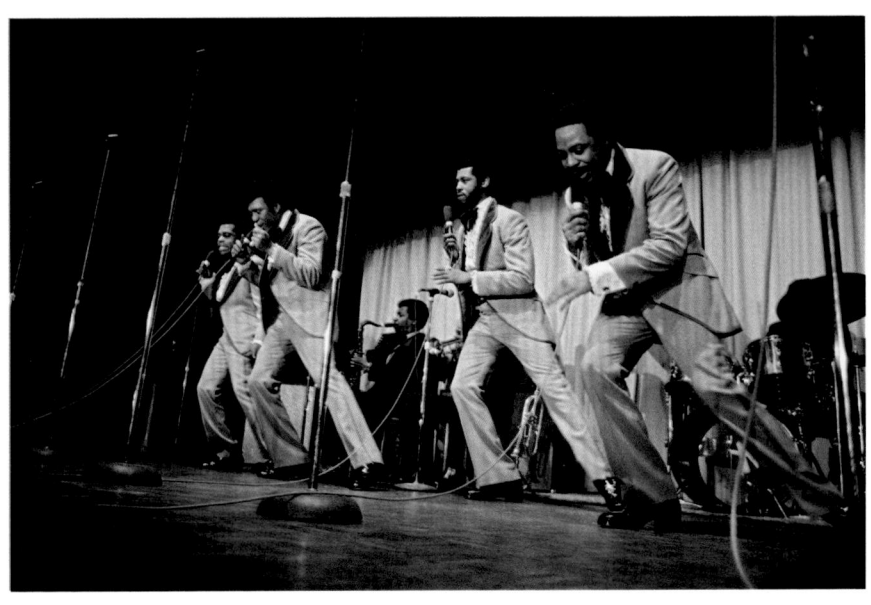

THE STYLISTICS
Los Angeles, 1974. (Opposite)
Possibly the sweetest of the Philadelphia singing groups, The Stylistics were fronted
by the finest falsetto in music, Russell Thompkins Jr. Their Thom Bell-produced,
ballad-heavy music garnered some of the biggest hits of the early 1970s. They were at
their peak with the smash "You Make Me Feel Brand New" when this photo was taken.

HAROLD MELVIN & THE BLUE NOTES
The Soul Train Club, Los Angeles, October 1973. (Above)
"Opening night for Don Cornelius' new nightclub venture, and The Blue Notes,
featuring a 23-year-old Teddy Pendergrass, were the main attraction. I remember
the powder-blue polyester tuxedos. I love the fact that I captured them midslide.
You don't see choreography like that anymore. It's a lost art." — Bruce Talamon

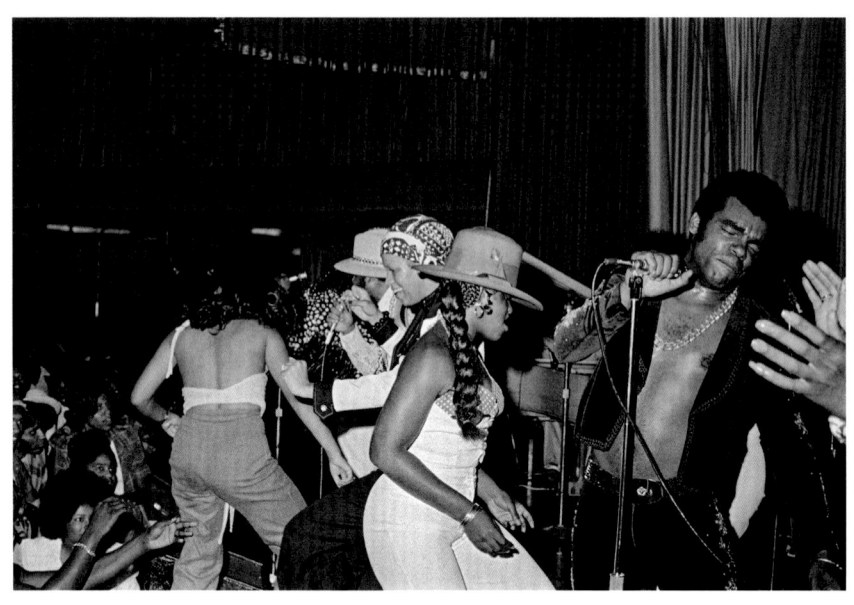

THE ISLEY BROTHERS
San Diego, California, 1973.
At the end of their show, Ronald Isley summoned girls one by one
to join the band onstage. Soon it was a crowded, chaotic celebration.

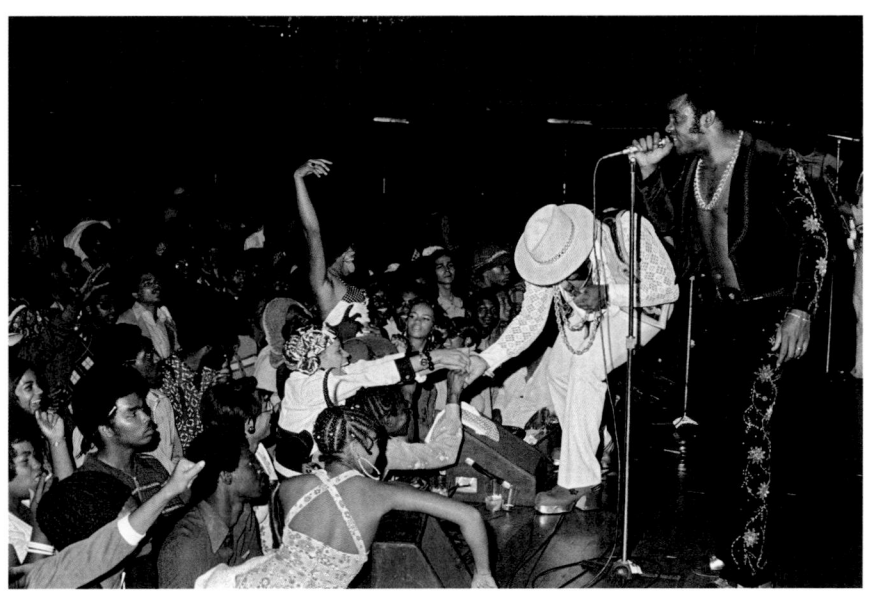

THE ISLEY BROTHERS
San Diego, California, 1973.
The Isley Brothers started in the late 1950s and have lasted 50 years.
Adding in-law and keyboardist Chris Jasper to the band in the early
1970s, along with brothers Marvin on bass and Ernie on guitar, led to
their most prolific, funky, and fruitful period.

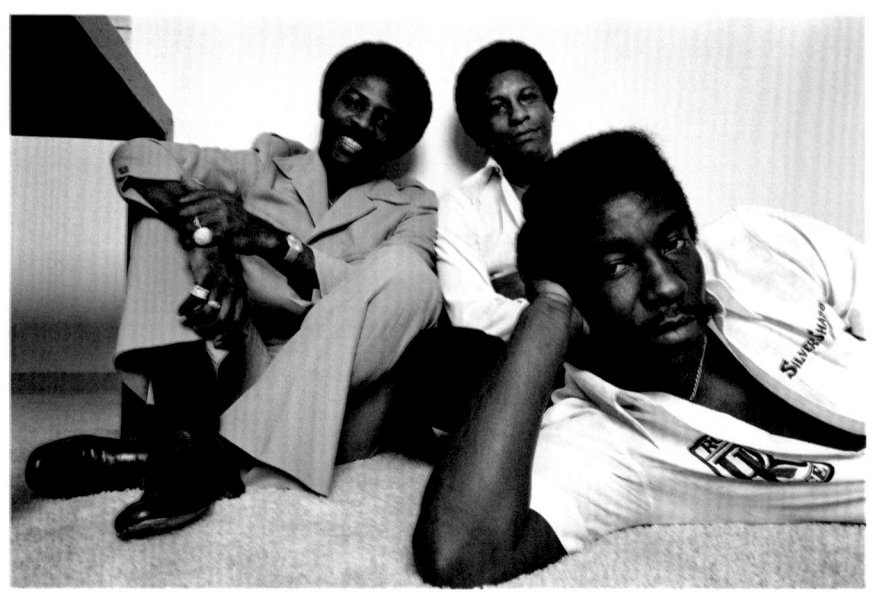

THE O'JAYS
Los Angeles, 1977. (Above)
The mighty O'Jays have recorded some of the most distinctive songs in the
Philadelphia soul catalog. Their chart-topping "Love Train," "For the Love of
Money," "Back Stabbers," and "Family Affair" embody the social-awareness side of
the legendary production and songwriting team of Kenny Gamble and Leon Huff.

The Forum, Inglewood, California, June 1977. (Opposite)
By the time the group gets to the end of their show, belting out "Love Train,"
Eddie Levert is in full flight.

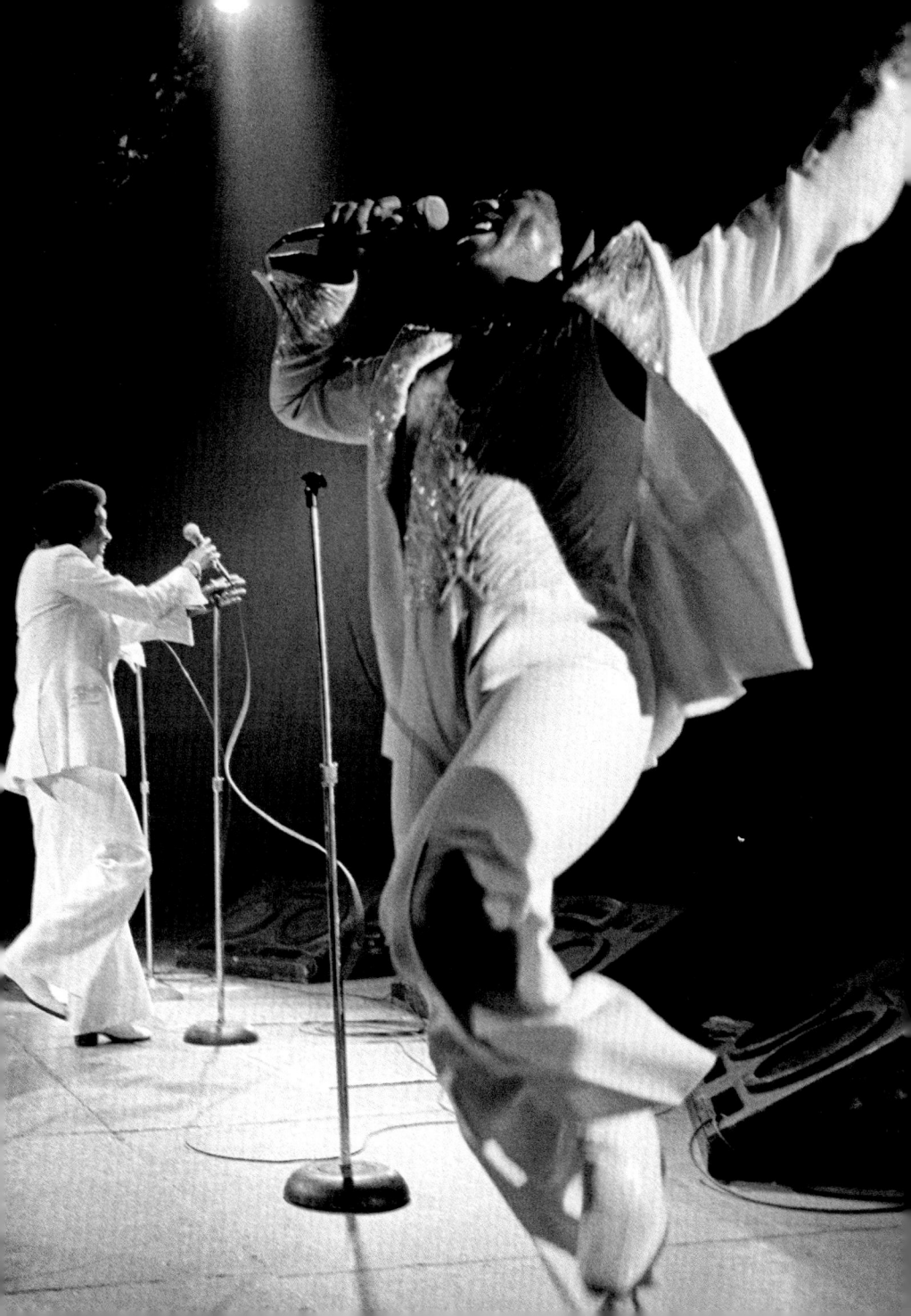

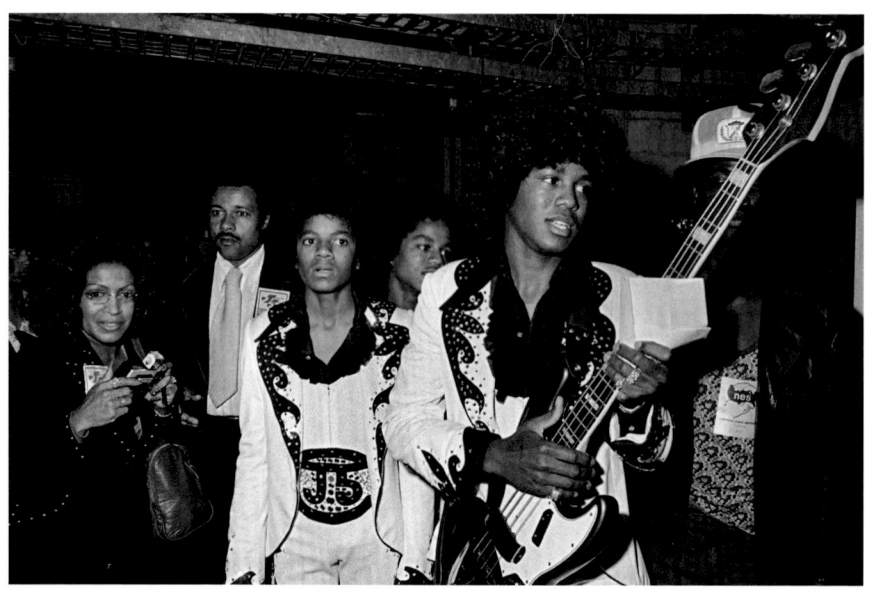

THE JACKSON 5

The Forum, Inglewood, California, June 1974.

It's showtime. Look at Michael's eyes. They missed nothing. The future
King of Pop knew early on that you had to bring down the house.

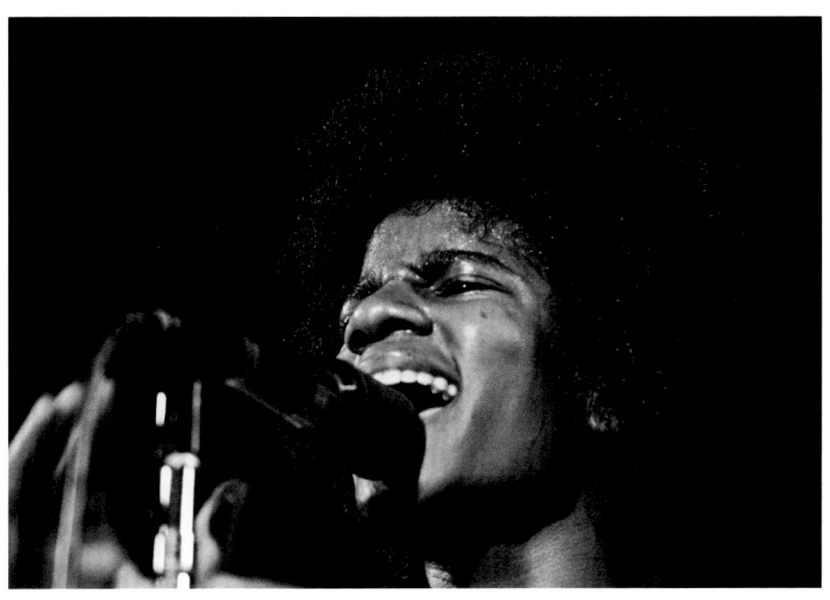

THE JACKSON 5
The Forum, Inglewood, California, June 1974. (Above)
The Michael Jackson story must be one of the most incredible
in show-business history. But it started with his voice.

The Forum, Inglewood, California, June 1974. (Pages 78–79)
Shell-shocked. The boundary between exhaustion and exhilaration
is blurred. Inside the limo after the performance.

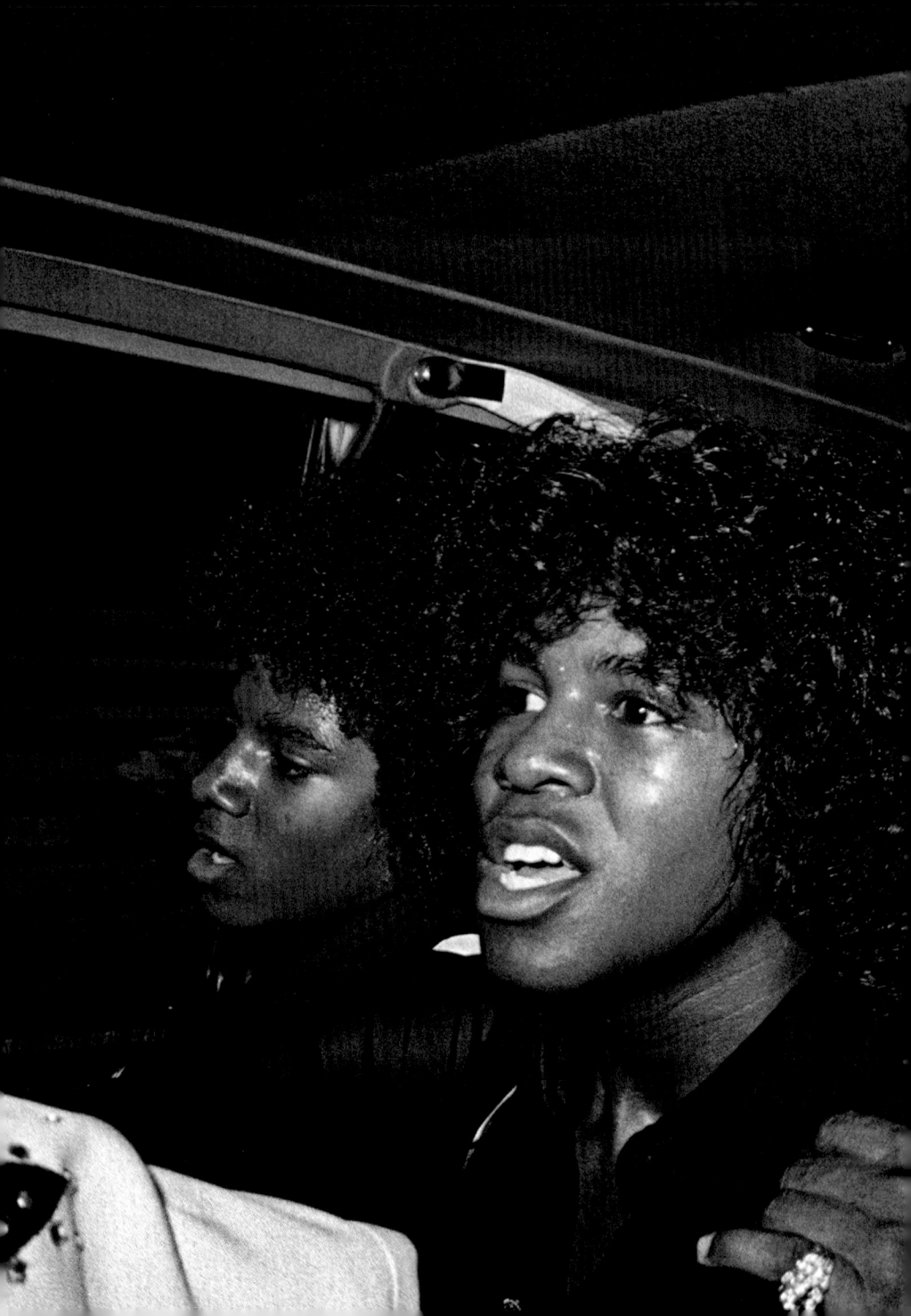

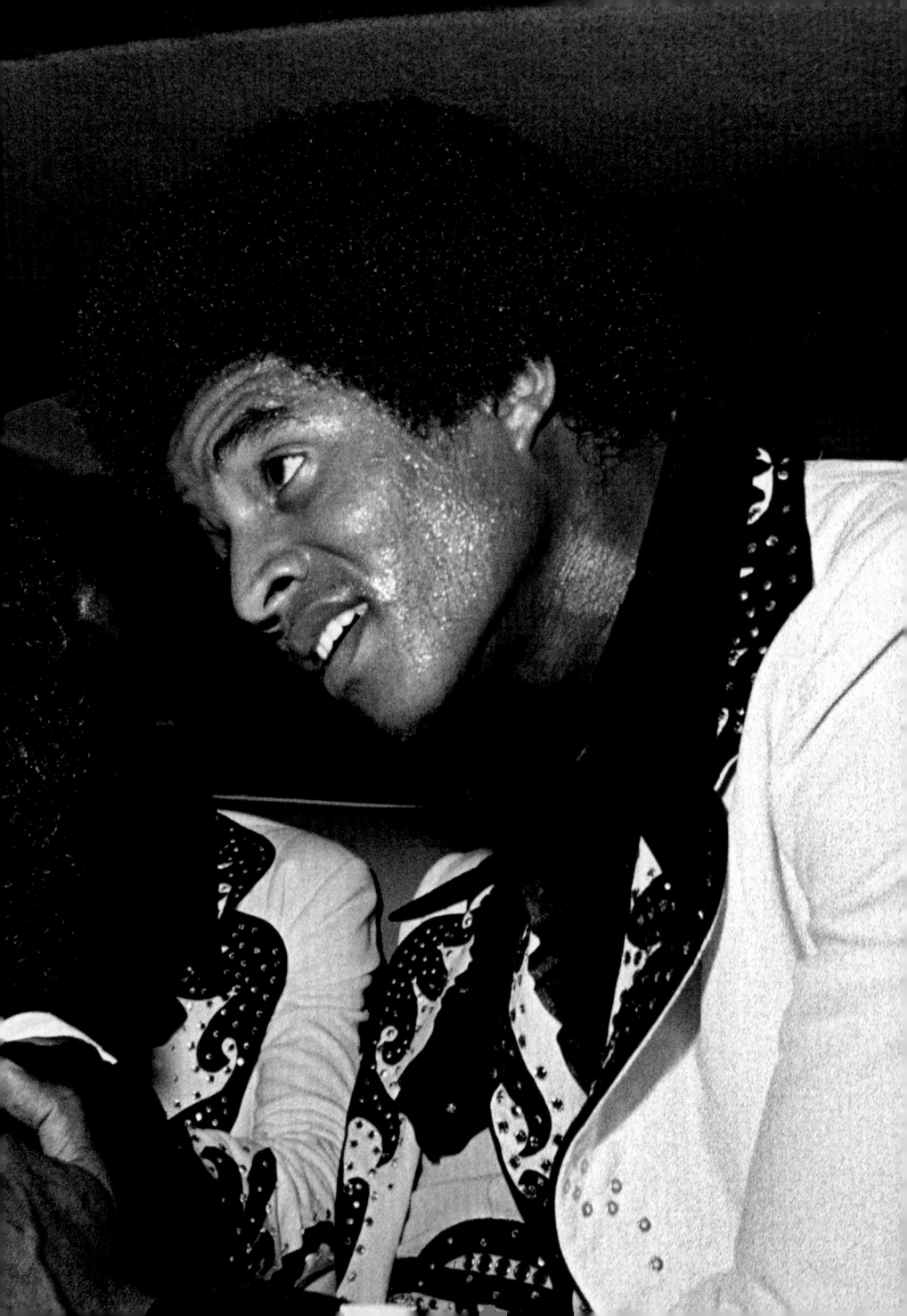

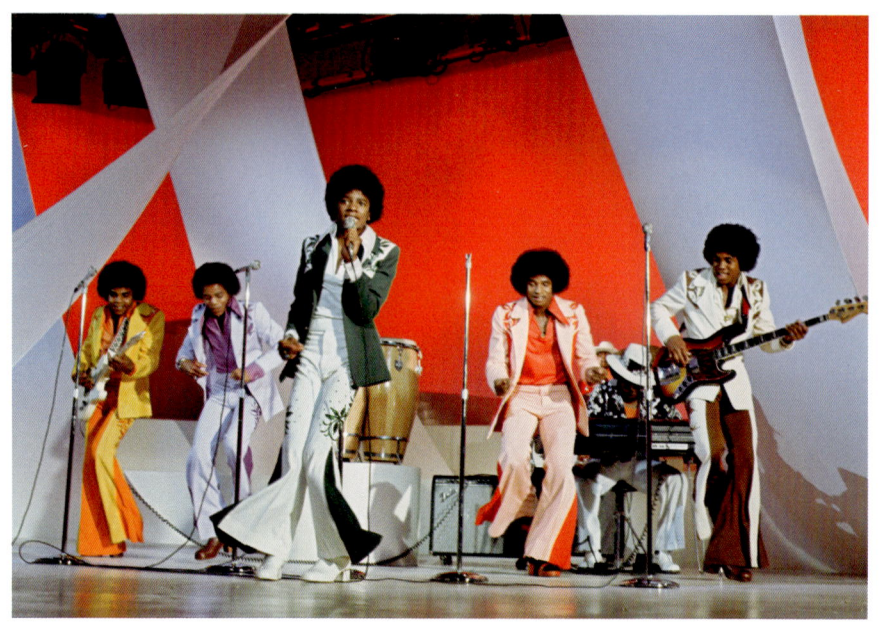

THE JACKSON 5
CBS Television Center, Los Angeles, 1974.

The Jackson 5 appeared endlessly on television between 1971 and
1975. On the short-lived CBS variety series *One More Time*, they
perform a medley of their hits attired in the hot colors of the 1970s.

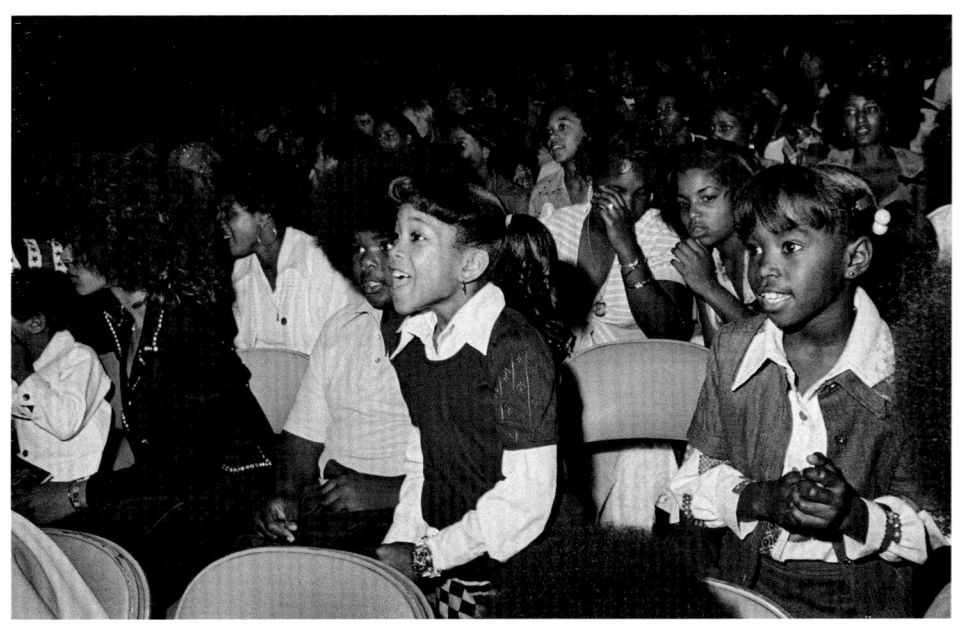

THE JACKSON 5
The Forum, Inglewood, California, 1974. (Above)
*"Before he conquered the world, Michael Jackson belonged to little black girls
from places like Chicago, Detroit, Harlem, Los Angeles, Houston, Atlanta,
Charlotte, and Memphis. Little black boys wanted to be Michael Jackson.
They learned the steps and played the 45s. If they were lucky, their heroes
came to town, and for that one night, it was magic."* — Bruce Talamon

Motown company basketball game, Los Angeles, 1974. (Pages 82–83)
Katherine, Janet, Michael, and Randy Jackson with Bill Bray. Bray was a
retired police officer when he began working as security chief for the J5 in the
early 1970s. He worked with Michael through his iconic *Thriller* days and beyond.

THE JACKSONS
Los Angeles, 1976. (Pages 84–85)

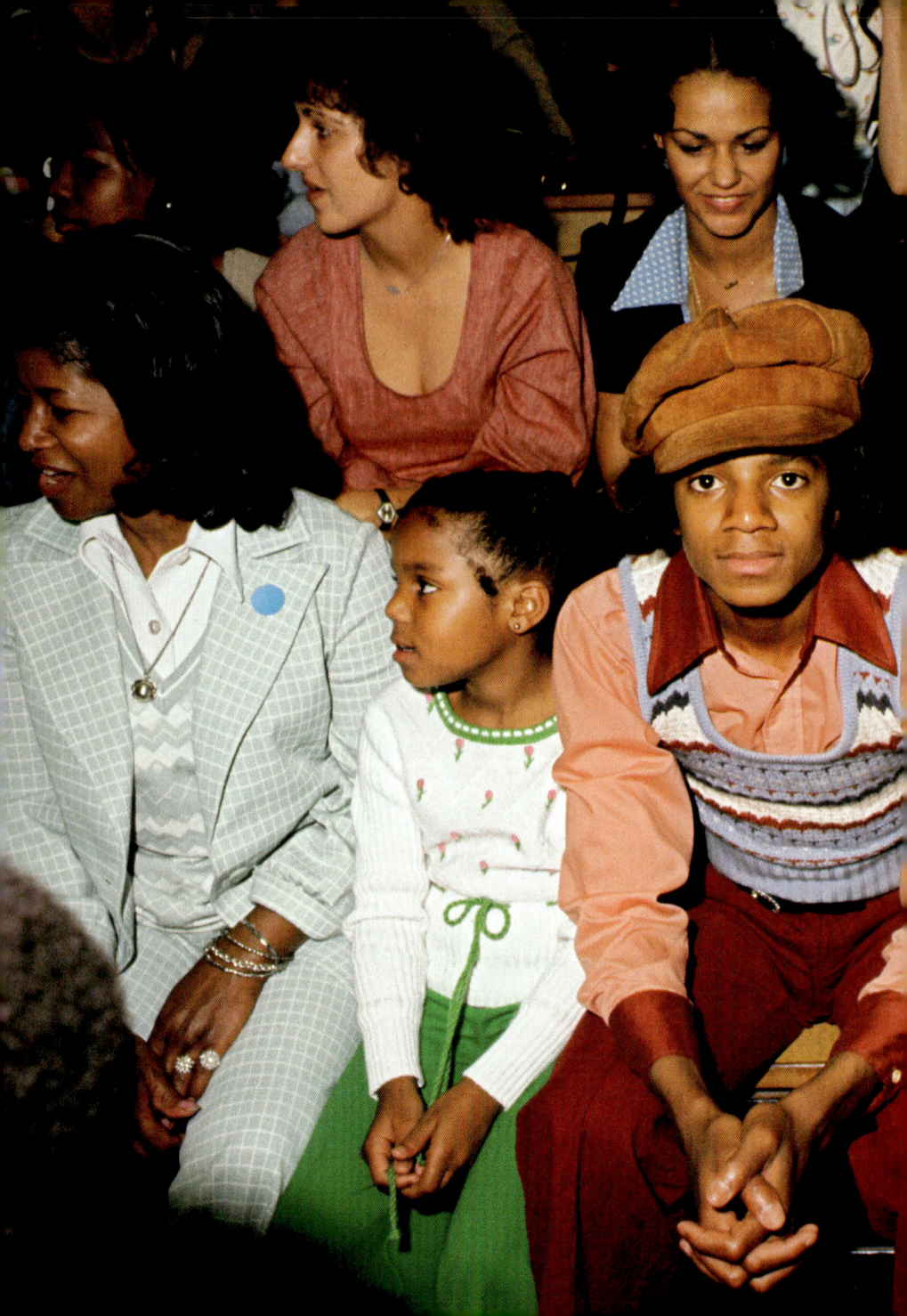

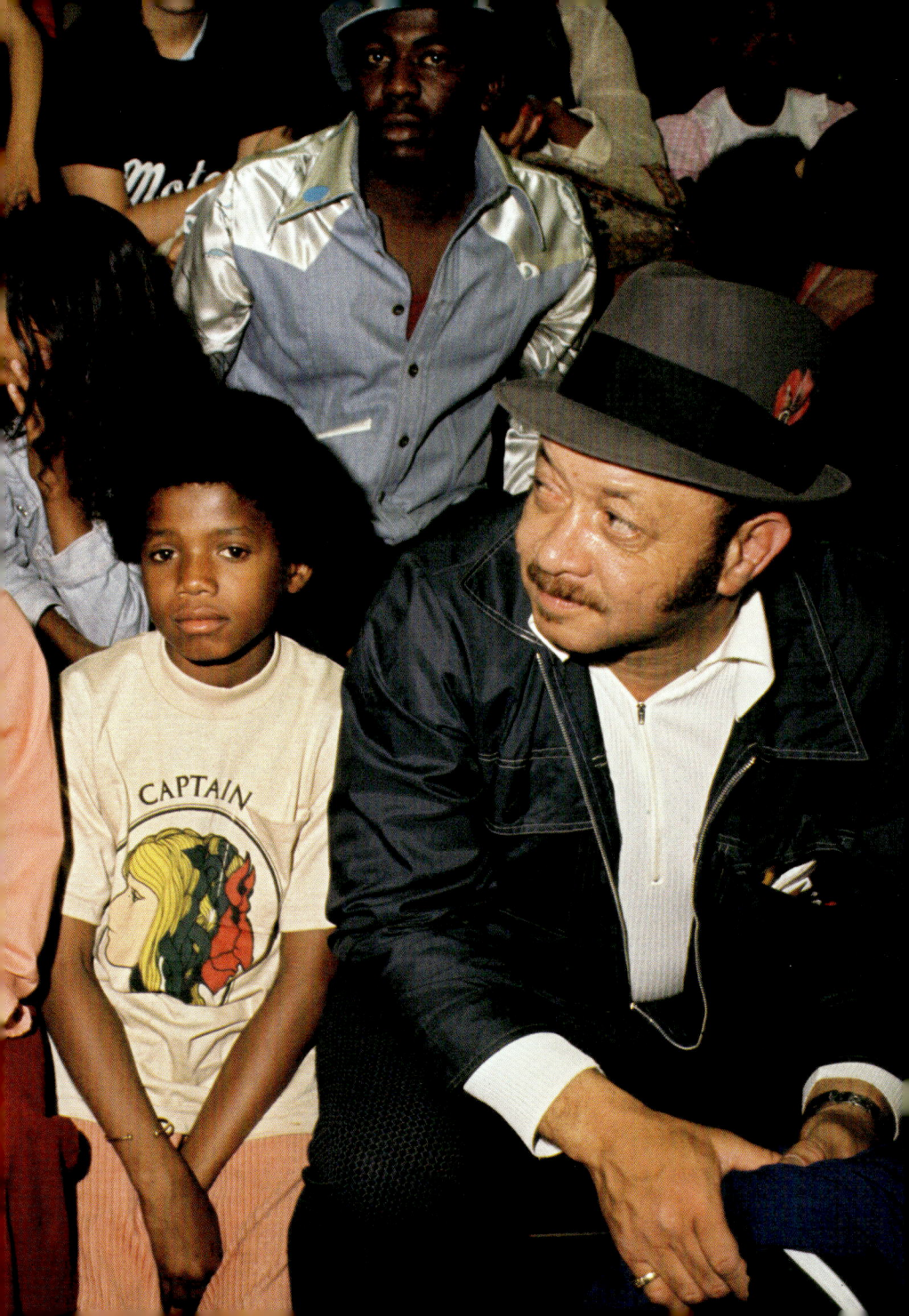

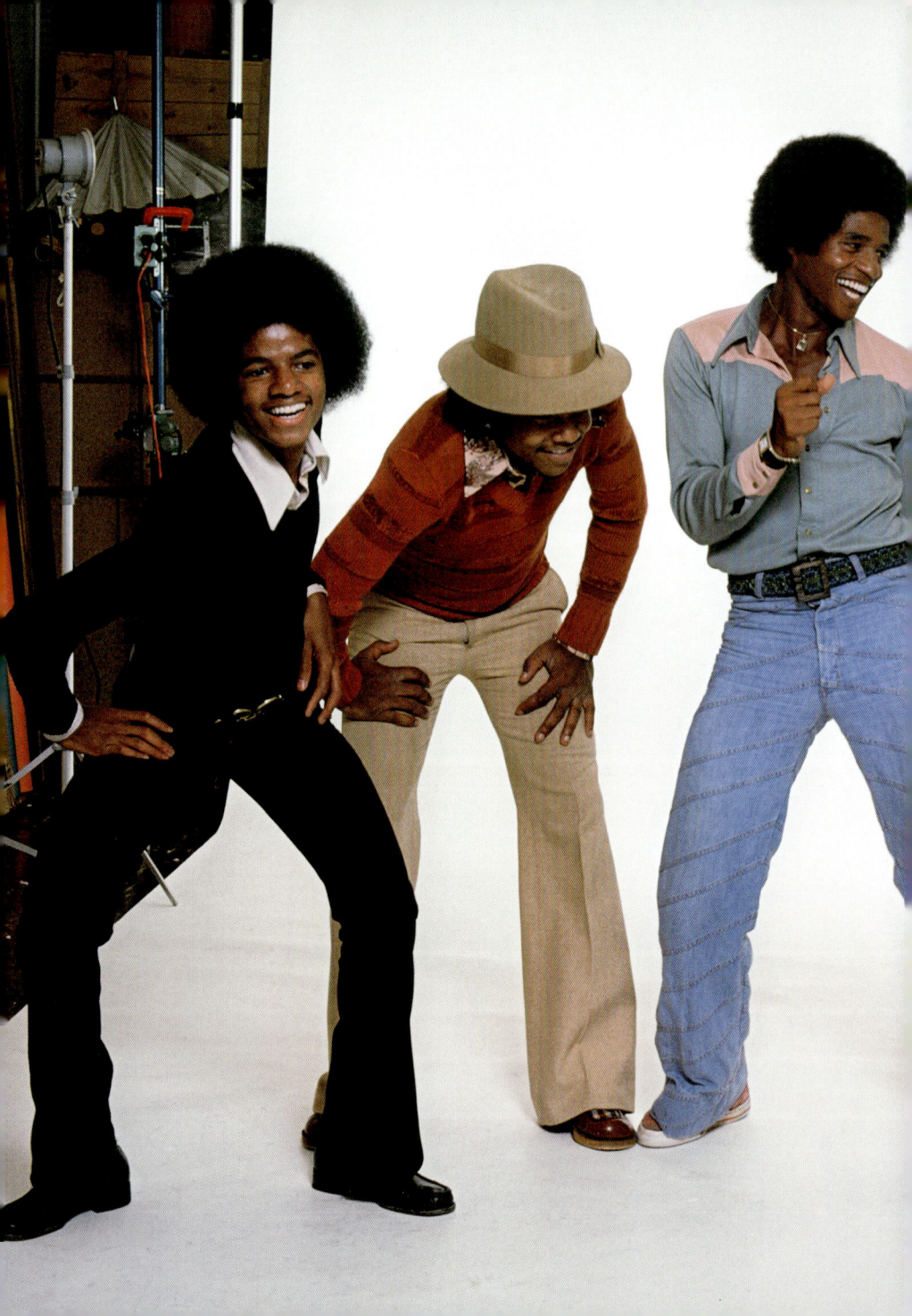

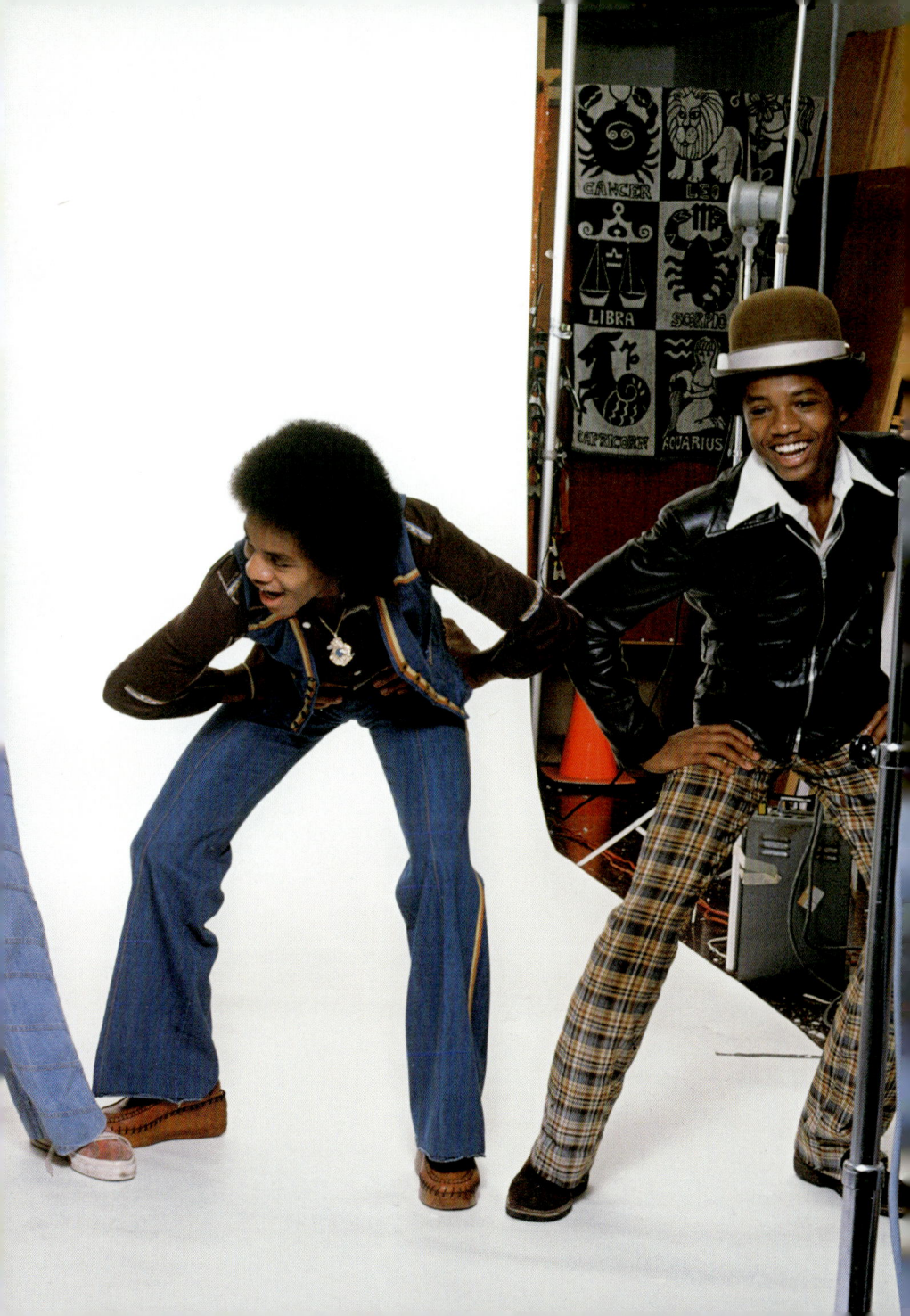

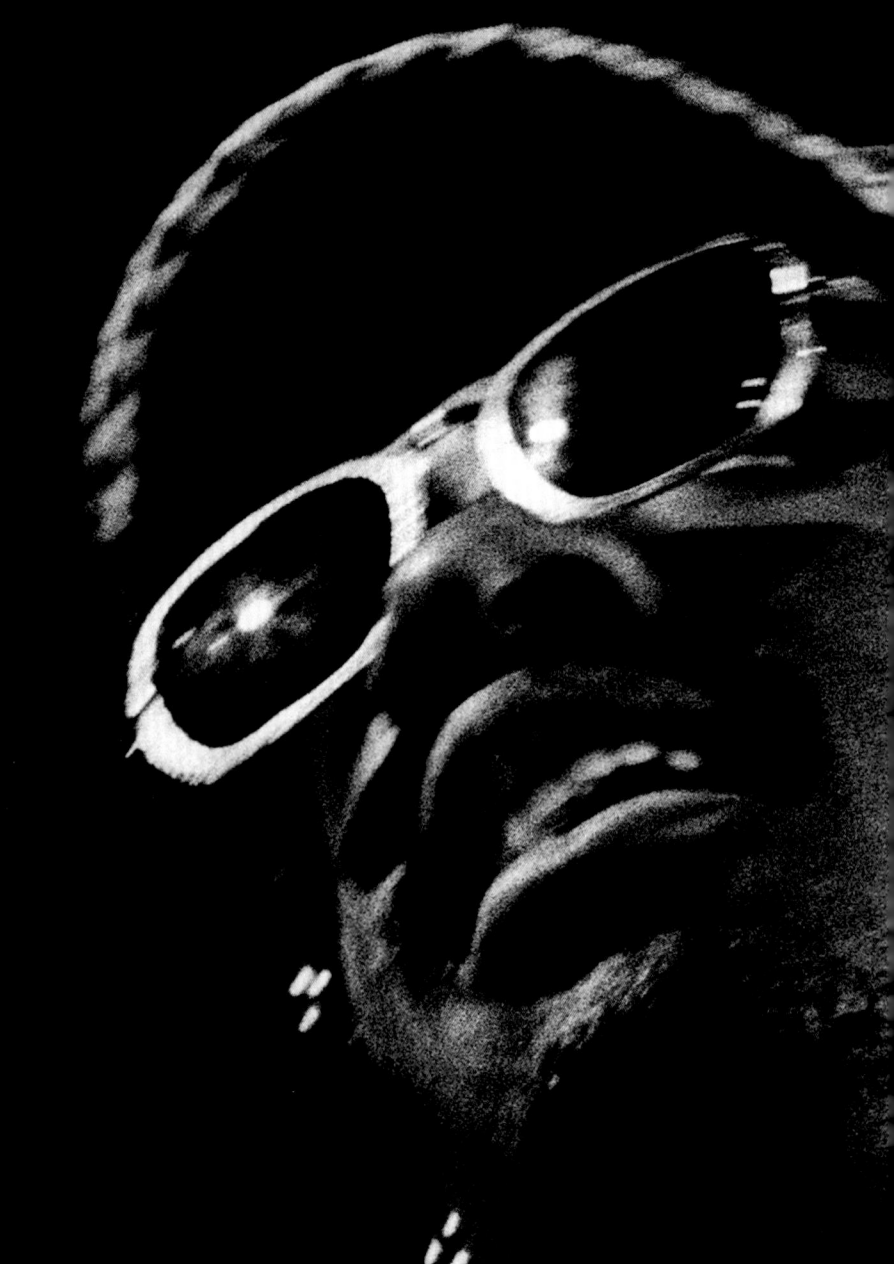

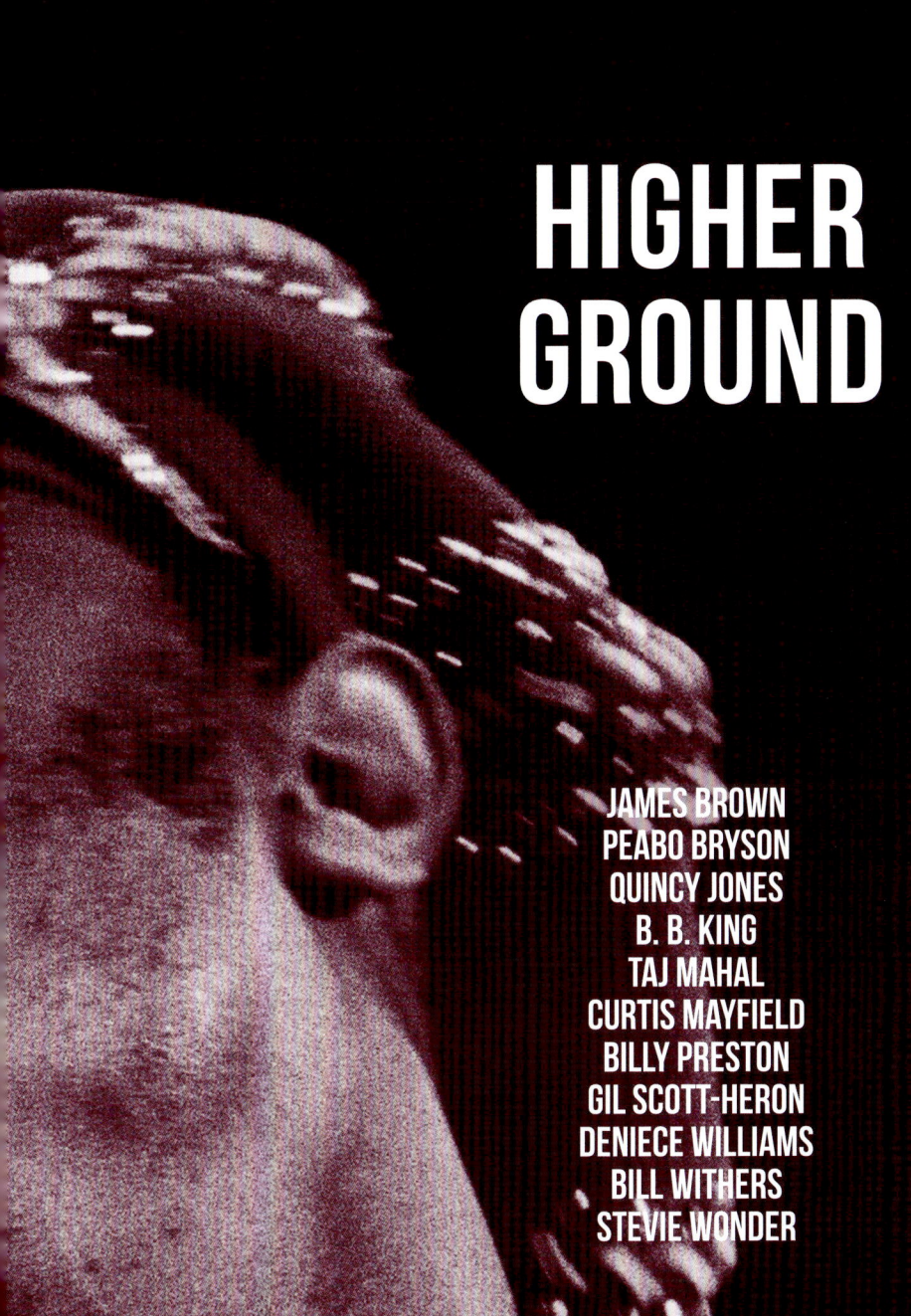

HIGHER
GROUND

JAMES BROWN
PEABO BRYSON
QUINCY JONES
B. B. KING
TAJ MAHAL
CURTIS MAYFIELD
BILLY PRESTON
GIL SCOTT-HERON
DENIECE WILLIAMS
BILL WITHERS
STEVIE WONDER

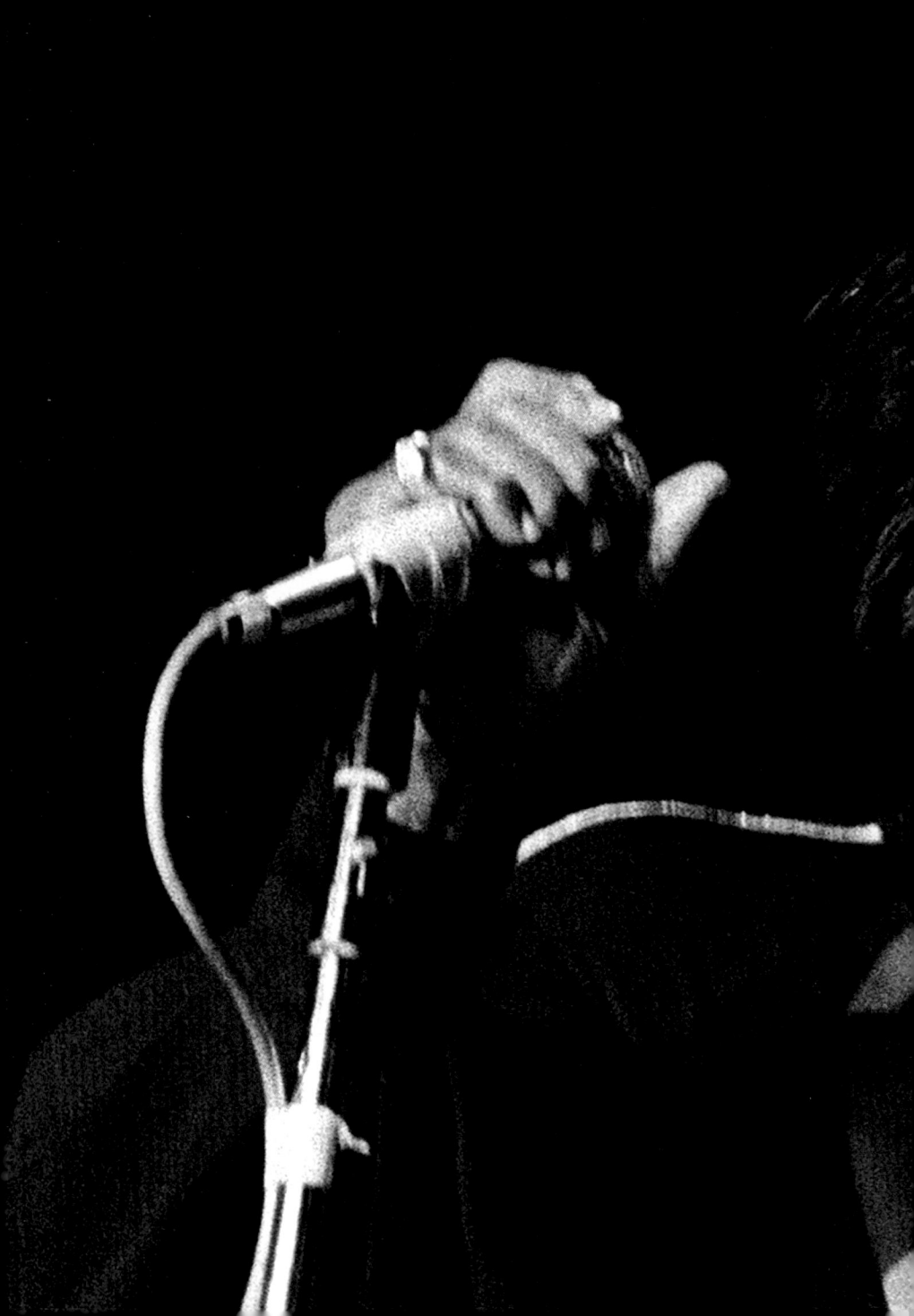

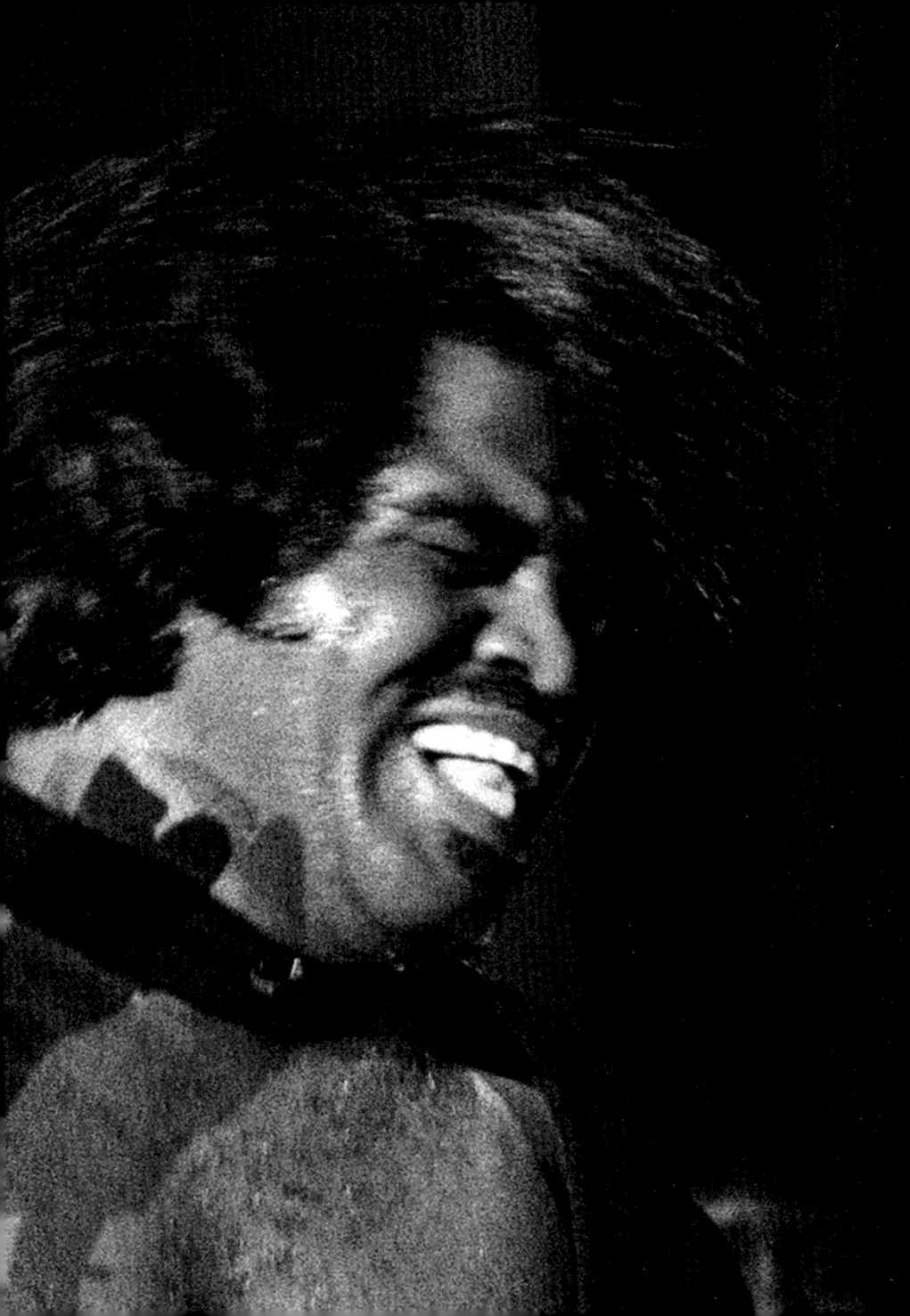

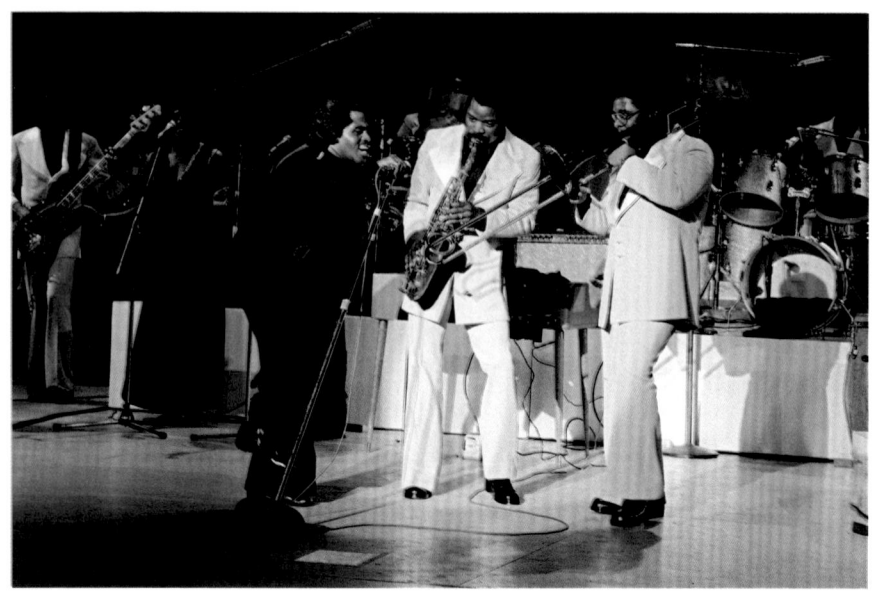

STEVIE WONDER
Los Angeles, 1974. (Pages 86–87)

JAMES BROWN
ABC Television Center, Hollywood, California, 1973. (Pages 88–89)
*"ABC censors sent word that James Brown had to change his costume or
he couldn't perform. Brown wore a black jumpsuit with an 8-inch-wide oval
stitched in white. In the middle of that oval were three letters: S-E-X.
What followed was a test of wills. Dick Clark versus James Brown. Finally, a
compromise: tape over the offending letters. Crisis averted."* — Bruce Talamon

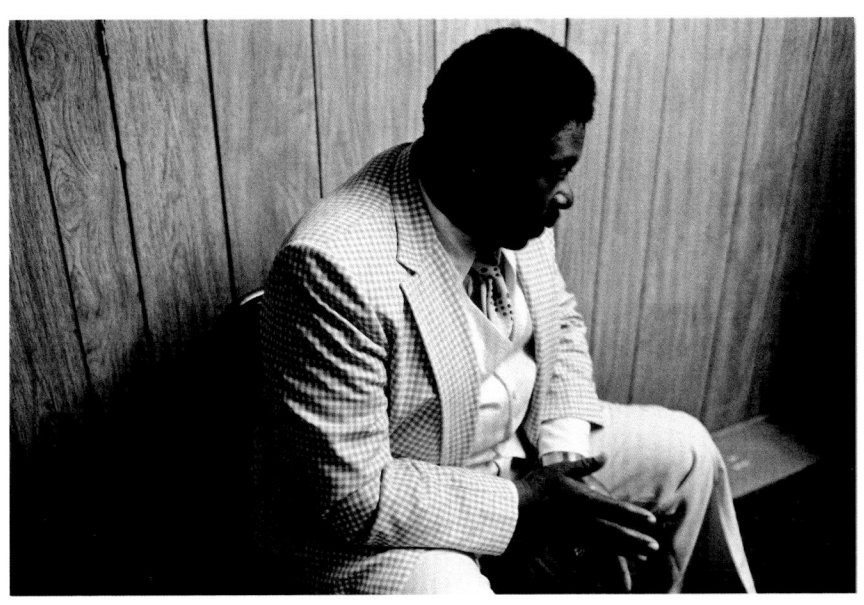

JAMES BROWN
ABC Television Center, In Concert, Hollywood, California, 1973. (Opposite)
Hit Me, Fred!: Fans of Brown knew who Maceo Parker and Fred Wesley were.
The Godfather of Soul would often shout out to them onstage and on recordings.

B. B. KING
The Roxy, West Hollywood, California, 1978. (Above)
King of the road: Starting in 1952 and ending around 2013, B. B. played
225 dates a year. That's 61 years. No one has even come close
to that amount of time spent on the road. Here, he has a quiet moment
before walking out to bring down the house yet again.

CURTIS MAYFIELD

**Santa Monica Civic Auditorium, Santa Monica,
California, 1972. (Opposite)**

An acknowledged masterpiece of the 1970s, Mayfield's *Superfly* film
score elevated him to superstar status as an artist, writer, and producer.
But Mayfield is also remembered for his earlier consciousness-raising
music with The Impressions.

GIL SCOTT-HERON, BRIAN JACKSON AND THE MIDNIGHT BAND

The Roxy, West Hollywood, California, 1978. (Pages 94–95)

BILLY PRESTON

**Santa Monica Civic Auditorium, Santa Monica,
California, 1974. (Pages 96–97)**

Sometimes called the Fifth Beatle or the Black Beatle, Preston was
so much more than his unique collaboration with the Fab Four. A child
prodigy on the organ, he would perform with Mahalia Jackson and
Nat King Cole, and tour with Little Richard. When this luminous
photo was taken, he was riding high with two number-one smash hits,
"Will It Go Round in Circles" and "Nothing from Nothing."

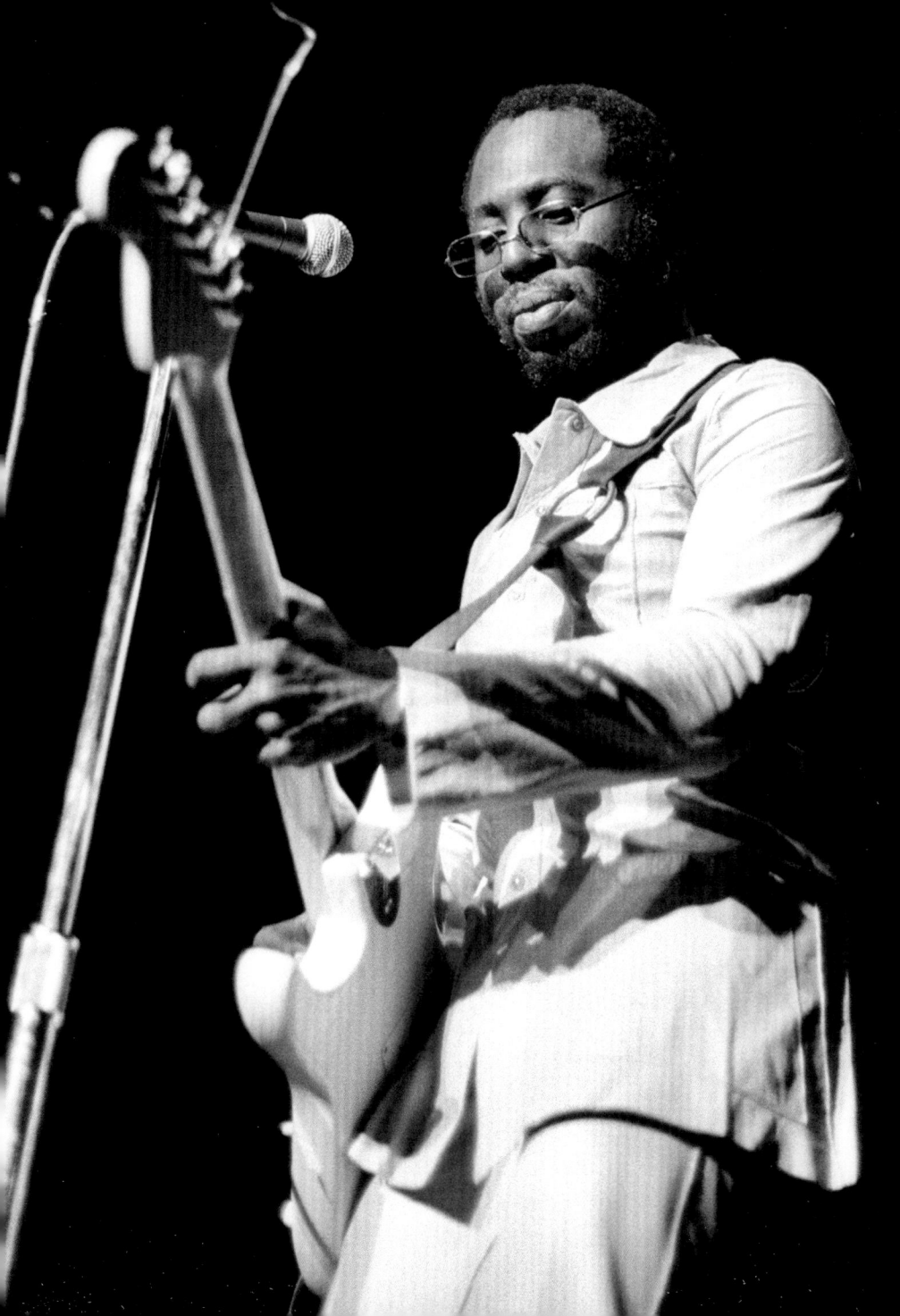

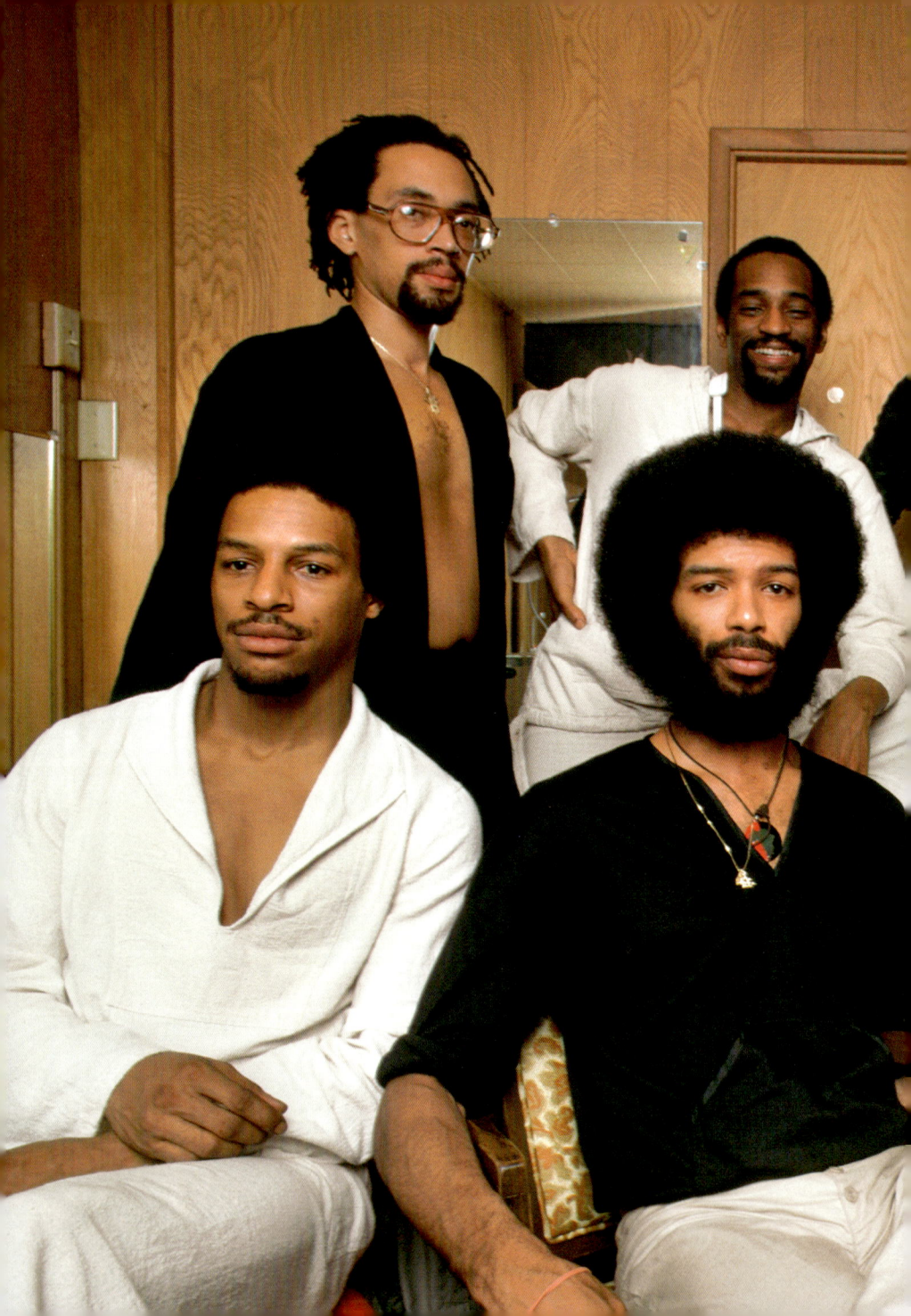

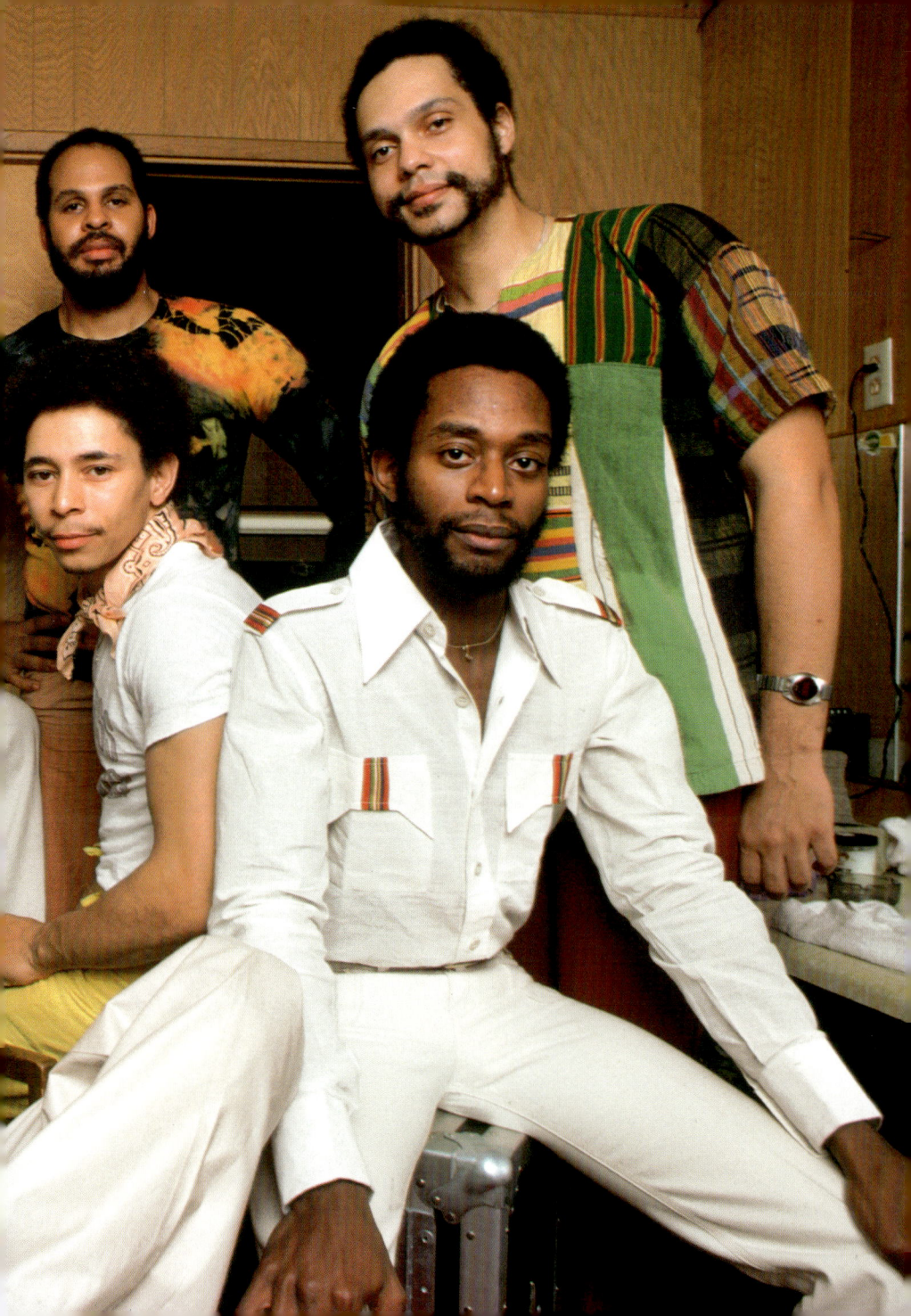

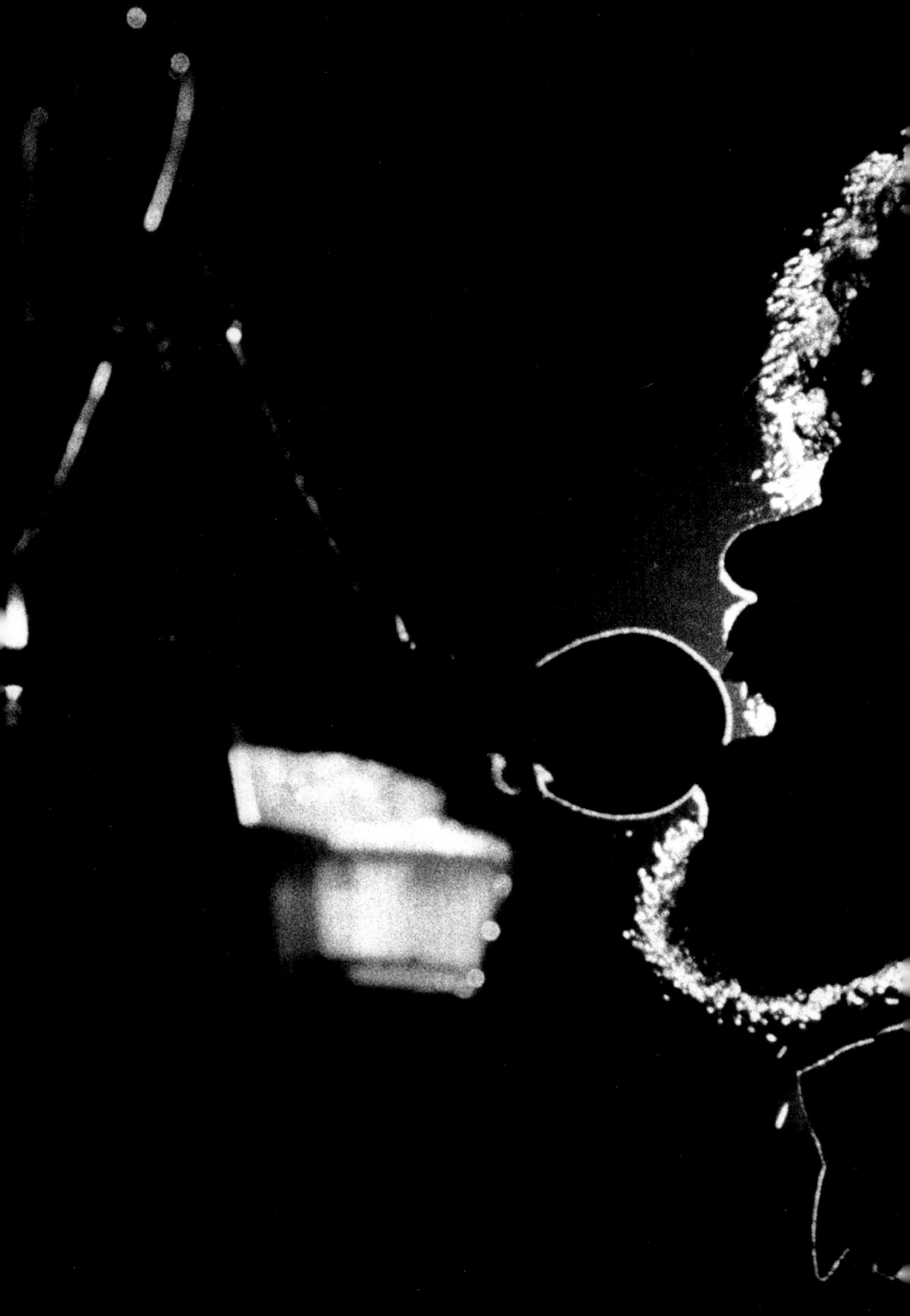

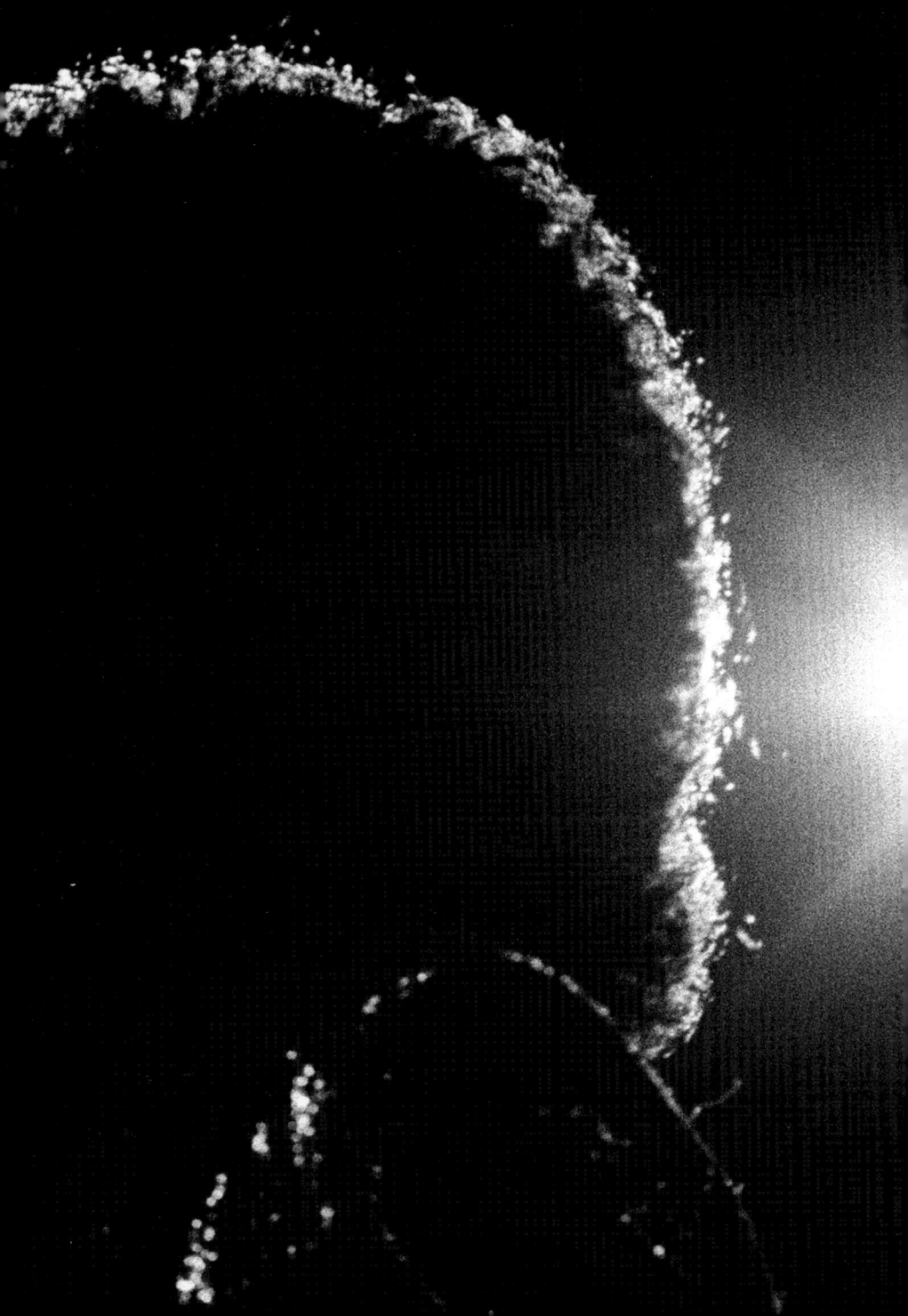

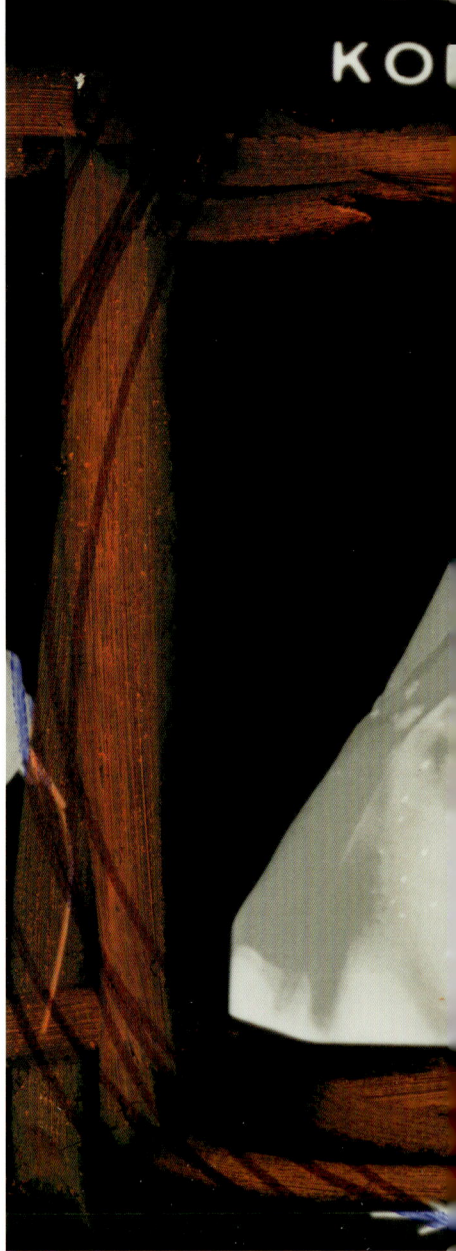

PEABO BRYSON
The Greek Theatre, Los Angeles, 1979.
(Opposite)
With a soulful yet piercing tenor voice, Bryson
exploded on the scene with the passionate R&B
ballads "Feel the Fire" and "I'm So Into You."
But it would be his Disney soundtrack duets with
Regina Belle and Celine Dion that would later
garner his pop success and two Grammy Awards.

BILL WITHERS
Los Angeles, November 1978. (Pages 100–101)
*"The session was at Bill's house. My equipment was
basic — a Norman 800D strobe pack, three heads,
and a red vinyl background. I used a ring light,
which produced a shadowless effect. Bill Withers
answered the door, and after a few seconds eyeing
my equipment, he invited me in. No assistants,
no hair or makeup. Just Bill and me. Before we
wrapped, I asked for one more photo. 'This time,
close your eyes and hug your guitar like it's your
woman.' He closed his eyes and smiled. That ended
up being my favorite."* — Bruce Talamon

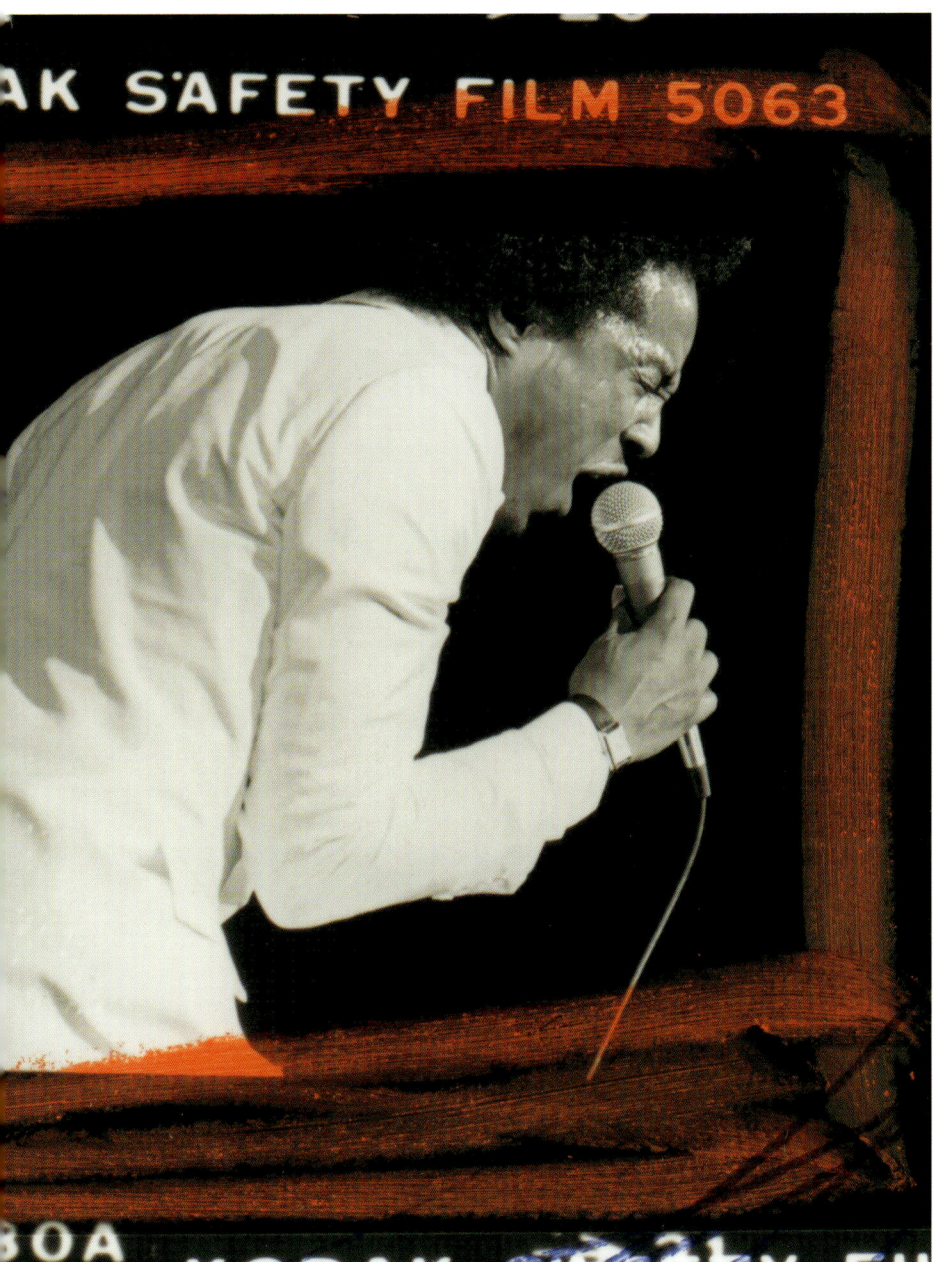

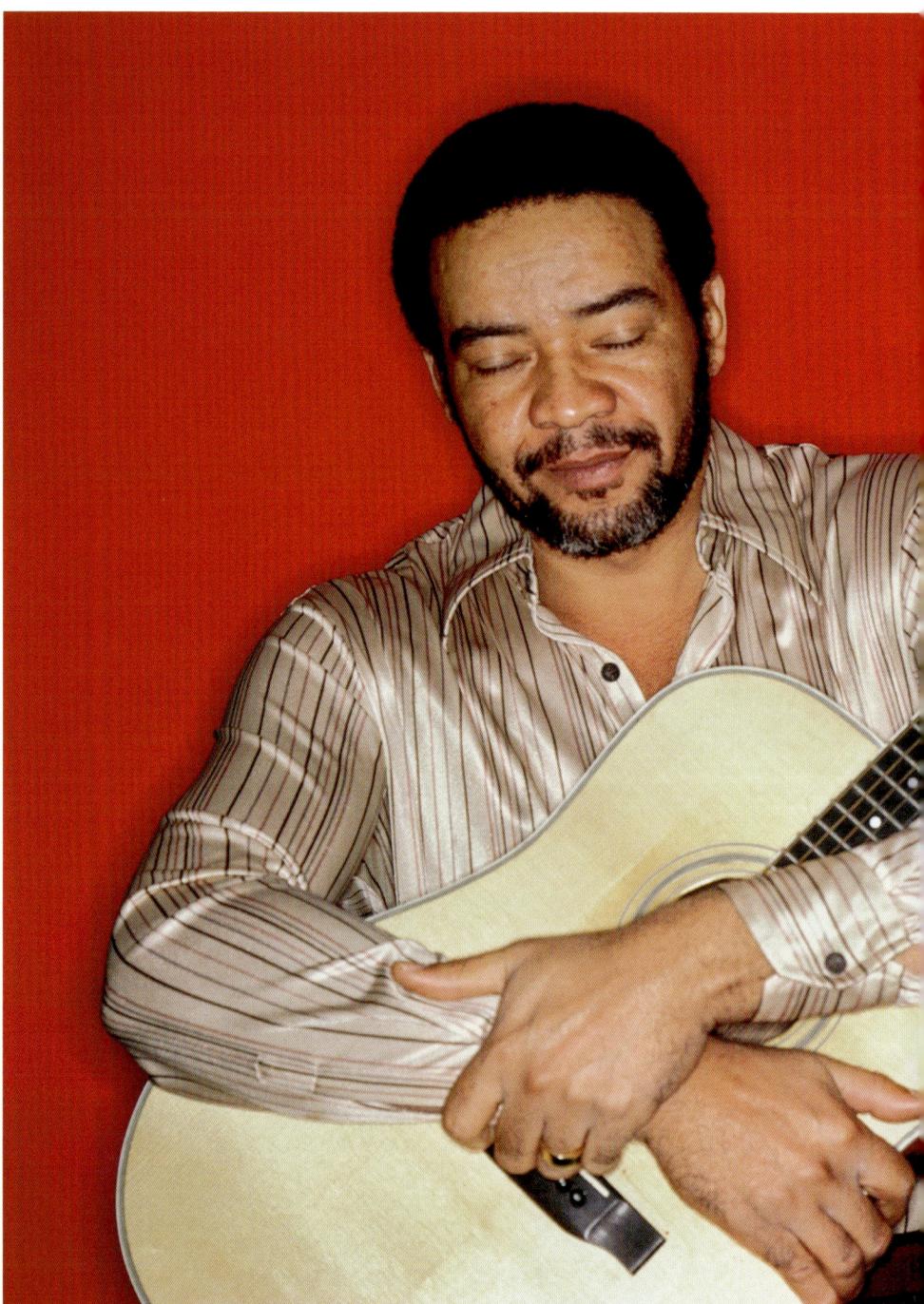

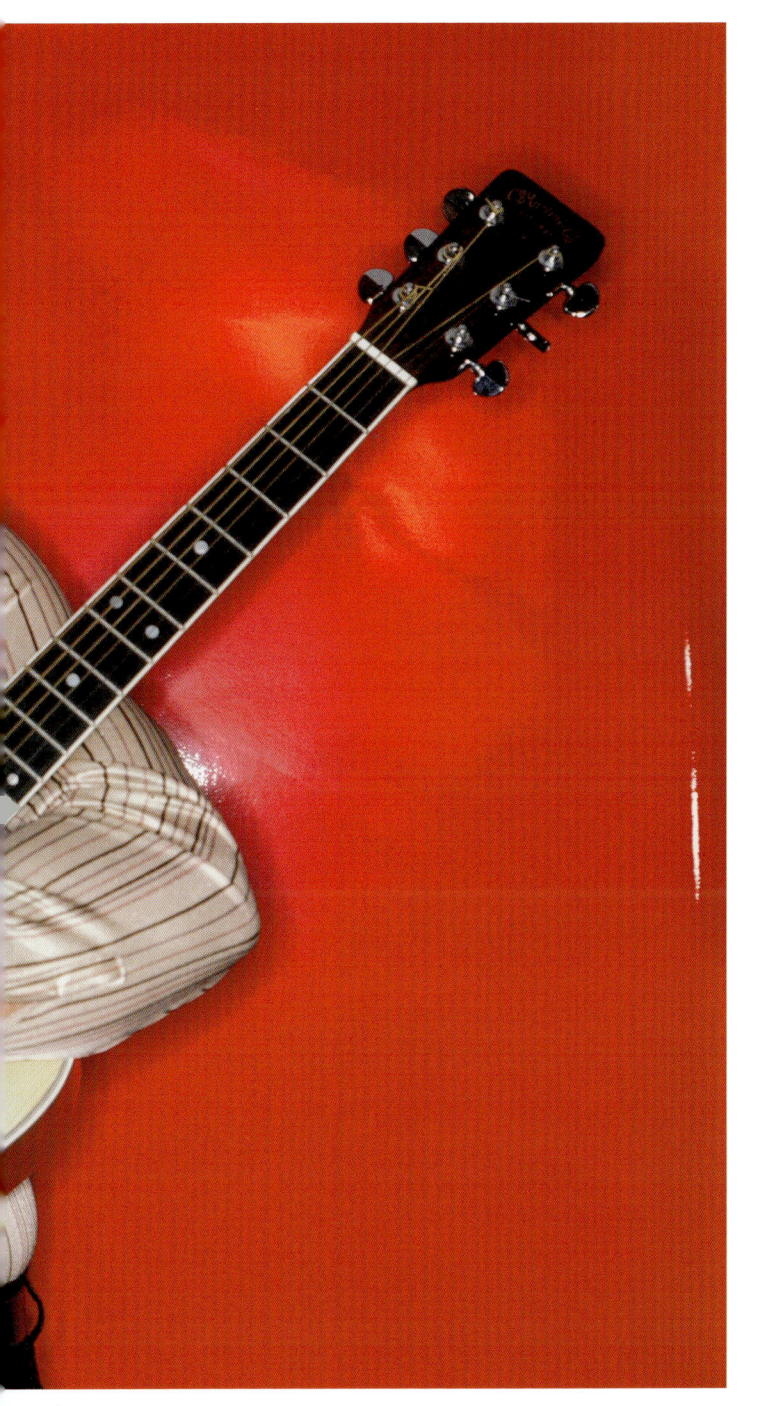

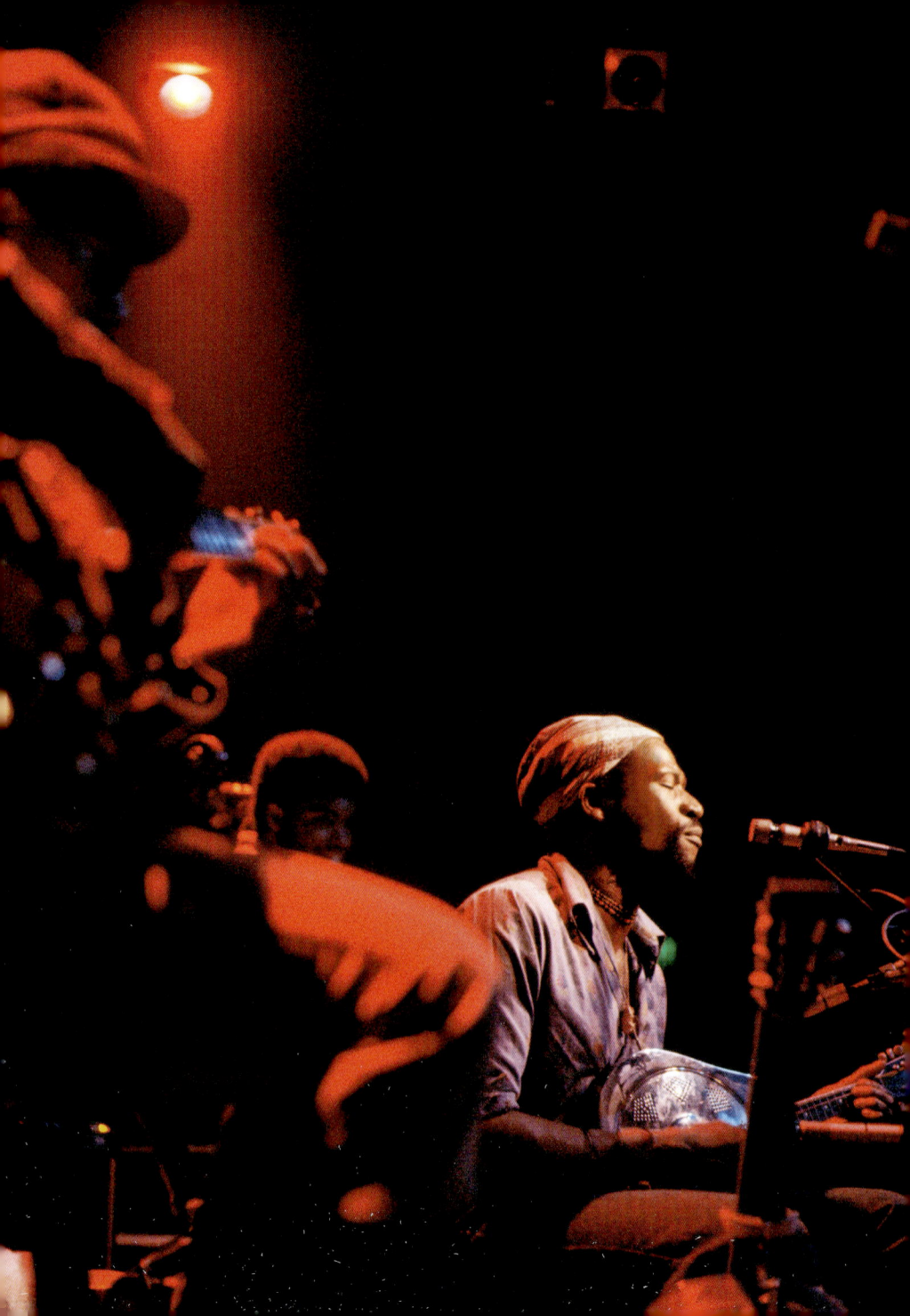

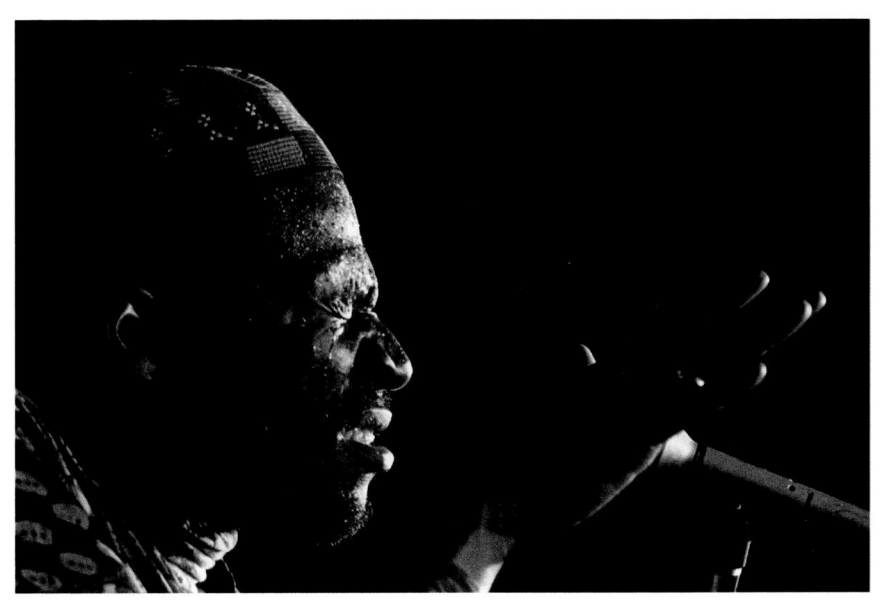

TAJ MAHAL
The Troubadour, Los Angeles, 1973. (Opposite)

The Hollywood Palladium, California, 1973. (Above)
Mahal says that he is a hunter-gatherer of music, which is why his own brand of blues, Americana, and world music has never been too far away from the roots of R&B. As a testament to being instrumental in revitalizing and maintaining interest in Americana music, the two-time Grammy winner received the Americana Music Association's Lifetime Achievement Award in 2014.

QUINCY JONES
A&M Recording Studios, Los Angeles, 1976. (Pages 104–105)
Player. Arranger. Bandleader. Record-company executive. Film composer. Record producer. Legend. Here, Q is engrossed in editing a music chart.

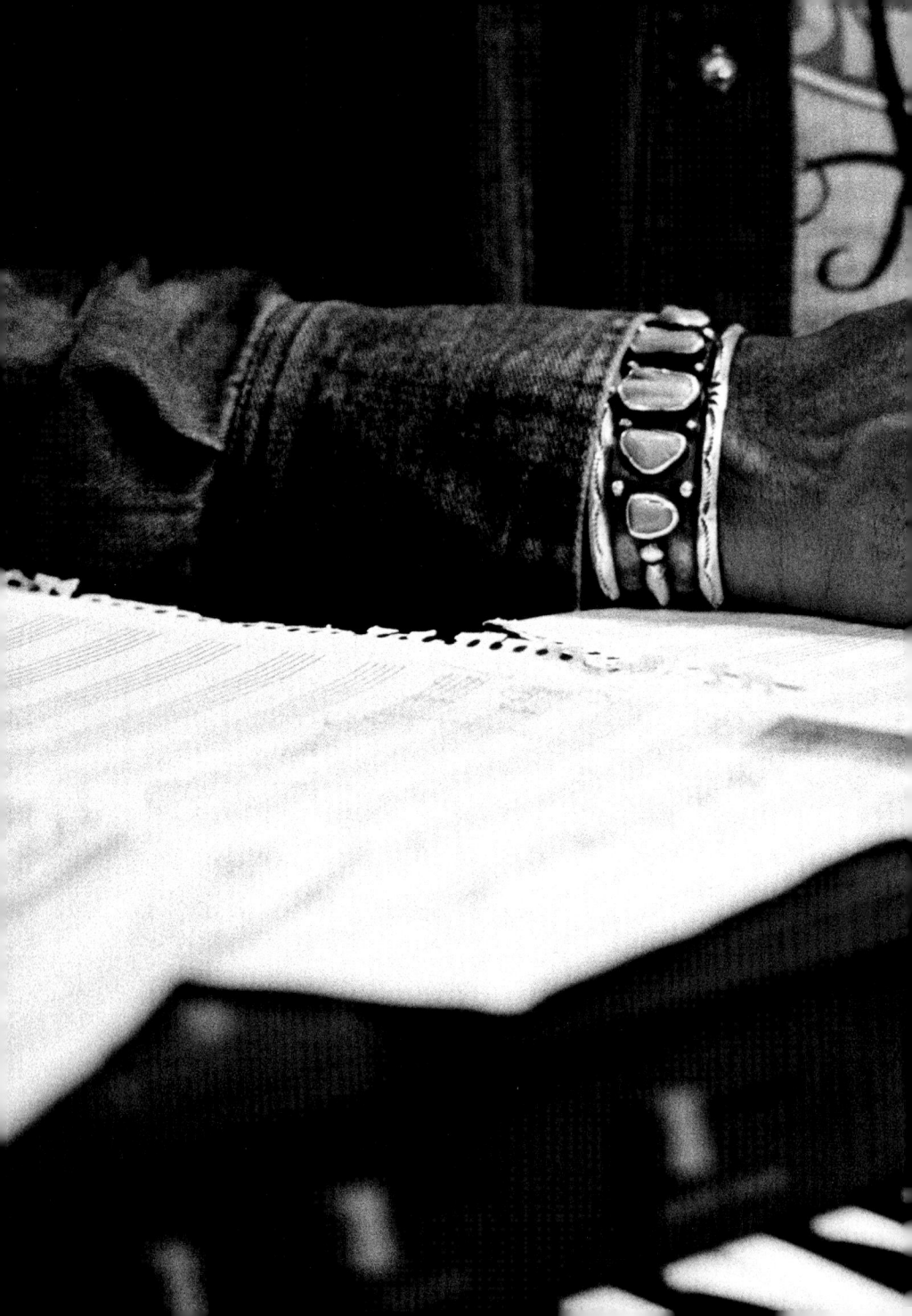

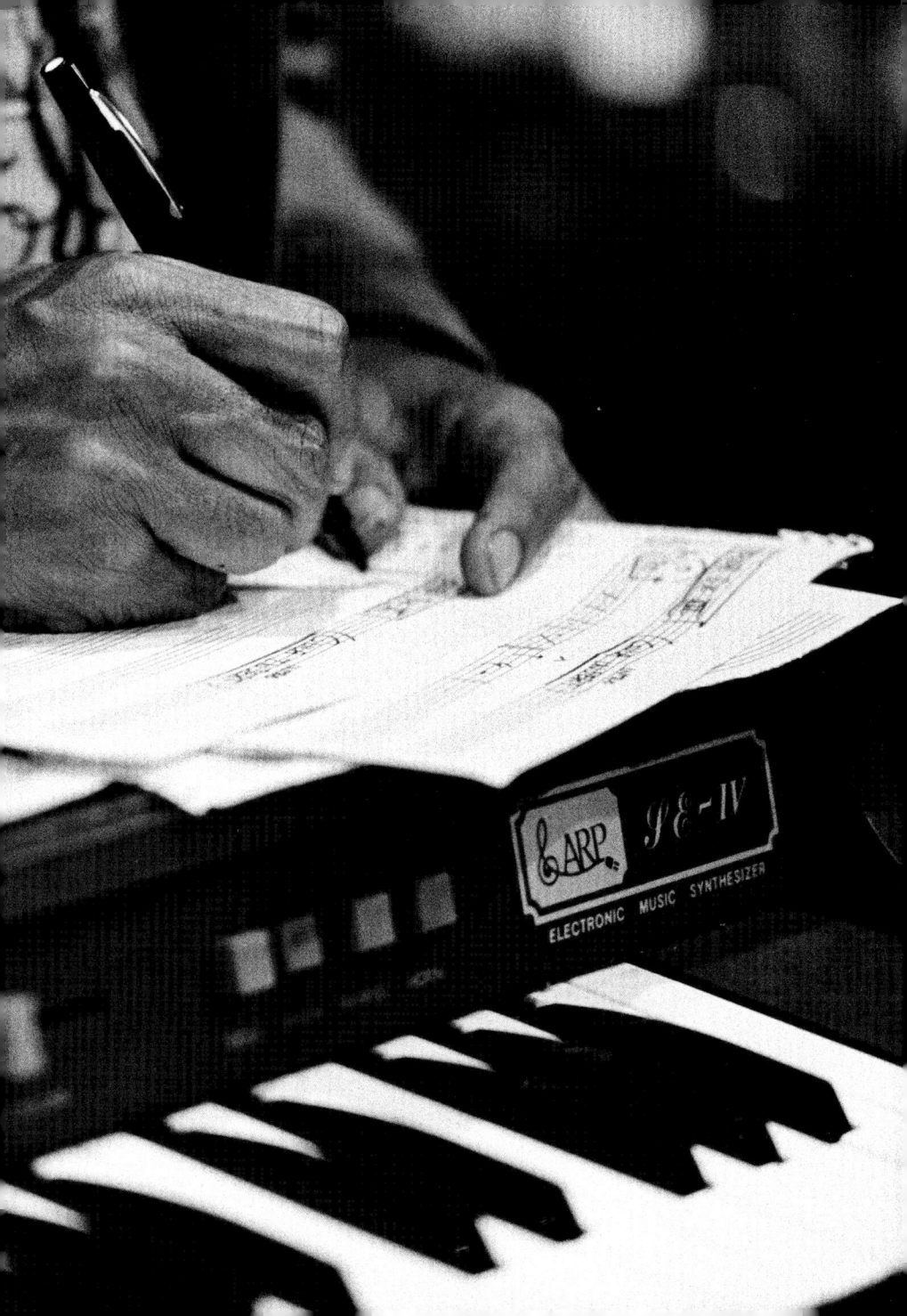

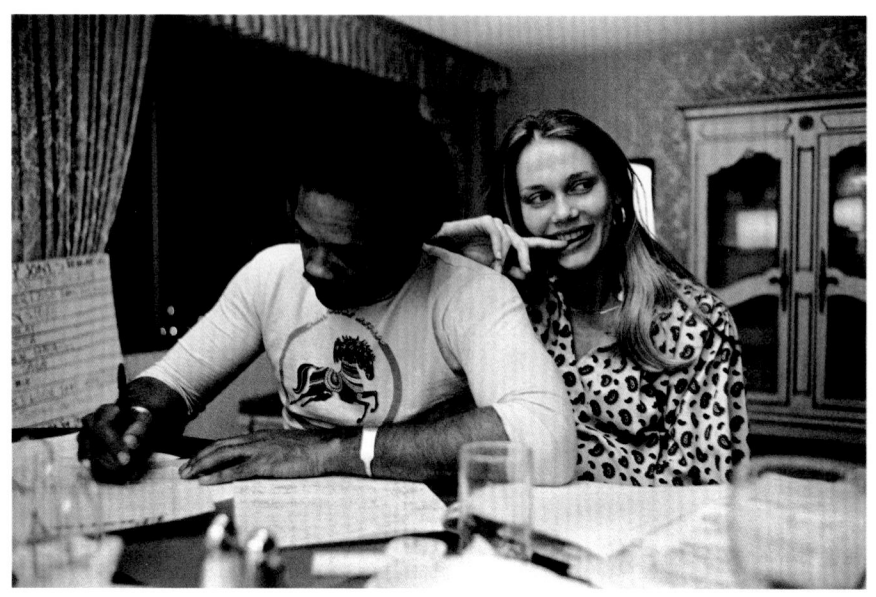

QUINCY JONES AND PEGGY LIPTON
The Fairmont Hotel, San Francisco, 1976.
In 1974, Q's R&B album *Body Heat* was his first big success as a recording artist.
Around the same time, he met and married actress Peggy Lipton, with whom he
would later have two children, one of whom is the actress, writer, and director
Rashida Jones. Not long after this photo was taken in 1976, Quincy would start
working on music for the groundbreaking television miniseries *Roots*.

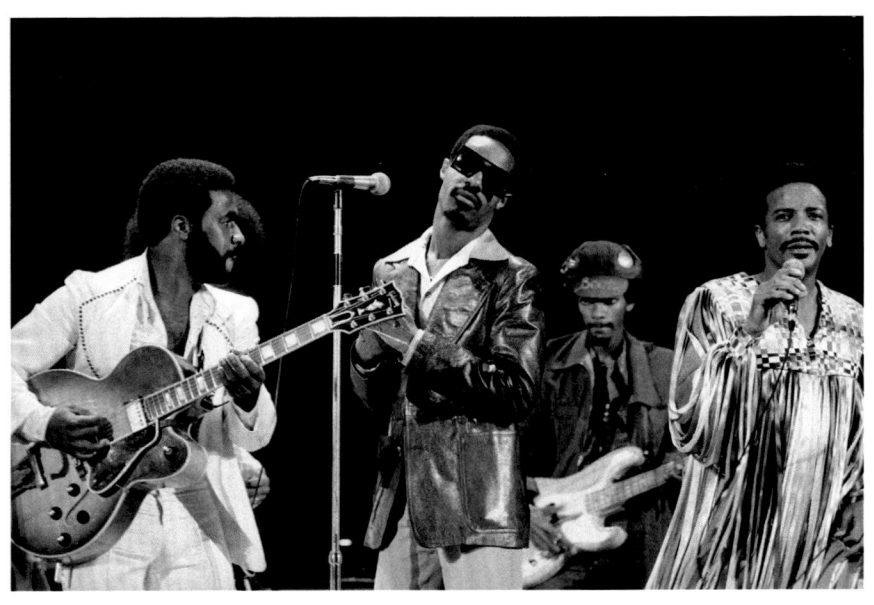

QUINCY JONES
The Cow Palace, San Francisco, 1976.
Needing to raise funds for Glide Memorial Church's new Center of
Self-Determination, the Reverend Cecil Williams recruited Q to put together
an all-star benefit concert. Guitar legend Wah Wah Watson, Stevie Wonder,
bassist Louis Johnson, and Q joined forces for the evening.

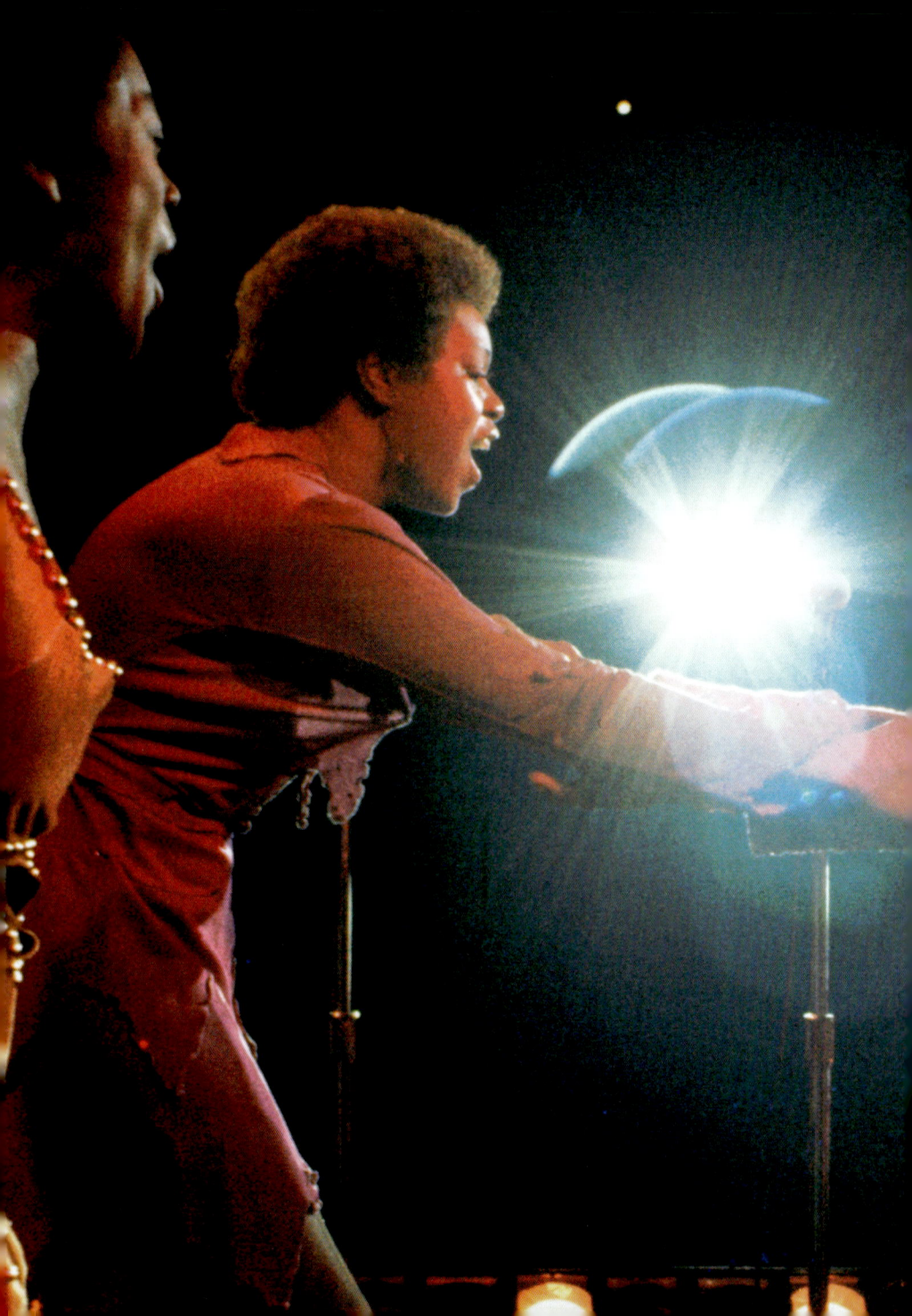

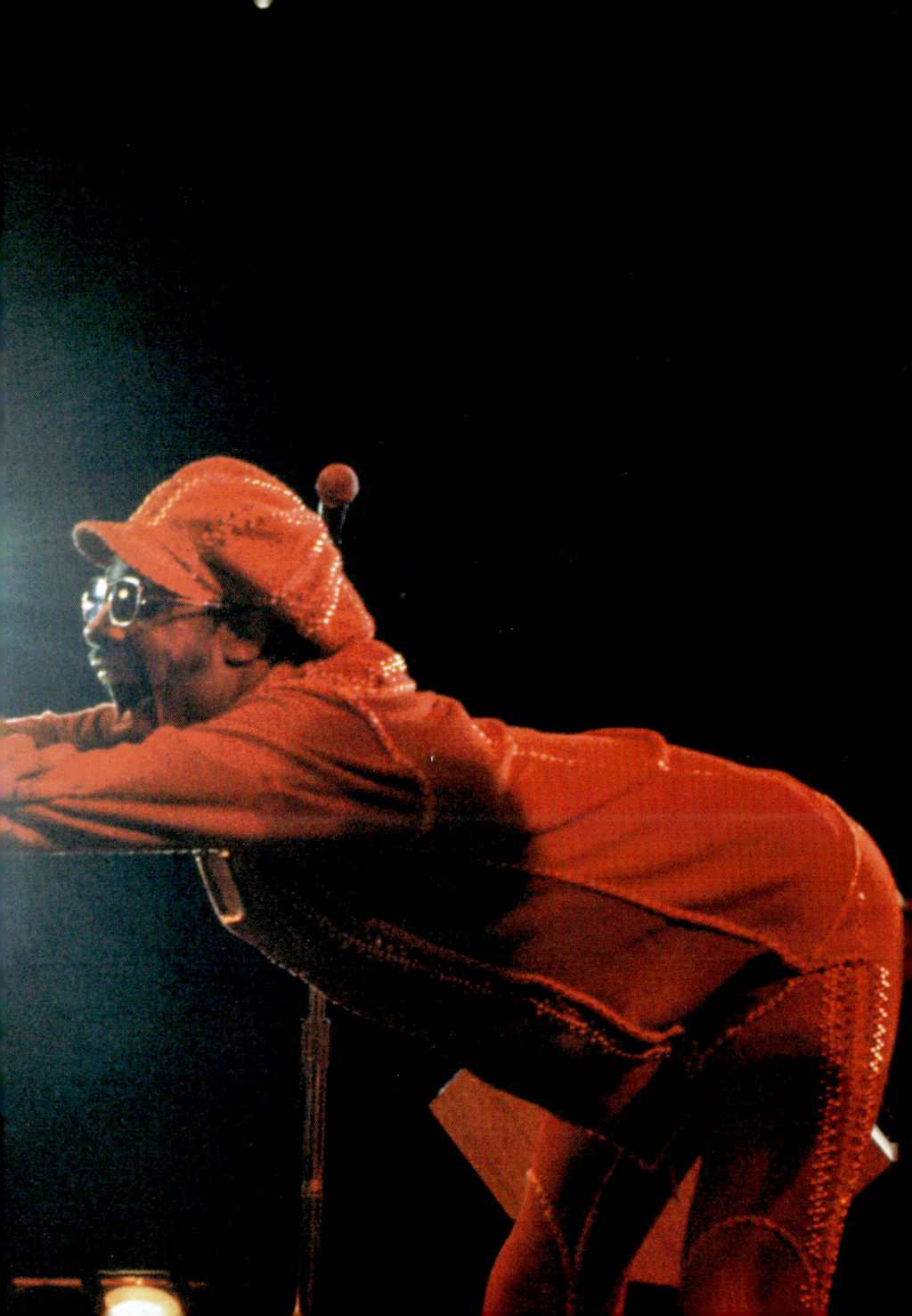

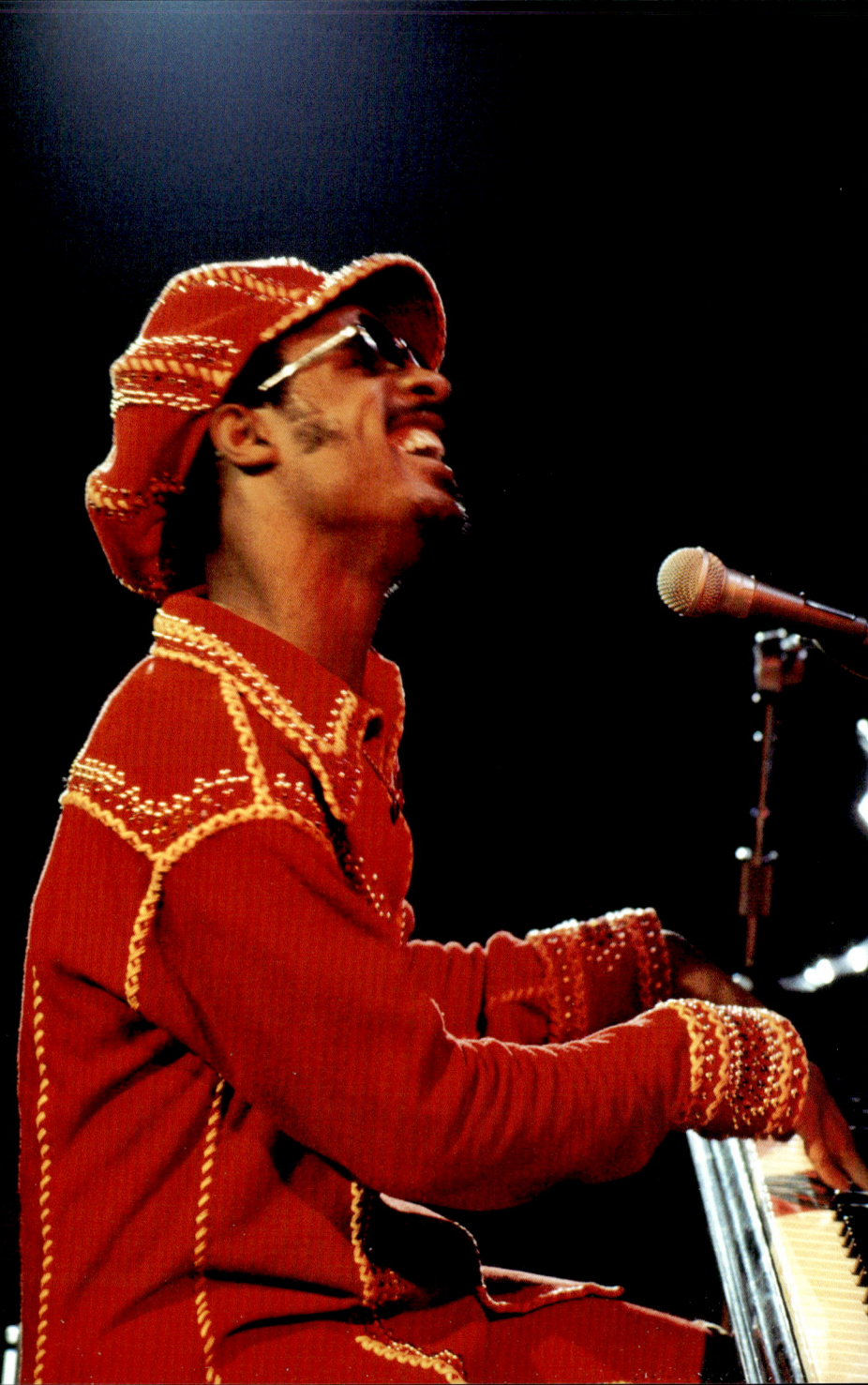

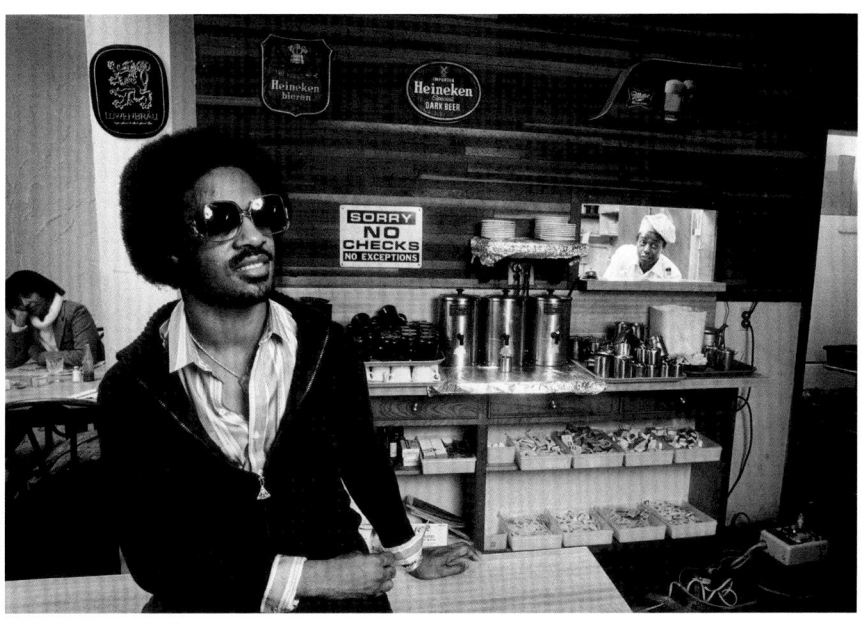

STEVIE WONDER AND DENIECE WILLIAMS
The Forum, Inglewood, California, 1974. (Pages 108-109)
With Susaye Greene looking on, this photo is a glorious celebration of the
musical relationship between Stevie and his backup singers in Wonderlove.

The Forum, Inglewood, California, 1974. (Opposite)

Hollywood, California, 1977. (Above)
Midnight at the original Roscoe's House of Chicken and Waffles on Gower
Street in Hollywood, as the cook looks on. *SOUL Newspaper* took over the
restaurant for the shoot — note the photo equipment in the shot. For celebrities
and noncelebrities alike, the L.A. restaurant is a cultural institution.

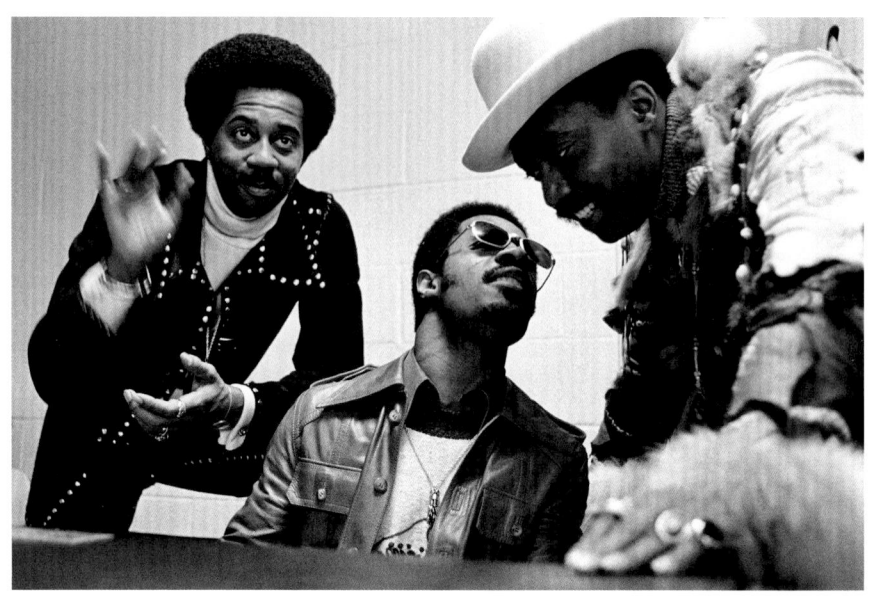

STEVIE WONDER AND THE TEMPTATIONS
The Forum, Inglewood, California, 1974. (Above)
As the nucleus of The Temptations, Otis Williams and Melvin Franklin's deep
friendship endured the ups and downs of the R&B music business for
40 years. Backstage, Stevie tests some new songs out on the stylish brothers
before he hits the stage.

STEVIE WONDER AND THE EMOTIONS
The Forum, Inglewood, California, October 1977. (Opposite)
Having just scored one of the biggest hits of the 1970s with "The Best of
My Love," the Chicago-born sister trio Wanda, Pam, and Sheila Hutchinson
are enthralled, hanging out backstage with Stevie Wonder. They
were successful, but this was Stevie. And, he had come to see them.

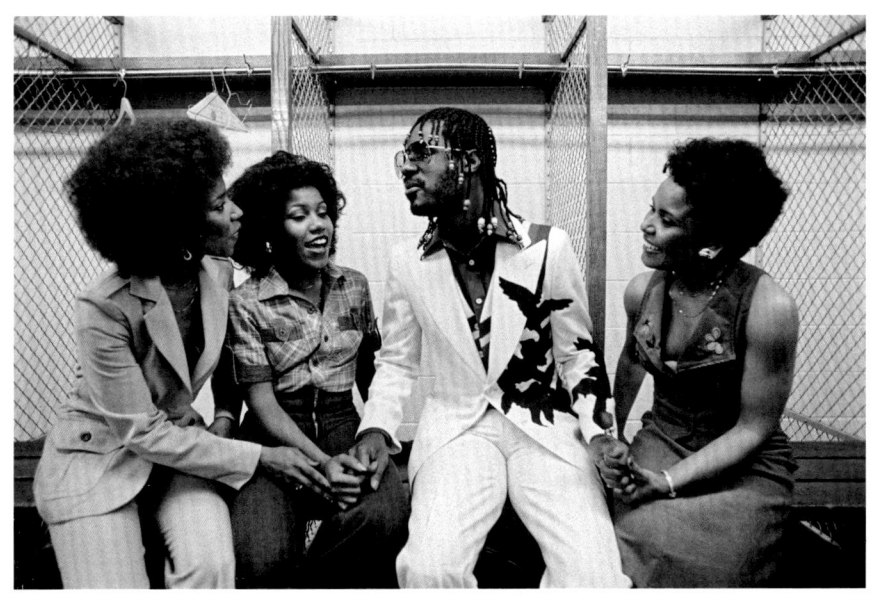

STEVIE WONDER

The Forum, Inglewood, California, December 1980. (Pages 114–115)

*"I had total access onstage during the set. After a couple of rolls of film,
I was confident that I had solid portraits. Now, I was looking for something exciting,
so sometimes you gotta kick the camera. Stevie moved his head from side to side
when he played. Experimenting with a low shutter speed, I used movement to
blur and essentially paint the photograph on the Ektachrome. This was done all in
the camera. No Photoshop."* — Bruce Talamon

BOBBY WOMACK, SLY STONE, AND B. B. KING

ABC Television Center, *In Concert*, Hollywood, California, 1973. (Pages 116–117)

B. B. was King of the Blues. Sly changed music forever. But the lesser-known Womack had
a revered career as well. Groomed by 1960s soul greats Sam Cooke and Wilson Pickett, he
played funky guitar behind Elvis, Aretha, Dusty Springfield, and Ray Charles. He made his
mark as an artist with the soul classics "Harry Hippie," "Across 110th Street," and "If You Think
You're Lonely Now." As a songwriter, he penned songs for Janis Joplin and George Benson,
and gave the Rolling Stones their first number-one U.K. hit in 1964 with "It's All Over Now."

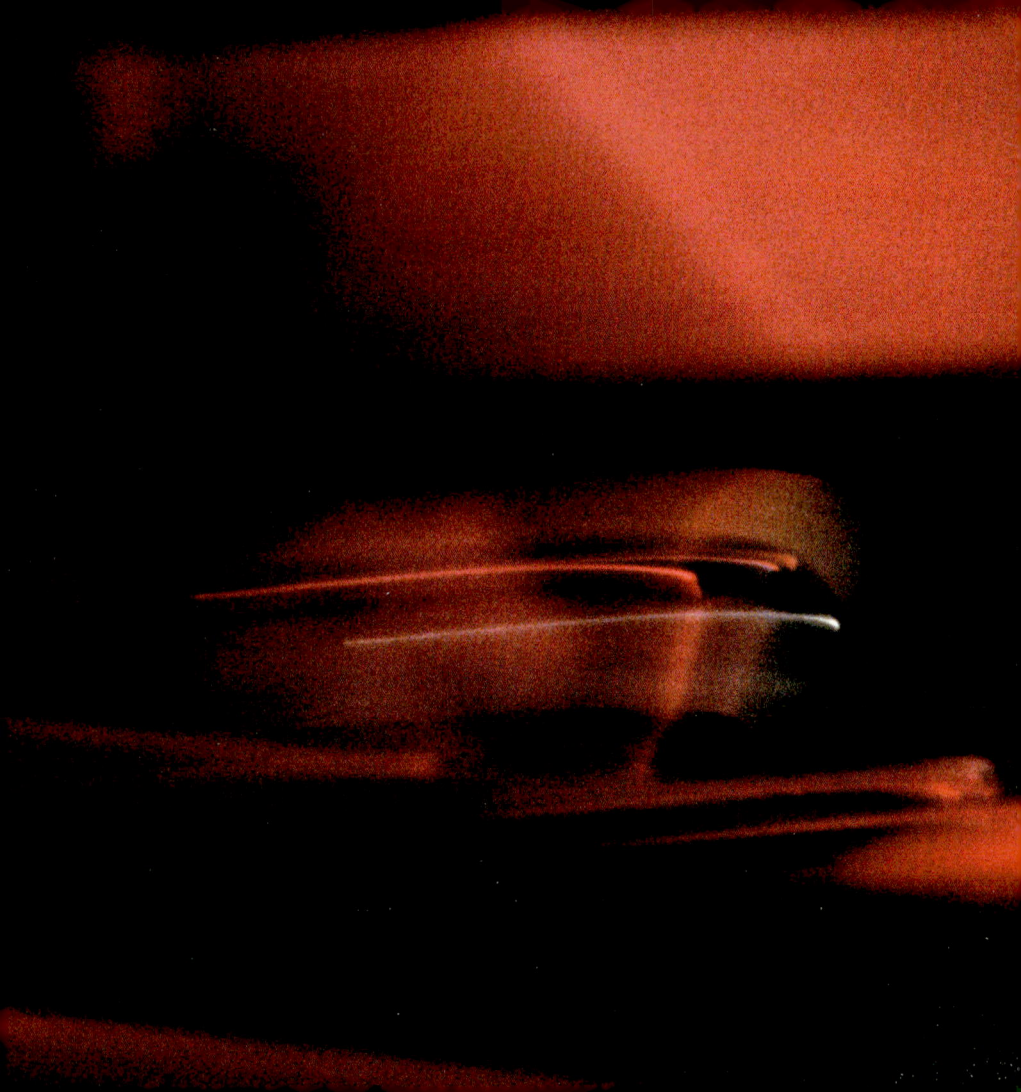

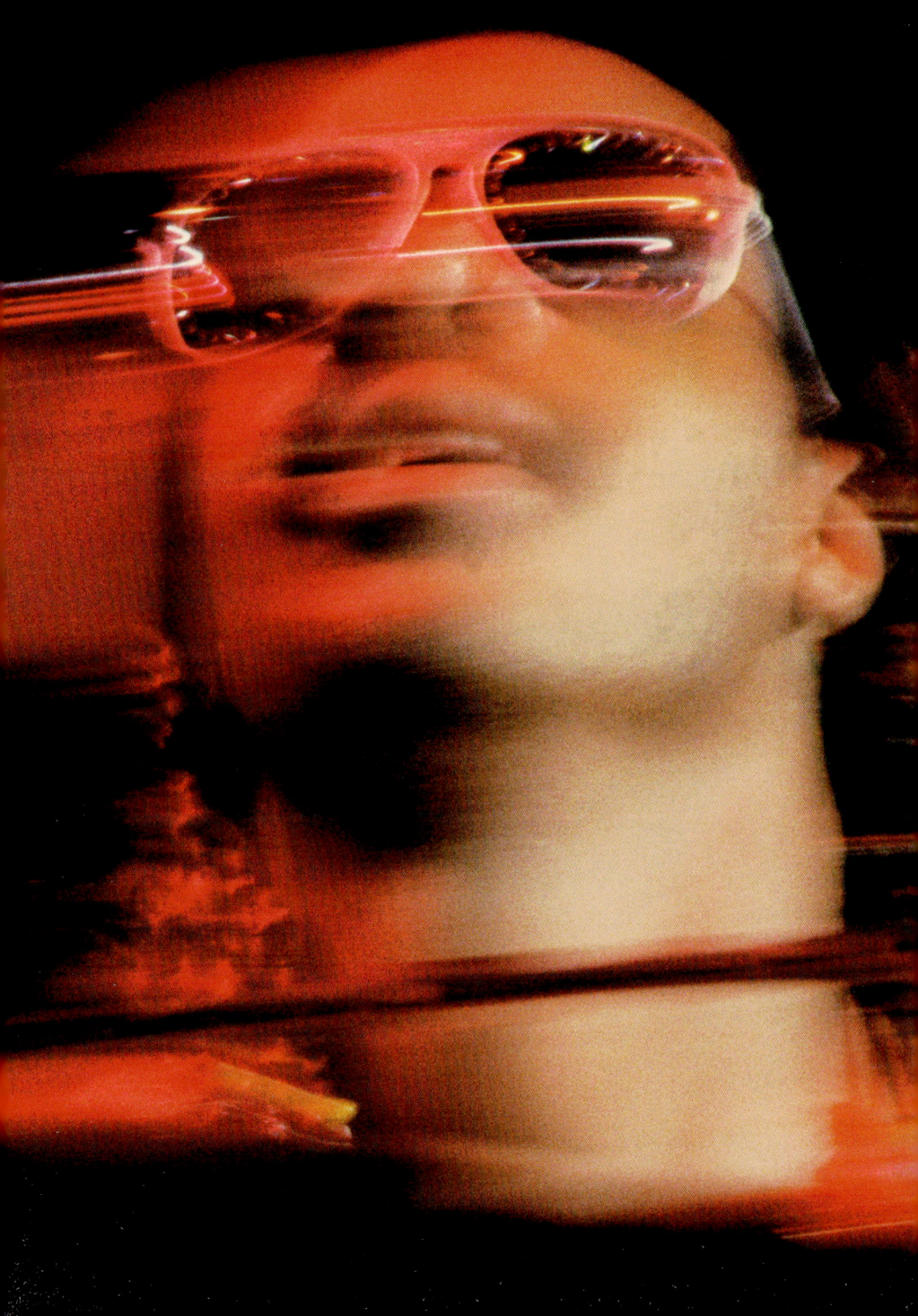

THE
SCENE

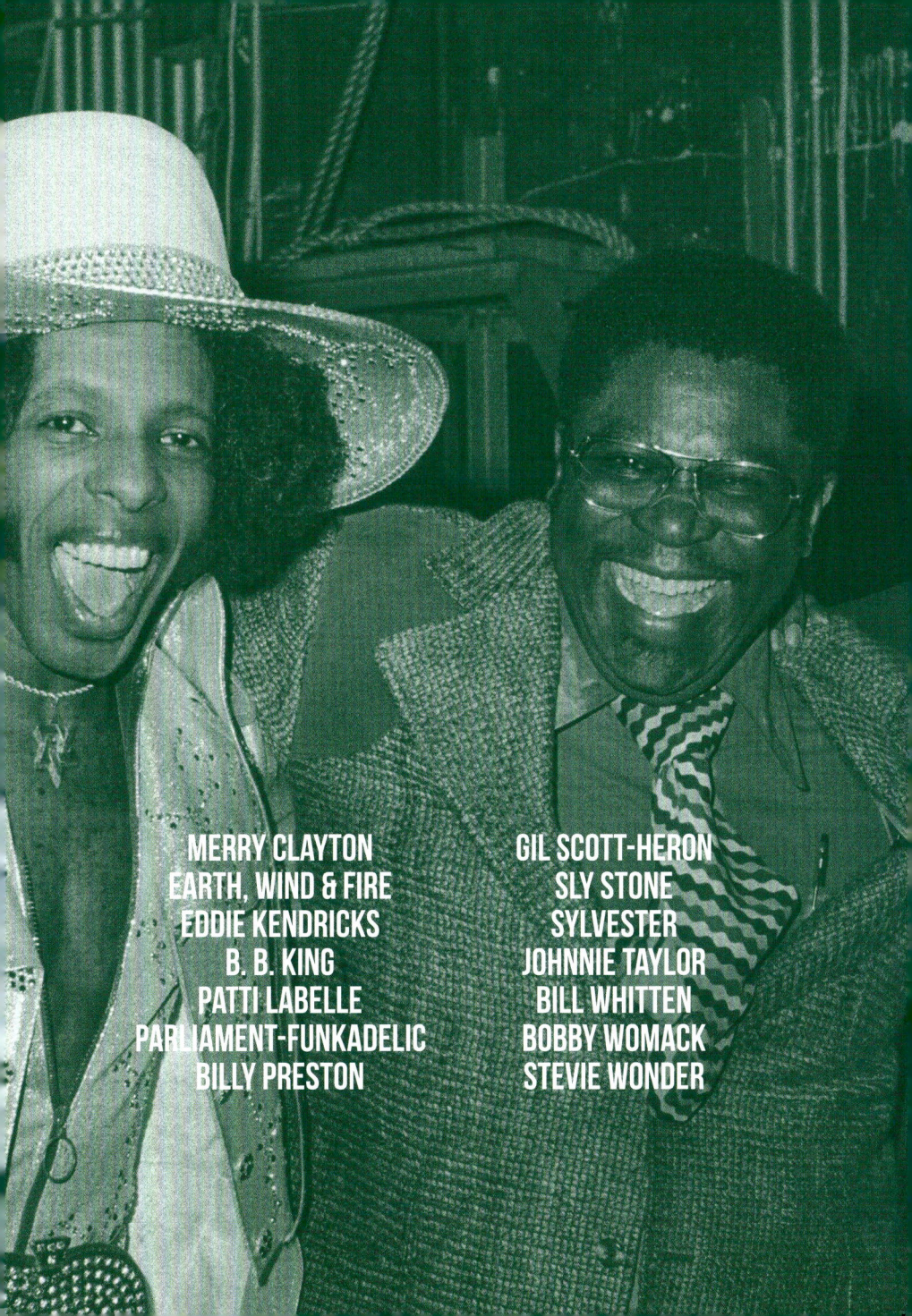

MERRY CLAYTON
EARTH, WIND & FIRE
EDDIE KENDRICKS
B. B. KING
PATTI LABELLE
PARLIAMENT-FUNKADELIC
BILLY PRESTON

GIL SCOTT-HERON
SLY STONE
SYLVESTER
JOHNNIE TAYLOR
BILL WHITTEN
BOBBY WOMACK
STEVIE WONDER

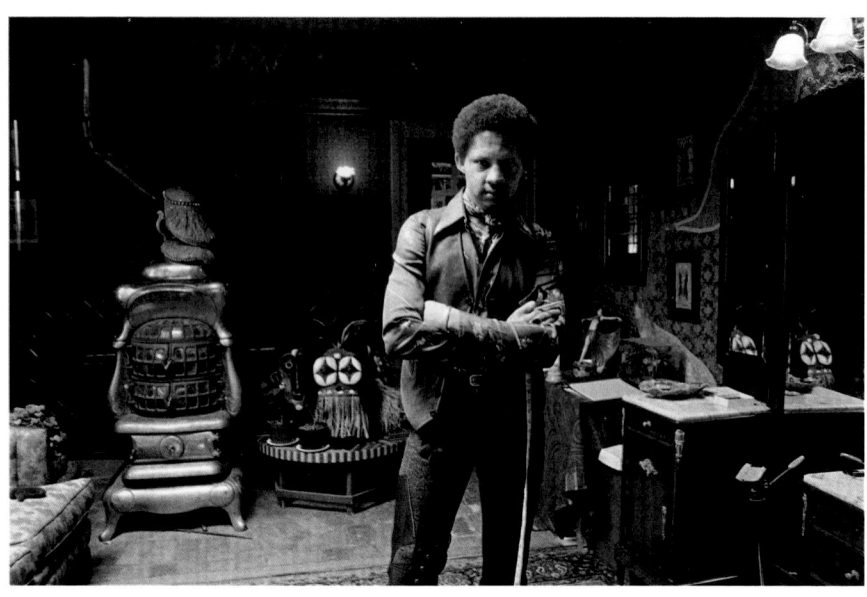

BILL WHITTEN
Workroom 27 (Whitten's studio), West Hollywood, California, 1975. (Above)
Any book about R&B music must address the issue of style. And in the 1970s, Bill Whitten led the way, designing for Earth, Wind & Fire; Stevie Wonder; The Jackson 5 (and later Michael's rhinestone glove); the Commodores; Eddie Kendricks; Elton John; and Neil Diamond. But, being fabulous came at a price. Maurice White's accountant said that when he saw the bill from Workroom 27 for the Earth, Wind & Fire costumes he cried.

EARTH, WIND & FIRE
Los Angeles, 1979. (Opposite)
Verdine White and Larry Dunn striking a pose in a Bill Whitten–designed wardrobe.

JOHNNIE TAYLOR
Parked at the curb, world-famous Pink's hot dog stand,
Los Angeles, 1977. (Pages 120–121)
At Stax Records in the mid-1960s, Johnnie Taylor had the hit "Who's Making Love." But after signing to Columbia Records, he had the smash of a lifetime with "Disco Lady." The song spent four weeks at number one on the Billboard Hot 100 chart. Lunch break: chili dog and a red soda.

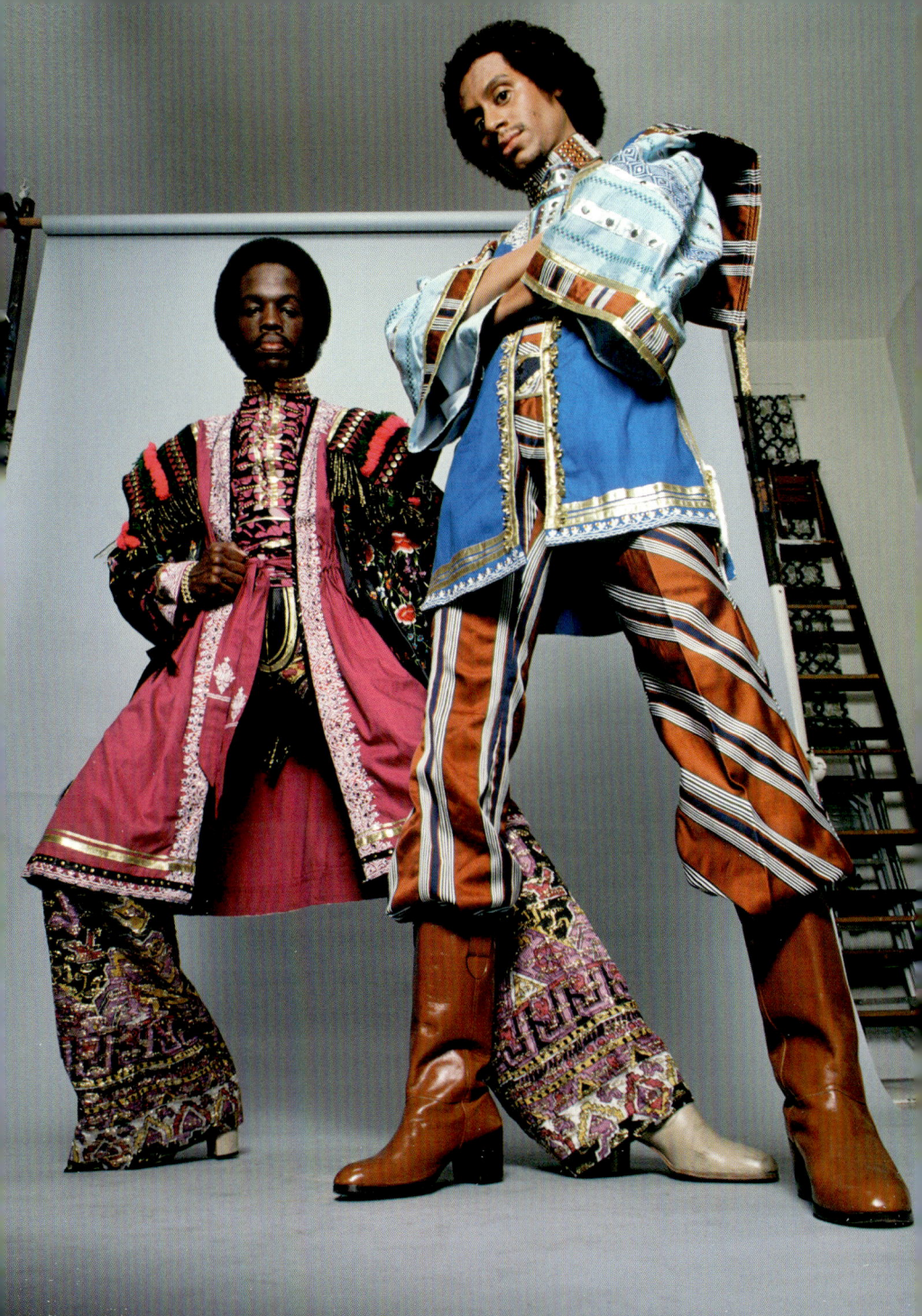

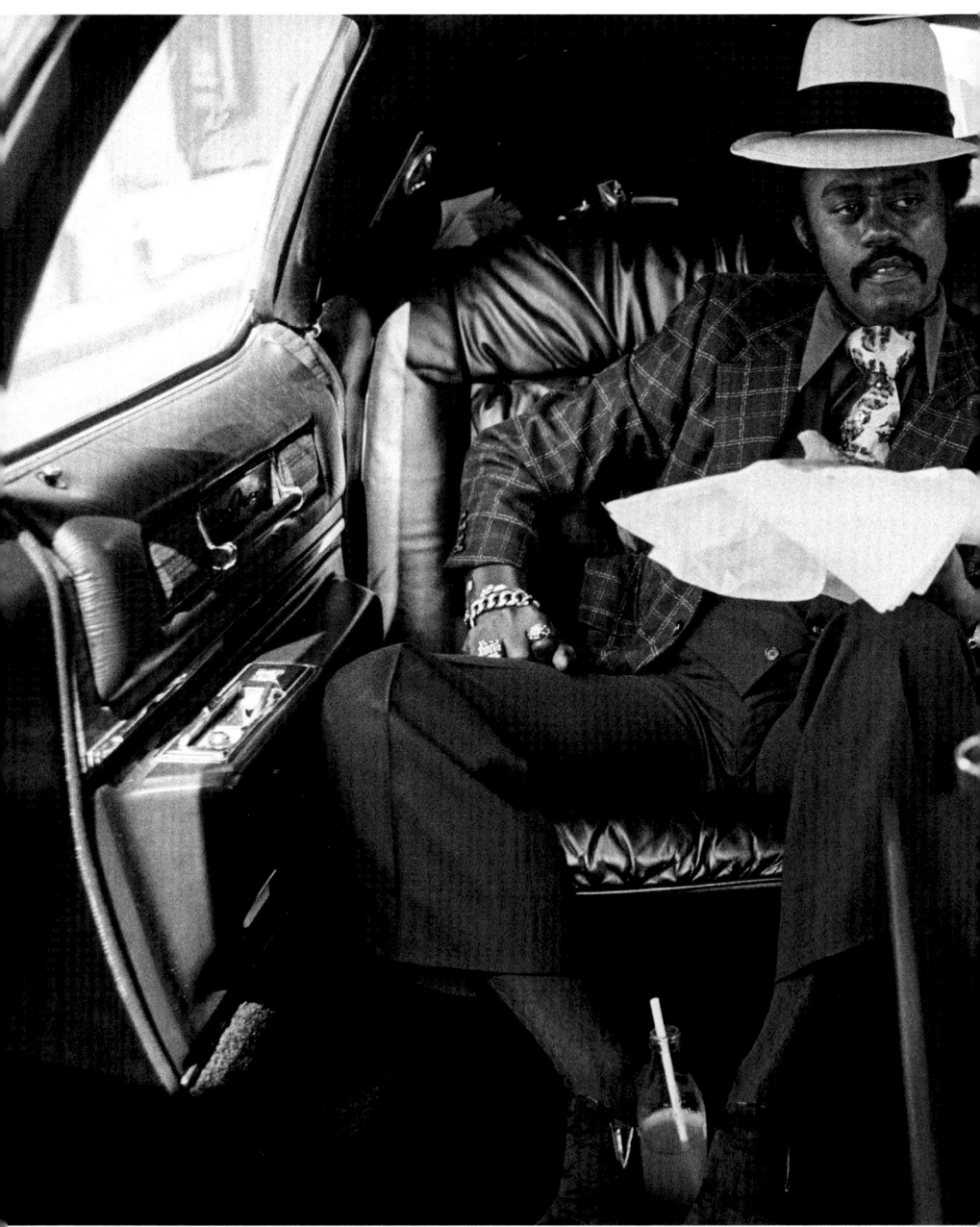

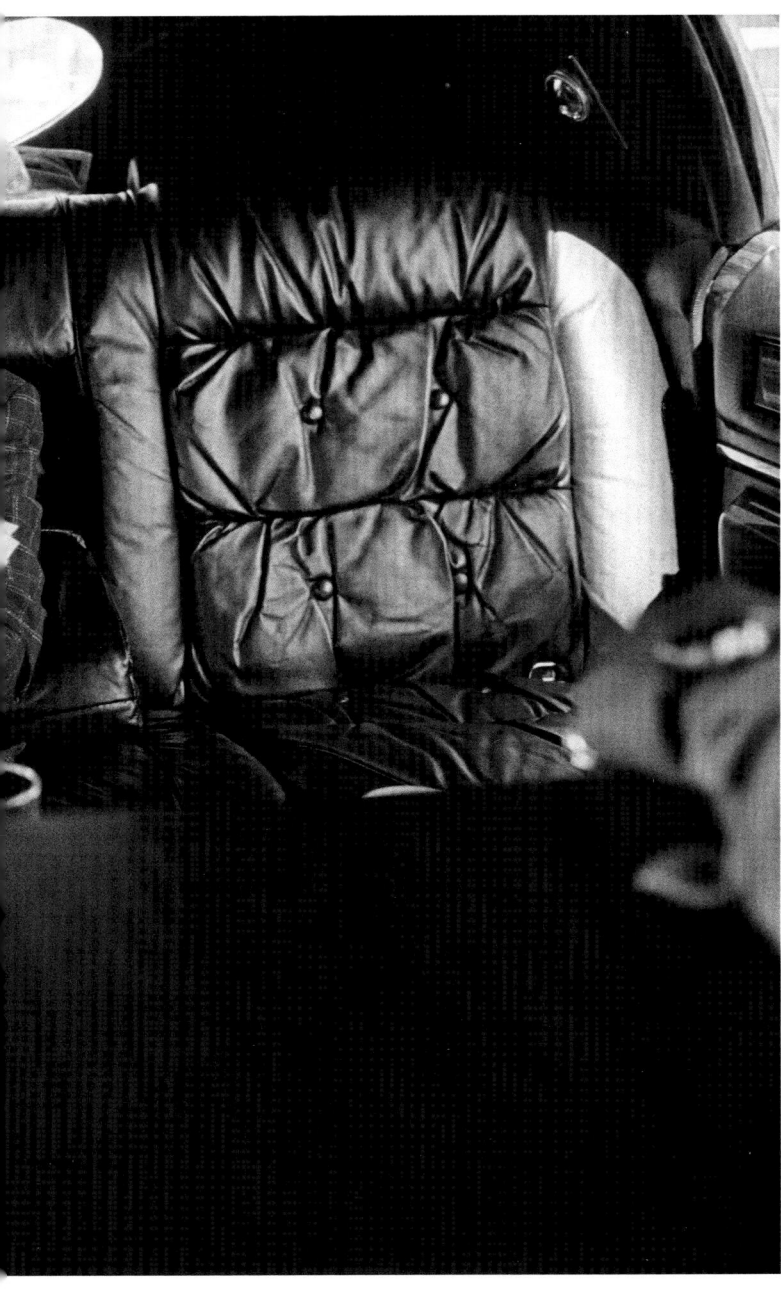

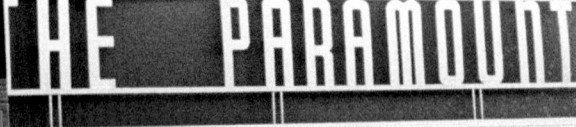

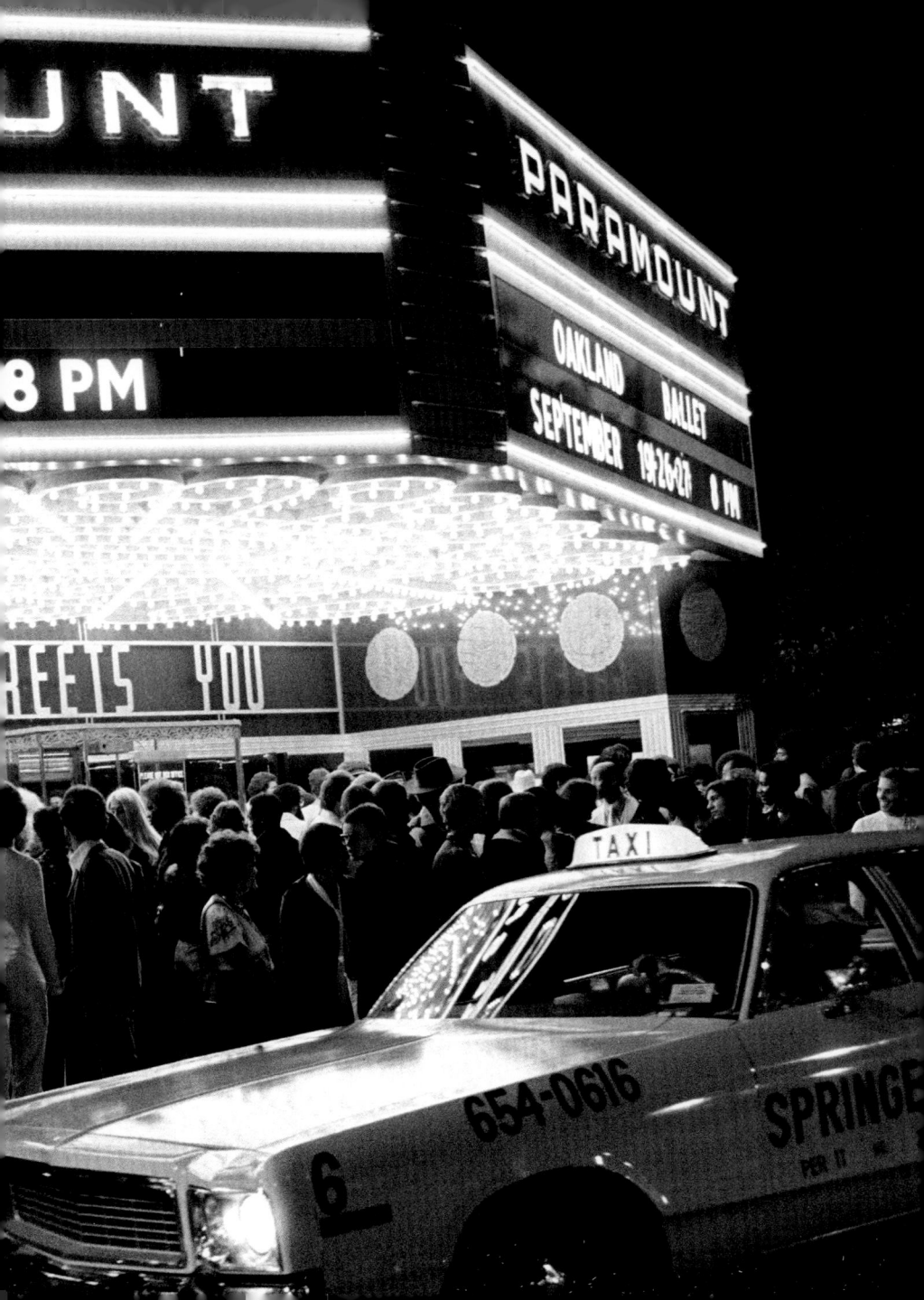

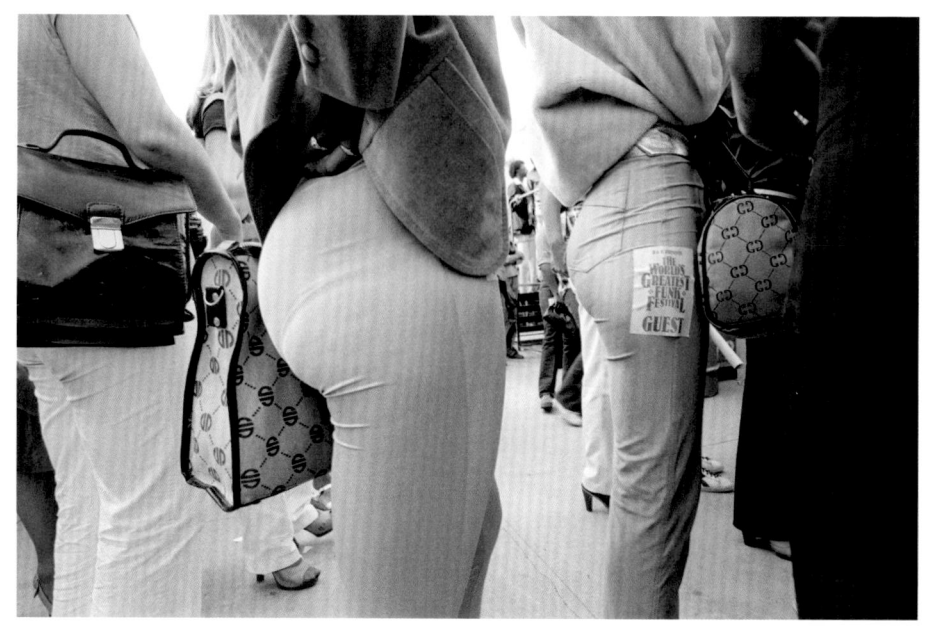

LABELLE
Paramount Theatre, Oakland, California, 1975. (Pages 122–123)

PARLIAMENT-FUNKADELIC
P-Funk Earth Tour, Funk Fest, Los Angeles Coliseum, 1977. (Above)
Seventies fashions and curves personified.

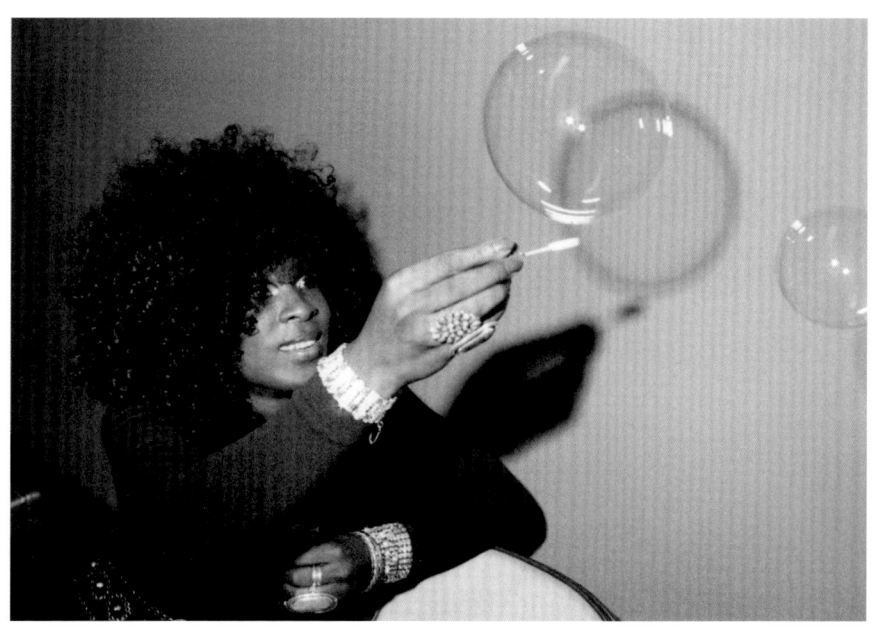

SYLVESTER
Santa Monica, California, 1973.
Making an unsung imprint on disco music's early electronic sound with "You Make Me Feel (Mighty Real)," the openly gay artist cultivated the euphoria of the discotheque world and was a vanguard of 1970s queer and drag culture.

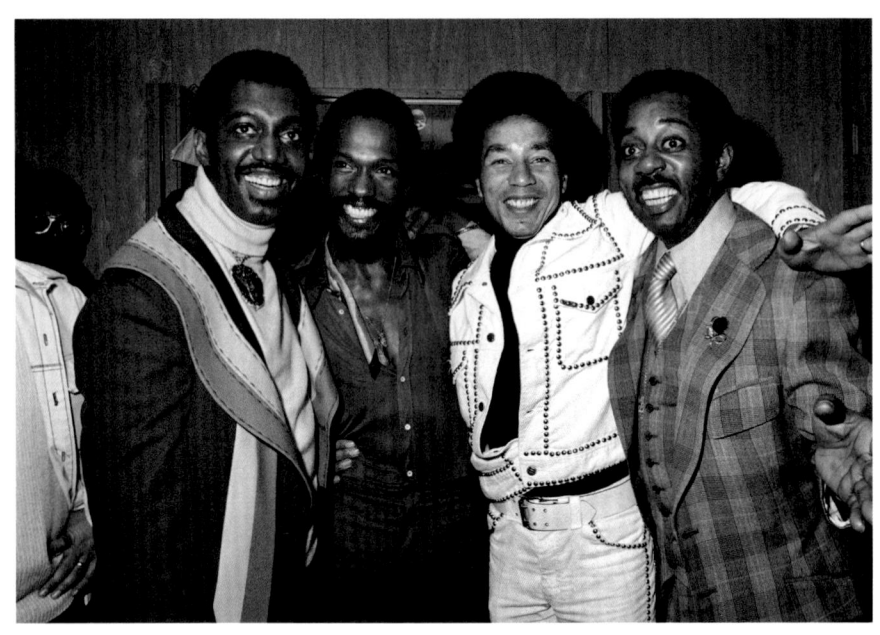

EDDIE KENDRICKS
The Roxy, West Hollywood, California, 1973.
While David Ruffin's departure from The Temptations was
acrimonious, Kendricks remained close with Smokey Robinson
and Temptations Otis Williams and Melvin Franklin.

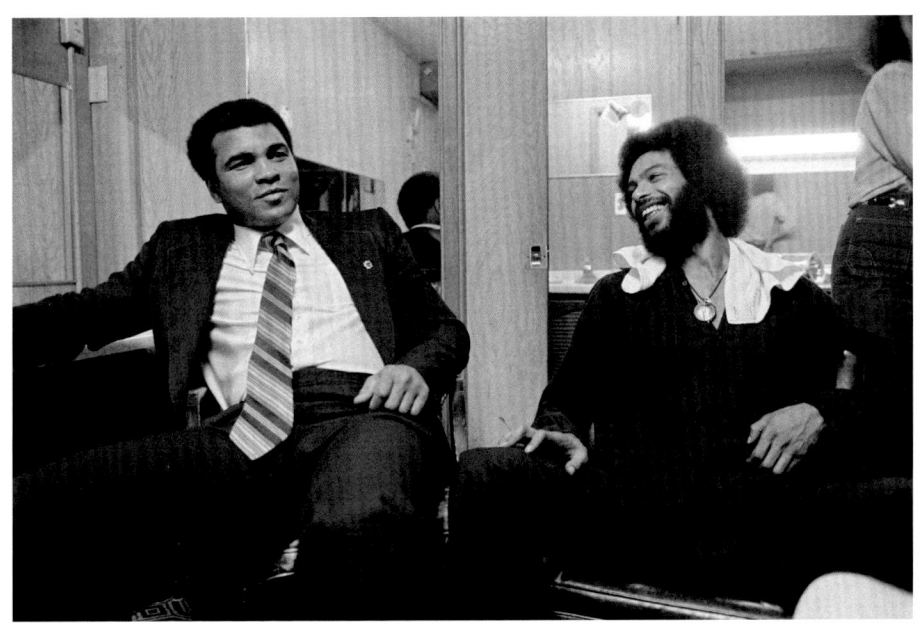

MUHAMMAD ALI AND GIL SCOTT-HERON
The Roxy, Los Angeles, 1977.

"That night they talked about ways to apply international pressure to protest for the release of Nelson Mandela. Gil and Ali were notorious with the ladies and big flirts, however, both had a long tradition of protest and understood that sometimes the music was about more than '…shakin' that ass.' Mandela served 27 years in prison and was finally released on February 11, 1990." — Bruce Talamon

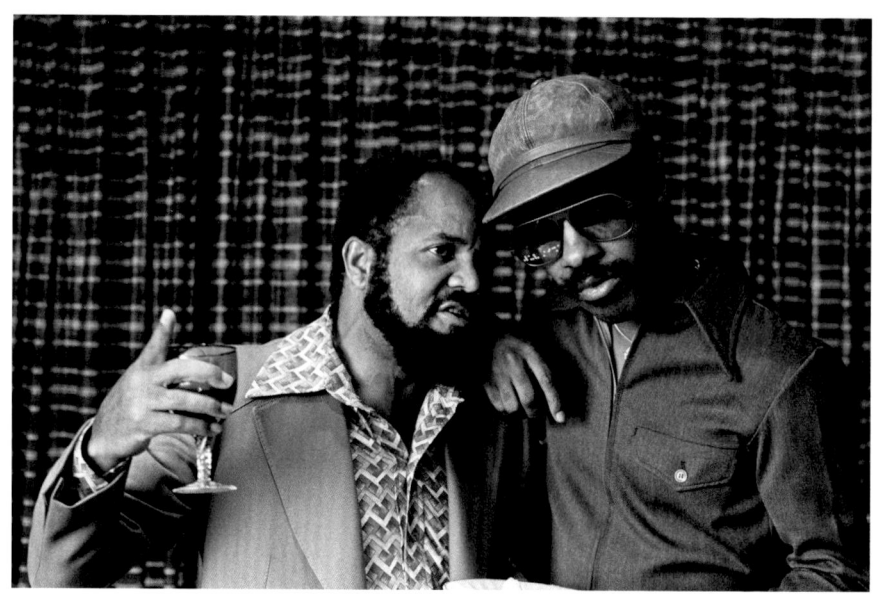

BERRY GORDY AND STEVIE WONDER

Motown Records office, Hollywood, California, March 1976. (Above)
A quiet moment between Berry Gordy and Stevie Wonder just after Stevie delivered
his finished tapes for *Songs in the Key of Life.* *"During Stevie Wonder's 24th birthday
party, the president of Motown, Ewart Abner, presented Stevie with a silver scroll
medallion inscribed in Braille. I always thought the gift was from Abner and was
curious about the inscription, so during research for the book I had it translated: 'Thank
you for being like you are—B.G. 5-13-74' Now I know it was from Berry Gordy."*
—Bruce Talamon

BILLY PRESTON AND MERRY CLAYTON

The Total Experience nightclub, Los Angeles, 1974. (Opposite & pages 130–131)
*"It was opening night and the band was on fire. Merry Clayton was in the front row,
along with a number of other celebrities, when Billy invited her up onstage near
the end of the set. Merry Clayton is famous as the background singer who sang
that memorable solo on the Rolling Stones' song 'Gimme Shelter.' When she sang
with Billy that night, they tore the house down."* —Bruce Talamon

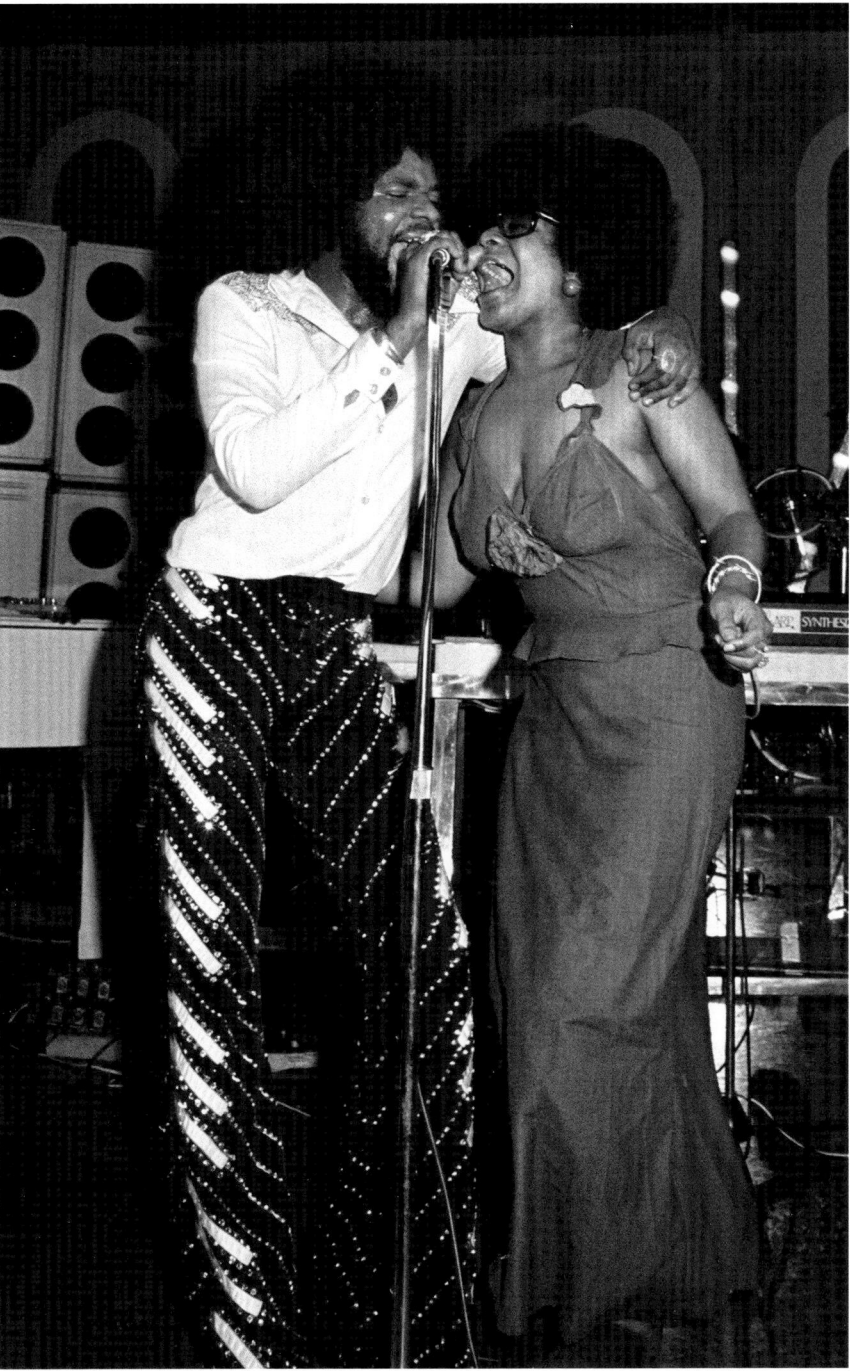

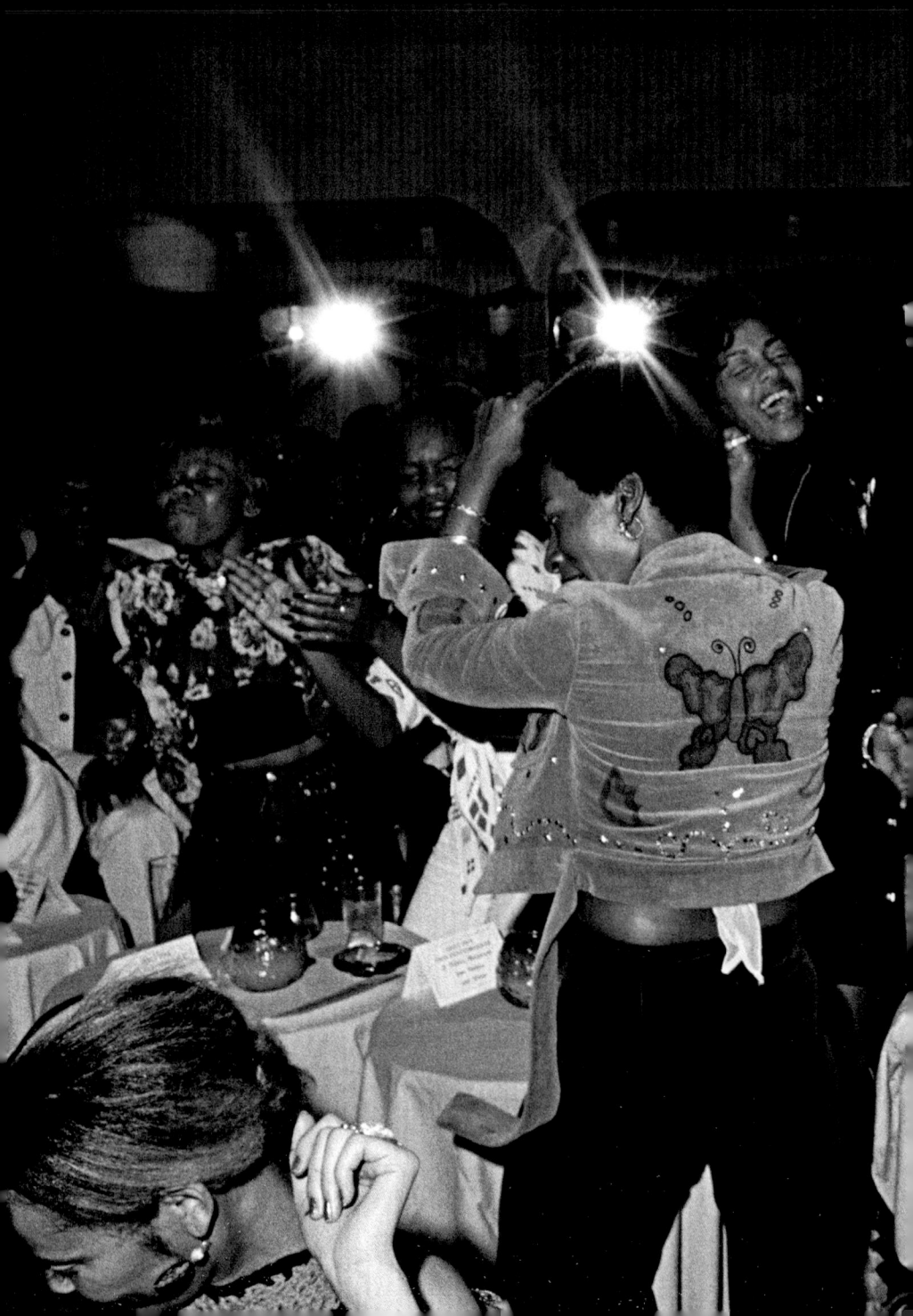

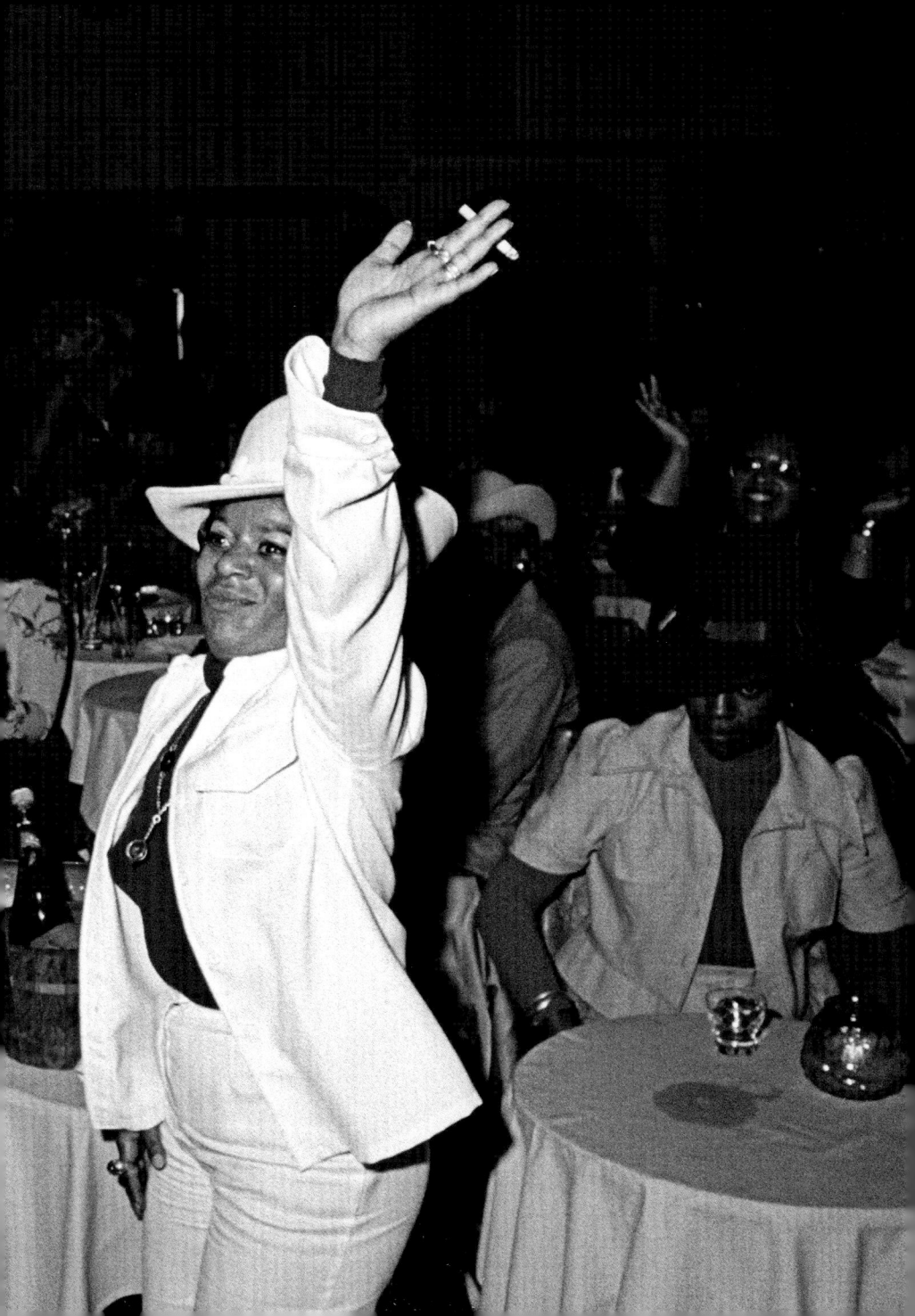

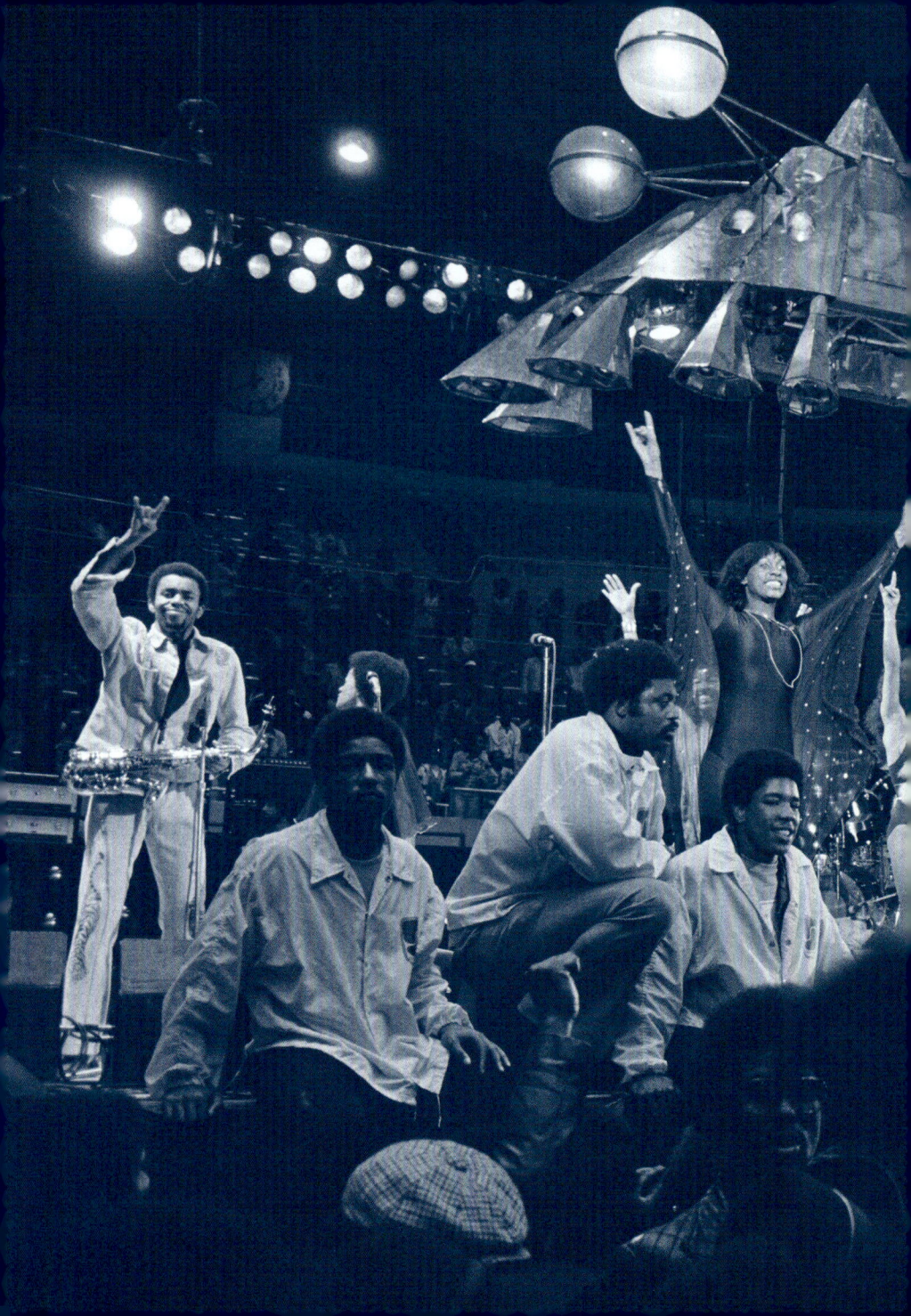

WE GOT THE FUNK

BOOTSY'S RUBBER BAND
THE BROTHERS JOHNSON
LARRY GRAHAM
EDDIE HAZEL
RICK JAMES
PARLIAMENT-FUNKADELIC
SLY STONE

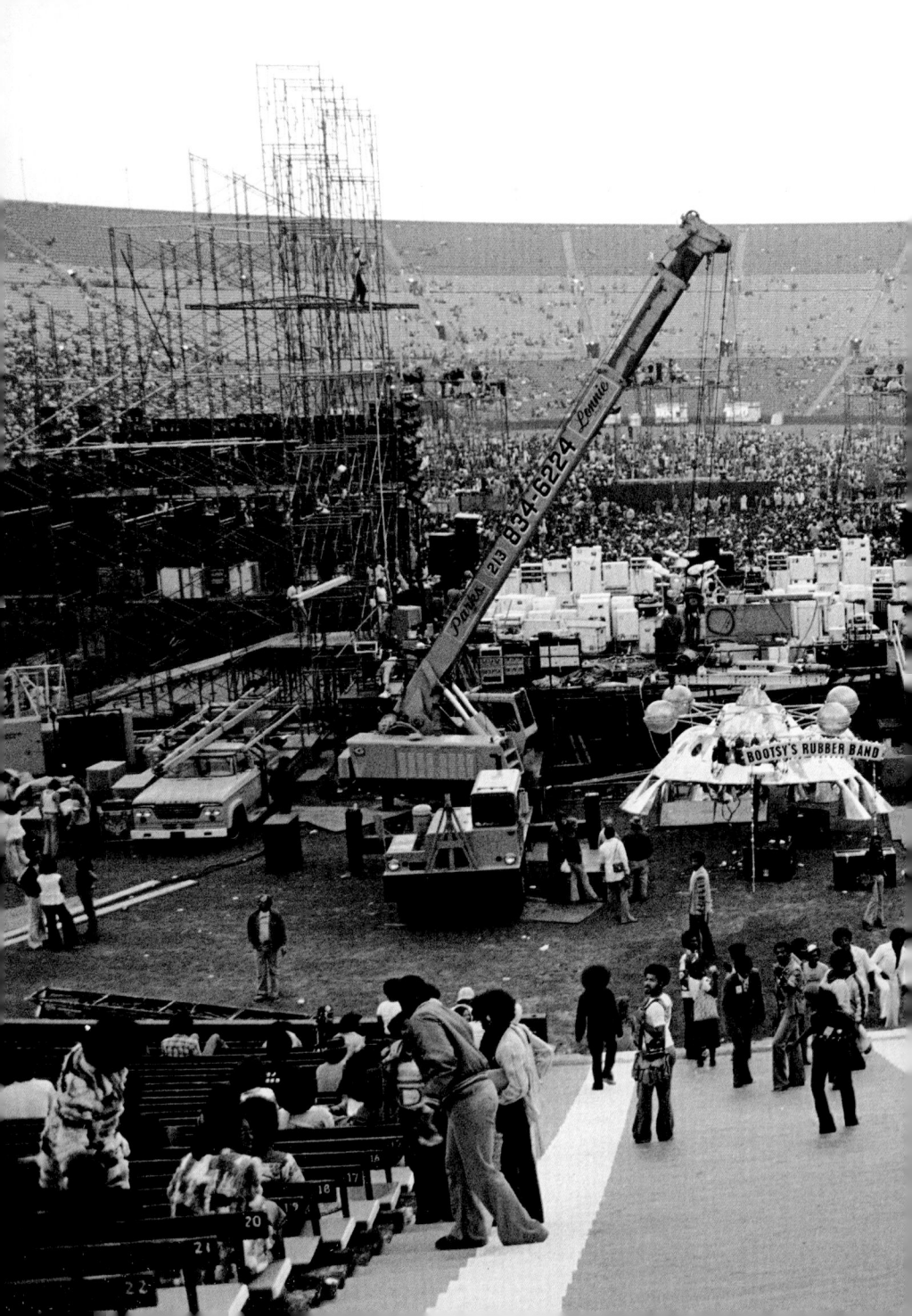

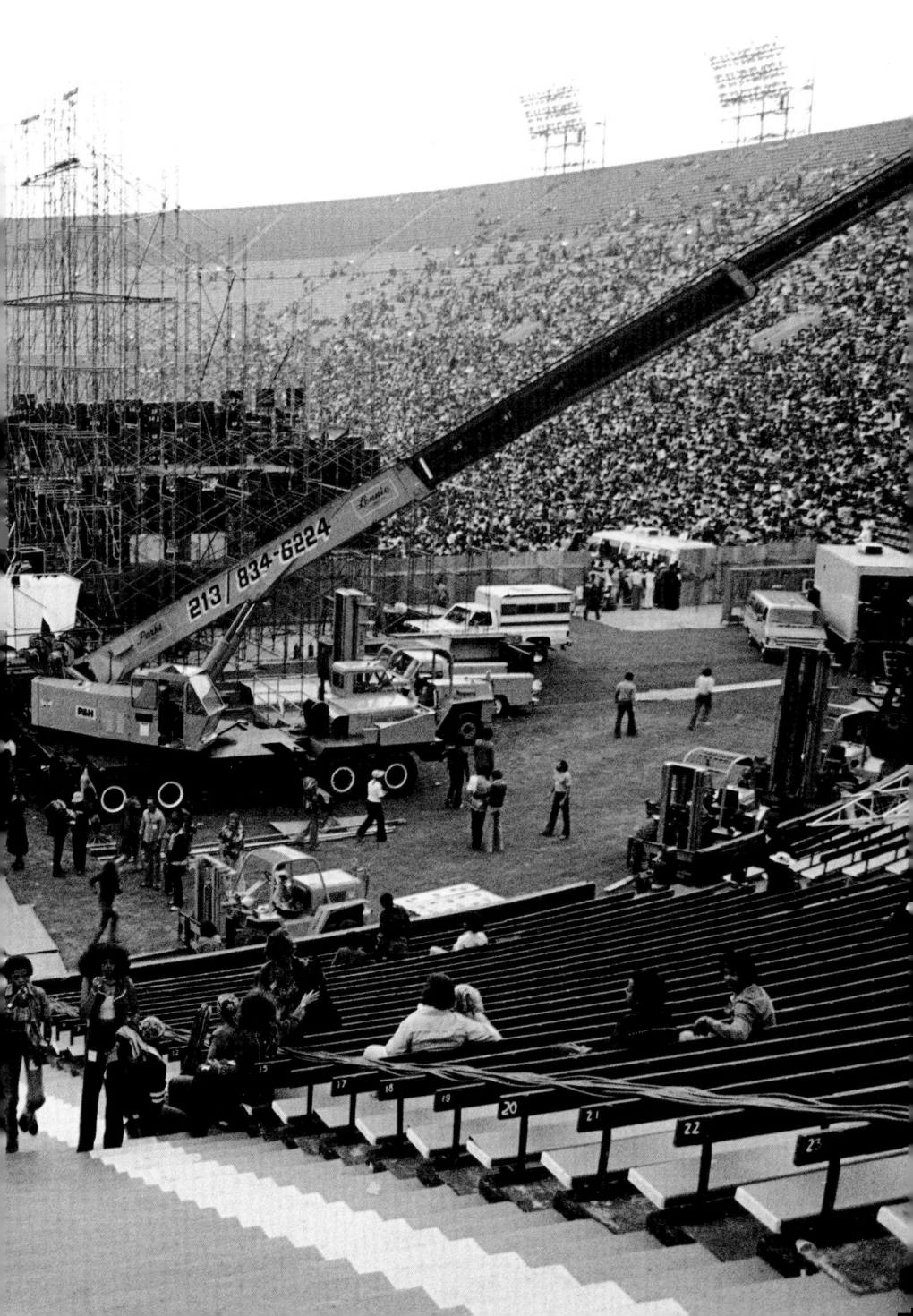

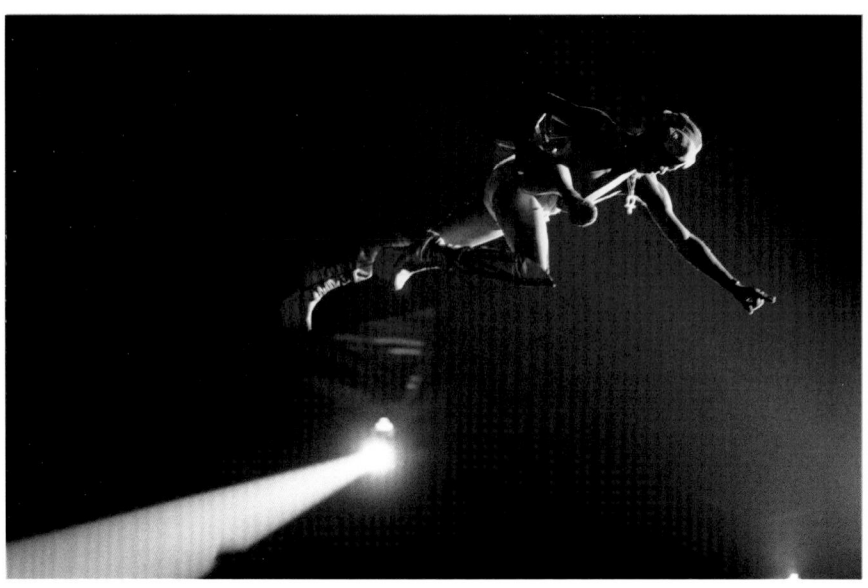

PARLIAMENT-FUNKADELIC

Los Angeles Sports Arena, 1977. (Pages 132–133)
The Mothership is one of the most iconic stage props in rock. The mystical spaceship would lower and deliver Dr. Funkenstein (George Clinton) to Earth at the beginning of a P-Funk concert. A replica of it now rightfully sits in the Smithsonian's National Museum of African American History and Culture.

P-Funk Earth Tour, Funk Fest, Los Angeles Coliseum, 1977. (Pages 134–135)
"One of George Clinton's road managers stated that George wanted to stage a 'black rock opera,' and he convinced Neil Bogart, president of Casablanca Records, to front $275,000, plus money for production costs. George hired the set designer Jules Fisher, who worked with the Rolling Stones. This photograph was taken the morning of June 4, 1977, during the P-Funk Earth Tour. The two giant construction cranes support the lighting and the Mothership. Here were black artists operating on such a grand scale. Rock 'n' roll dipped in funk, with crowds of black fans regularly reaching 100,000 or more. Eventually the funk had to stop. Rumor has it that in 1982, the Mothership was unceremoniously kicked off the back of a flatbed truck into a landfill in Seat Pleasant, Maryland, for nonpayment of storage fees. Coincidentally, 1982 was when I stopped shooting R&B." — Bruce Talamon

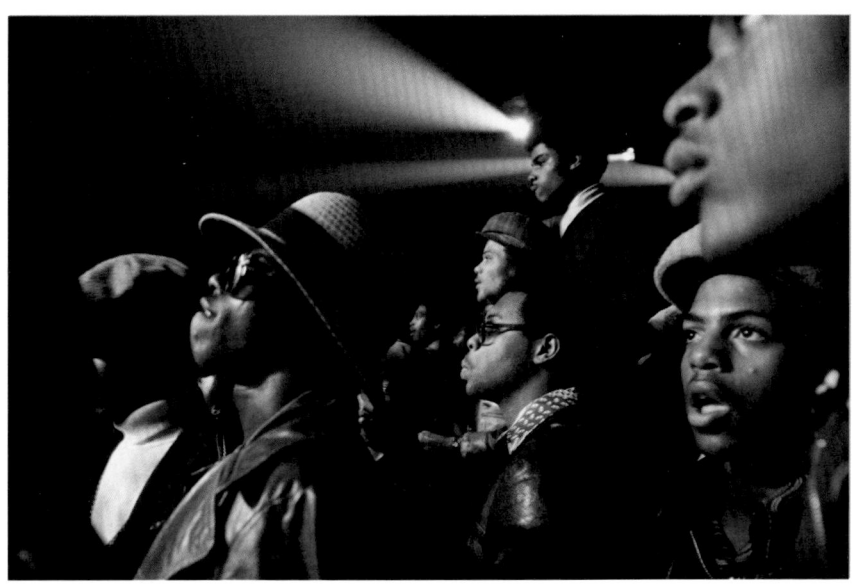

PARLIAMENT-FUNKADELIC
Los Angeles Sports Arena, 1977. (Opposite)
Platform shoes intact, Garry Shider takes flight high above the stage.

Los Angeles Sports Arena, 1977. (Above)
Not unlike the Grateful Dead's Deadheads, hardcore
fans of P-Funk feel a special kindred spirit to the music. The crowd
reacts in awe and disbelief to the Mothership as it lands.

Los Angeles Sports Arena, 1977. (Page 138)
George Clinton aka Dr. Funkenstein.

BOOTSY'S RUBBER BAND
The Forum, Inglewood, California, 1978. (Page 139)
Ahh...The Name Is Bootsy, Baby!

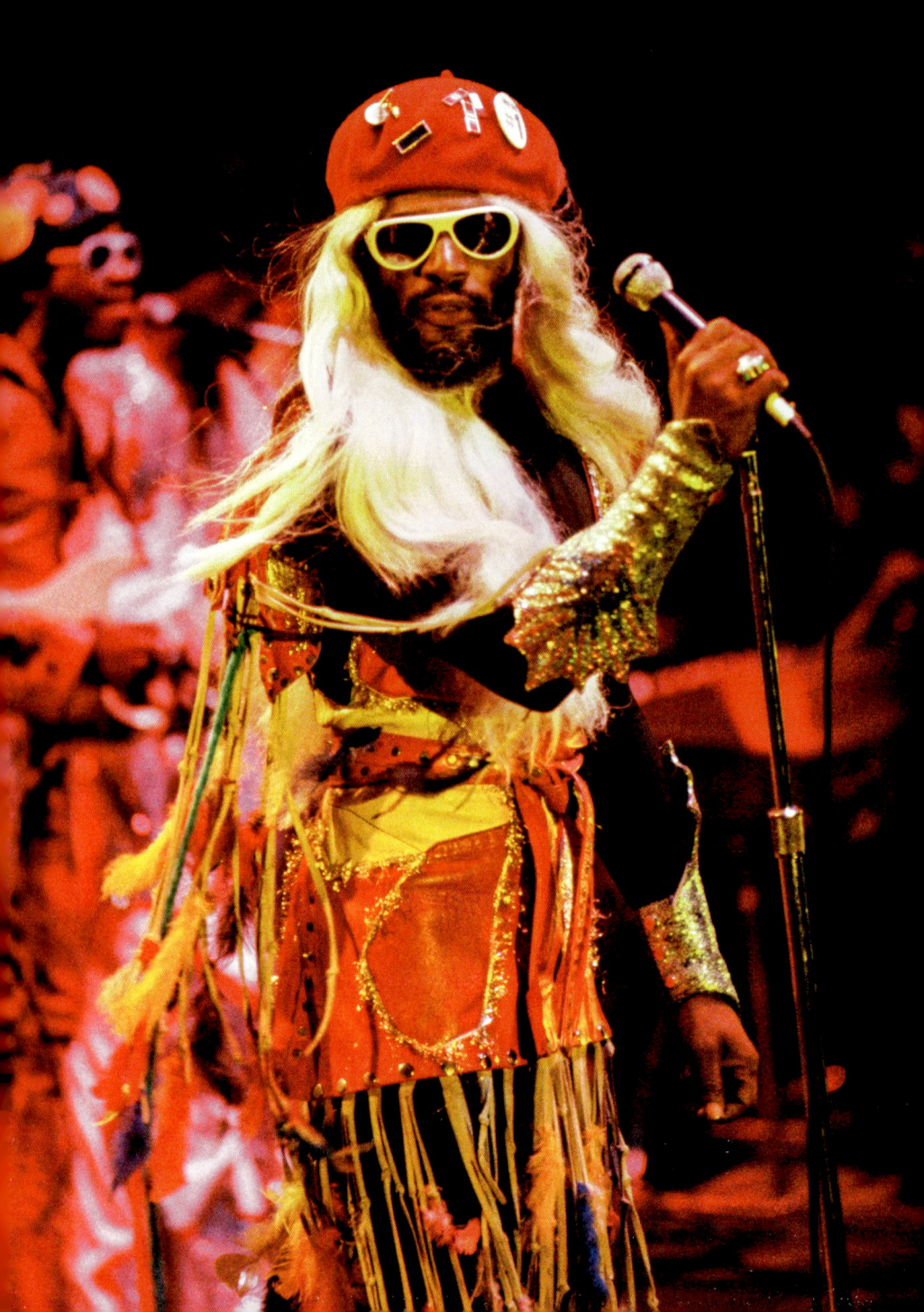

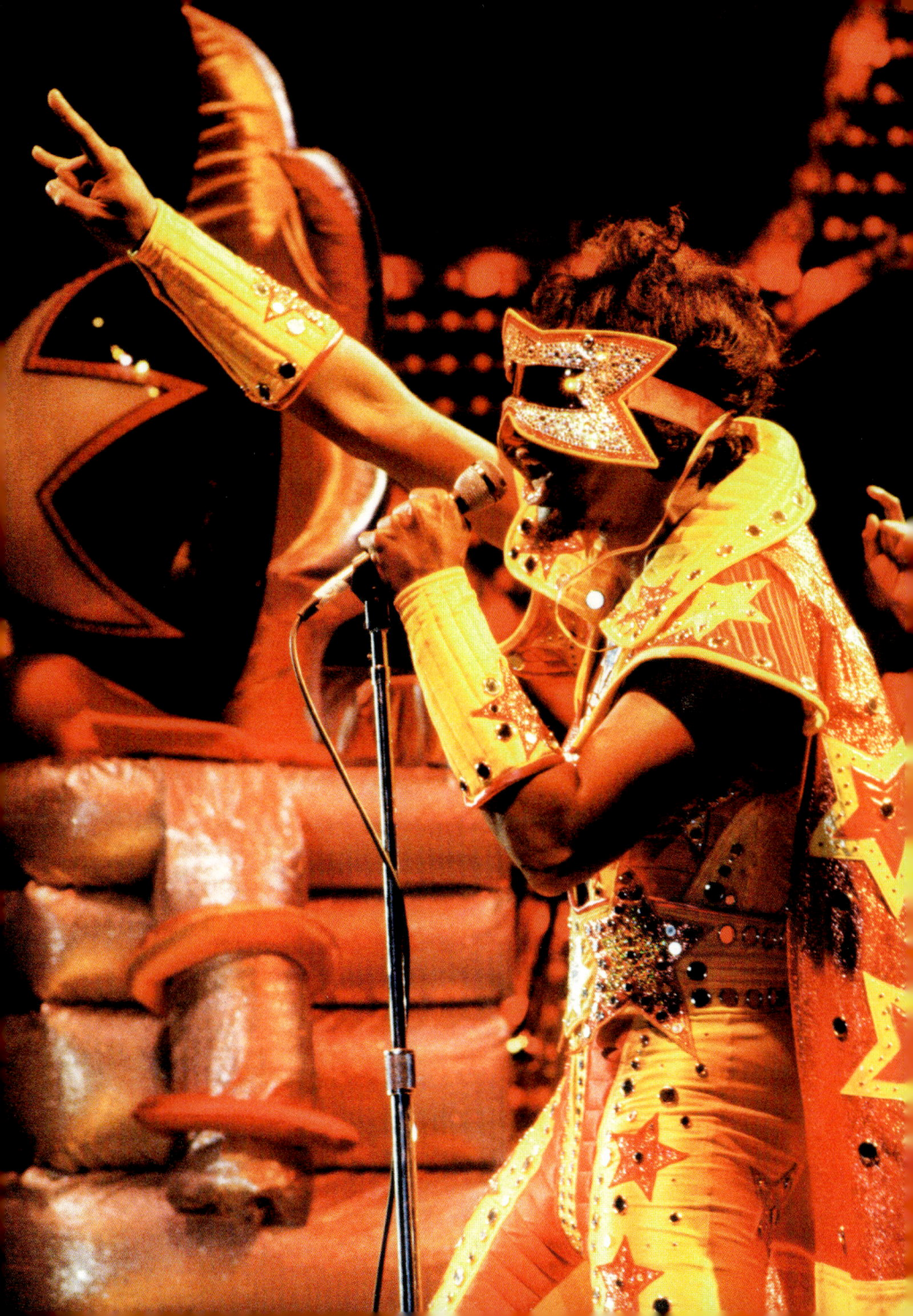

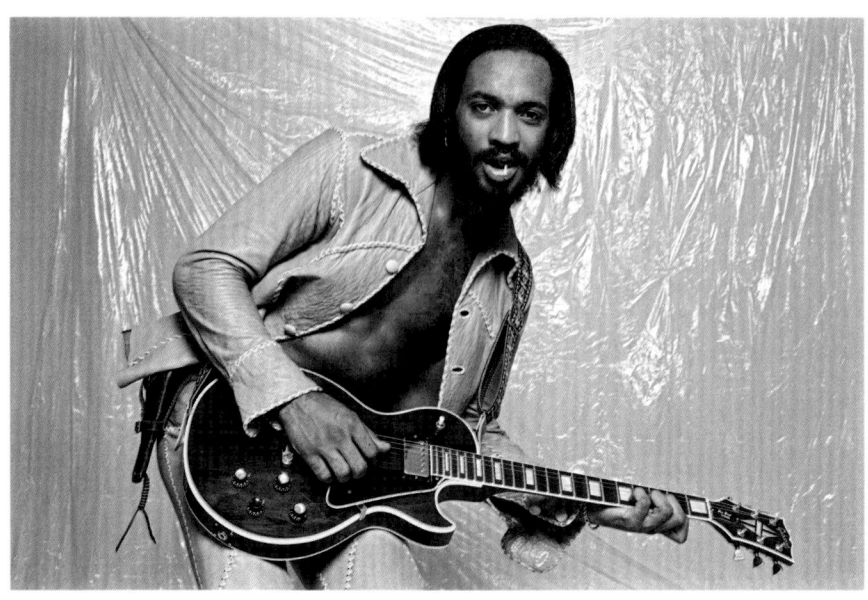

EDDIE HAZEL
Los Angeles, 1977. (Above)
Hazel was a guitar god. His 10-minute, fuzzbox-laden solo on "Maggot Brain" is considered one of the all-time great guitar performances. His contribution to the song helped it become Parliament-Funkadelic's magnum opus of psychedelic expression.

PARLIAMENT-FUNKADELIC
Los Angeles, 1977. (Opposite)
George Clinton brought funk to a whole new generation. But overlooking him as a master conceptual artist would not be giving him his due.

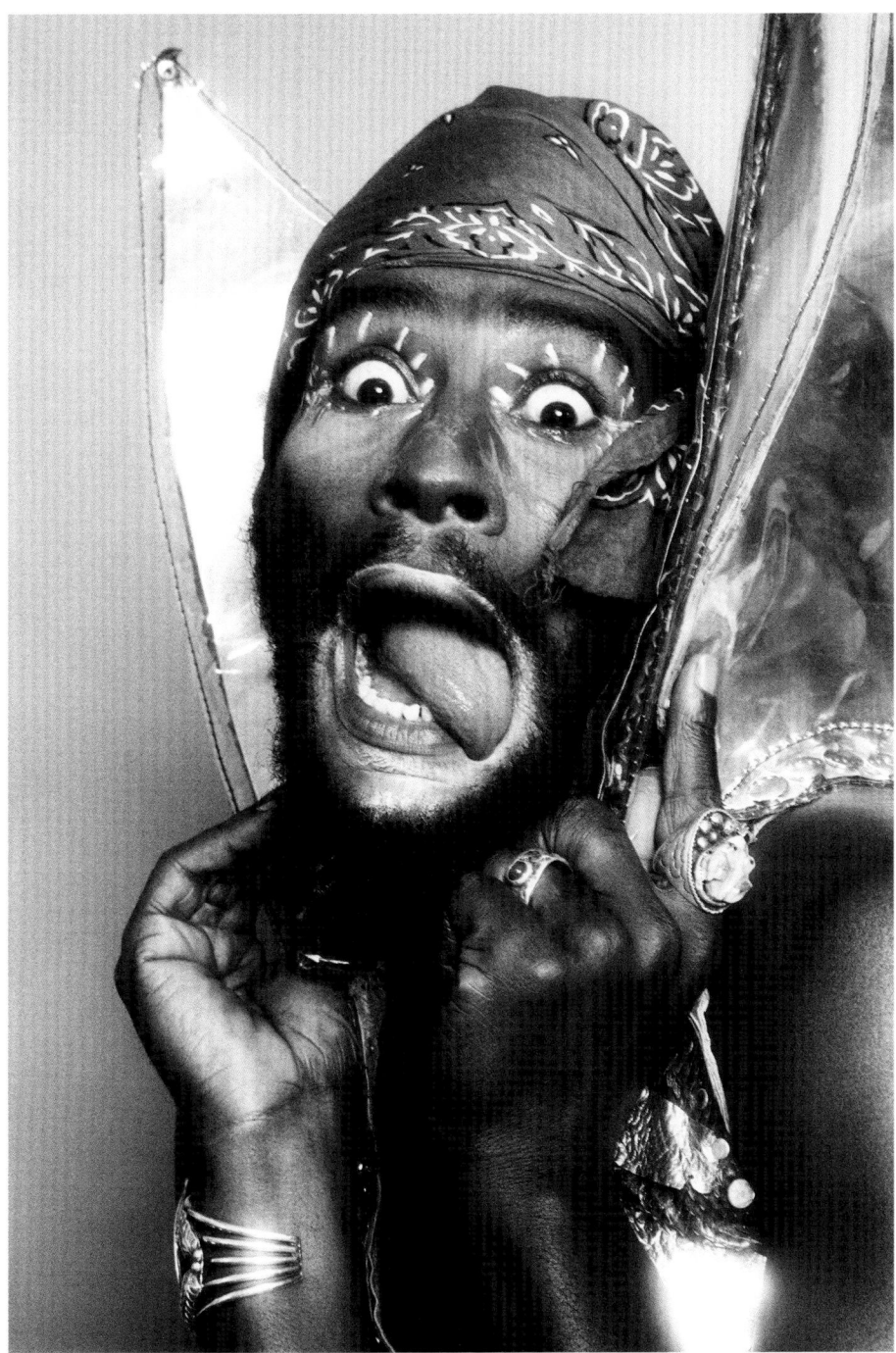

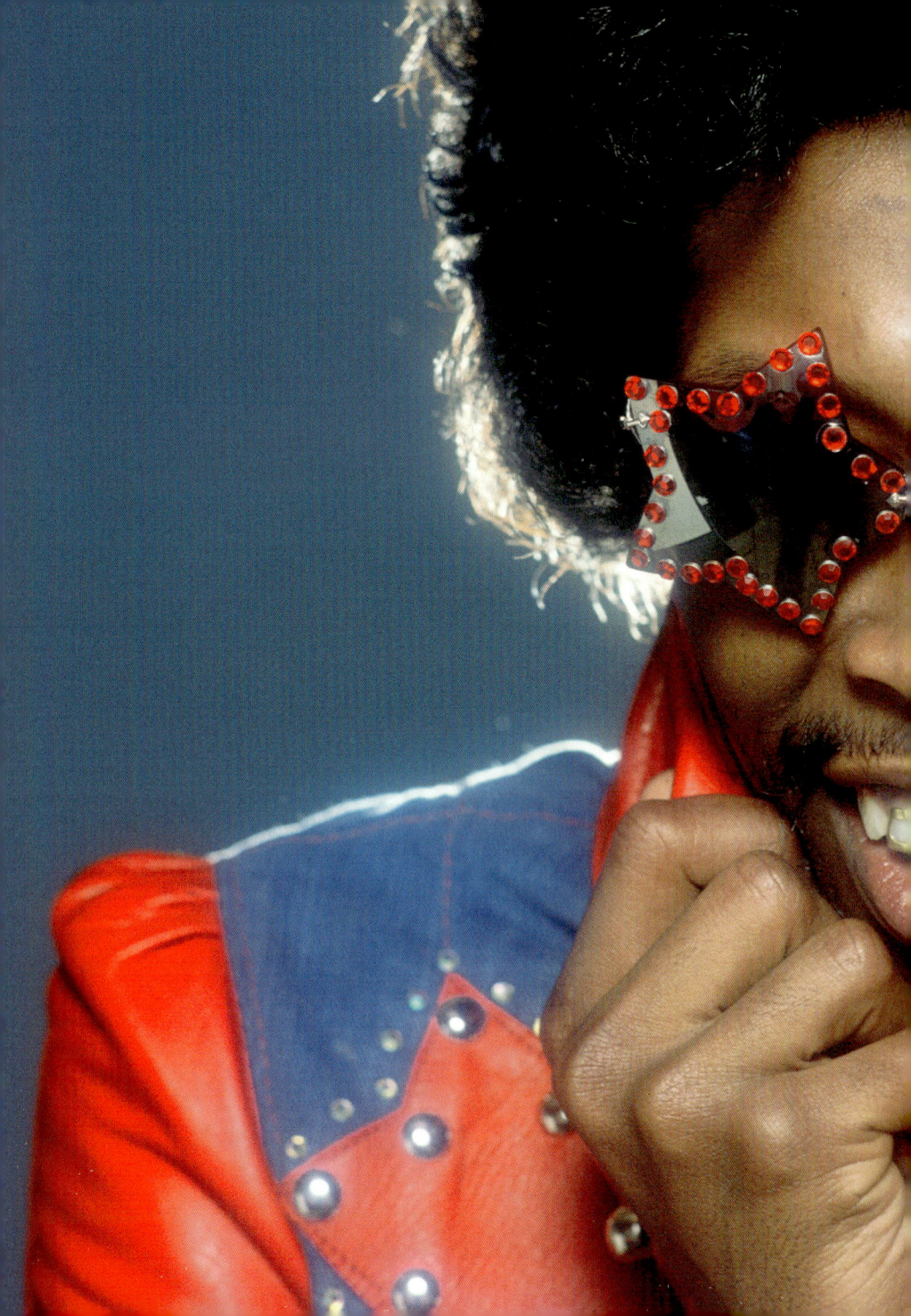

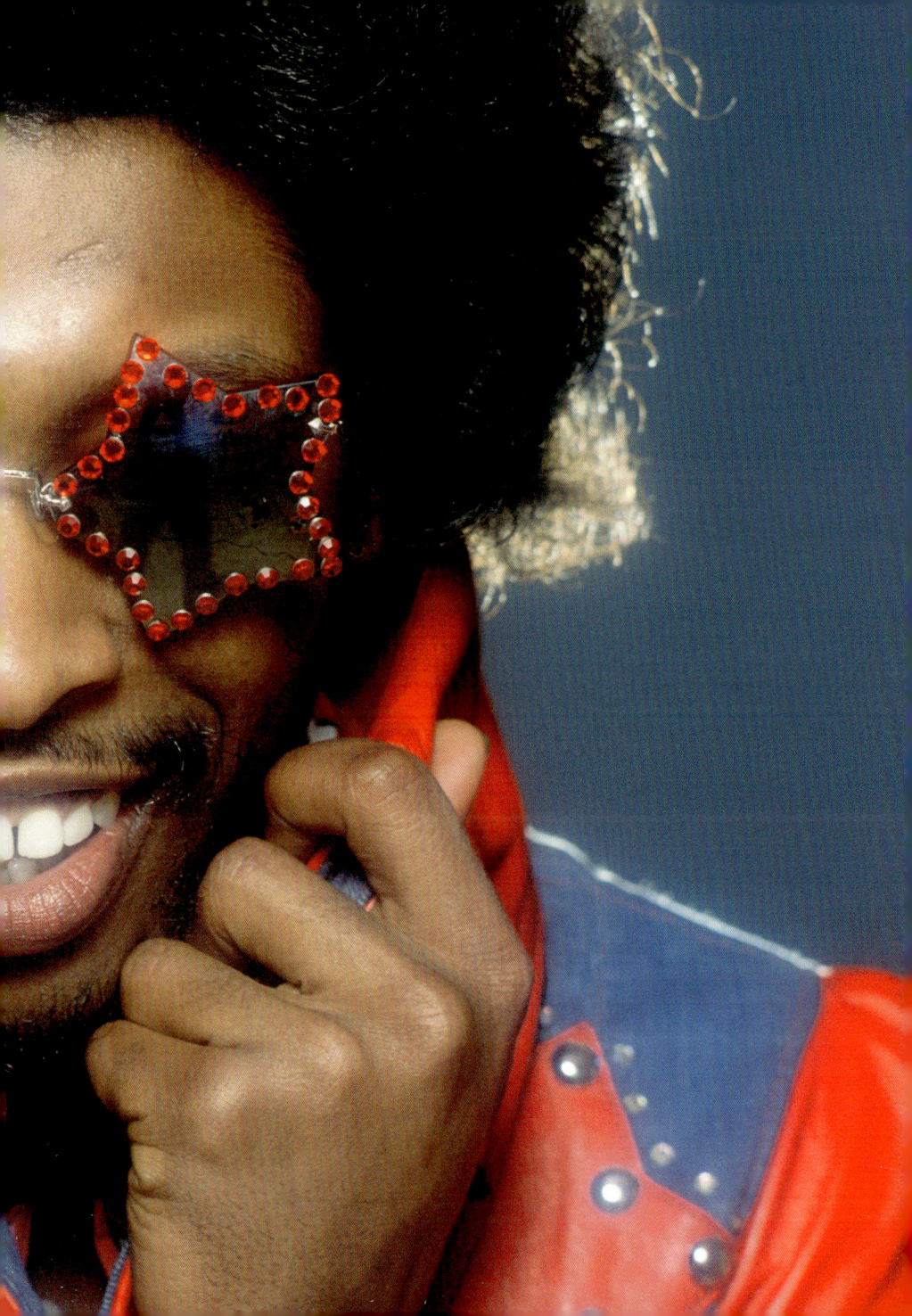

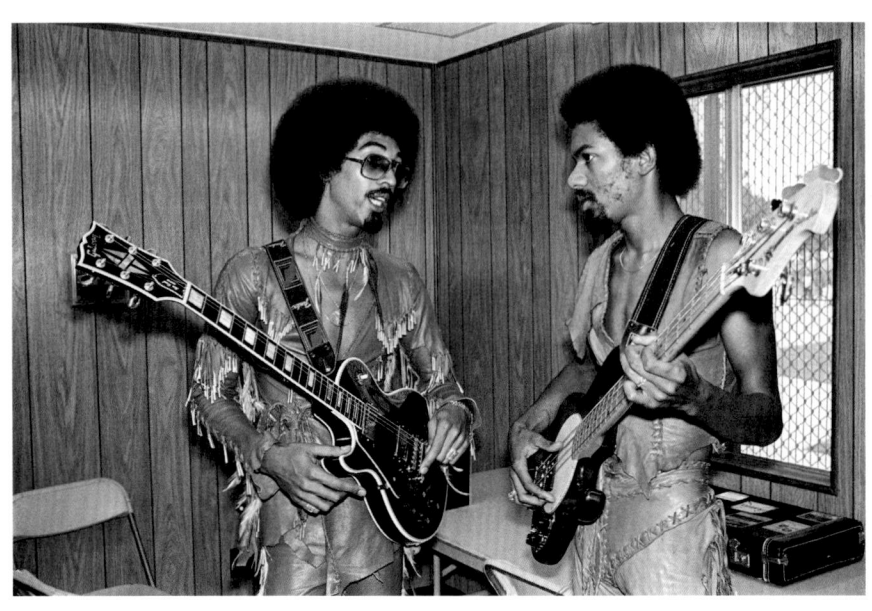

BOOTSY'S RUBBER BAND
Warner Bros. Records, Burbank, California, 1977. (Pages 142–143)
William Earl "Bootsy" Collins.

THE BROTHERS JOHNSON
Funk Fest, Los Angeles Coliseum, 1977. (Above)
Brothers George and Louis discuss their set before taking the stage.

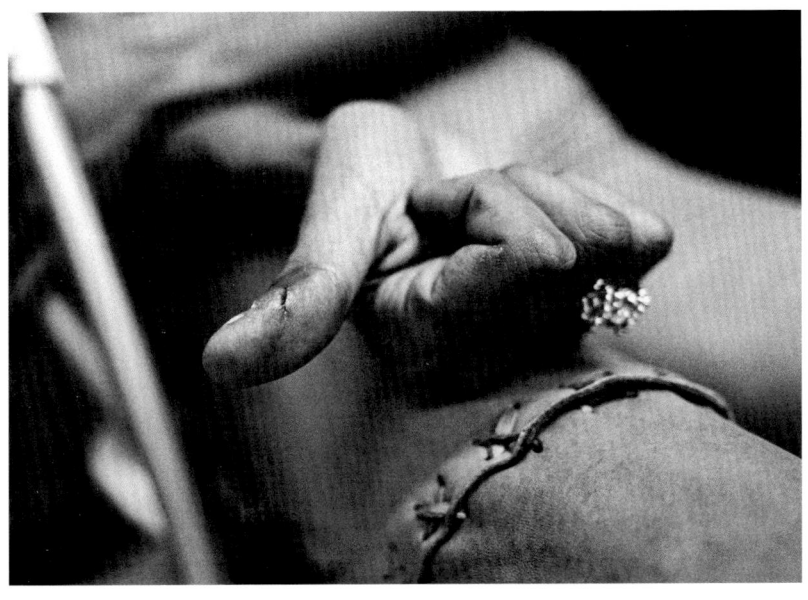

THE BROTHERS JOHNSON
Funk Fest, Los Angeles Coliseum, 1977.
*"This is a close-up of Louis Johnson's blistered thumb after performing at the
P-Funk Earth Tour. This is one of those moments where we see exactly what
the artist has to give to get that great performance. I had followed Louis and
George offstage after their set. Louis mentioned that he had shredded his thumb
during their set, and then he turned to me and grinned."* —Bruce Talamon

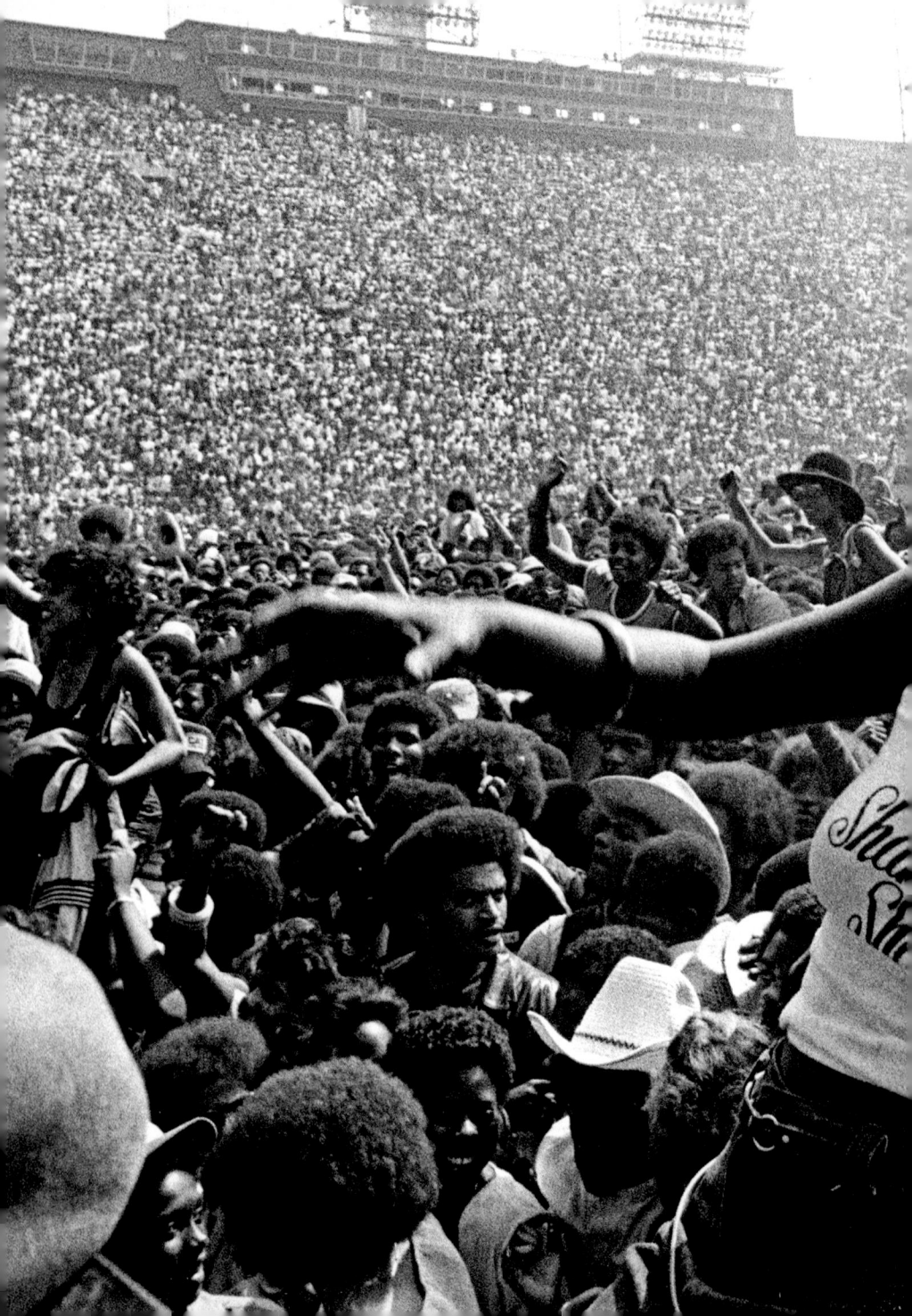

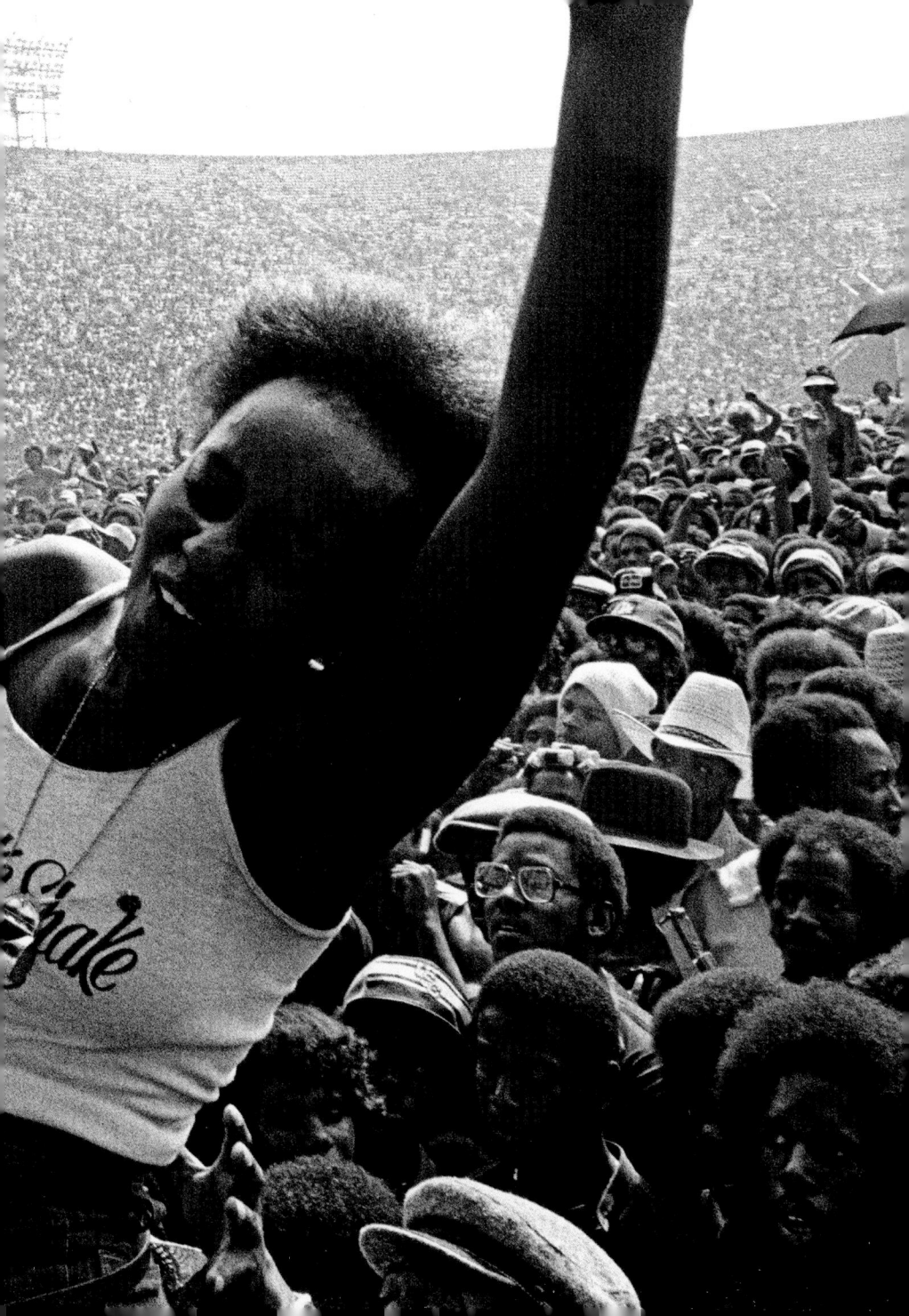

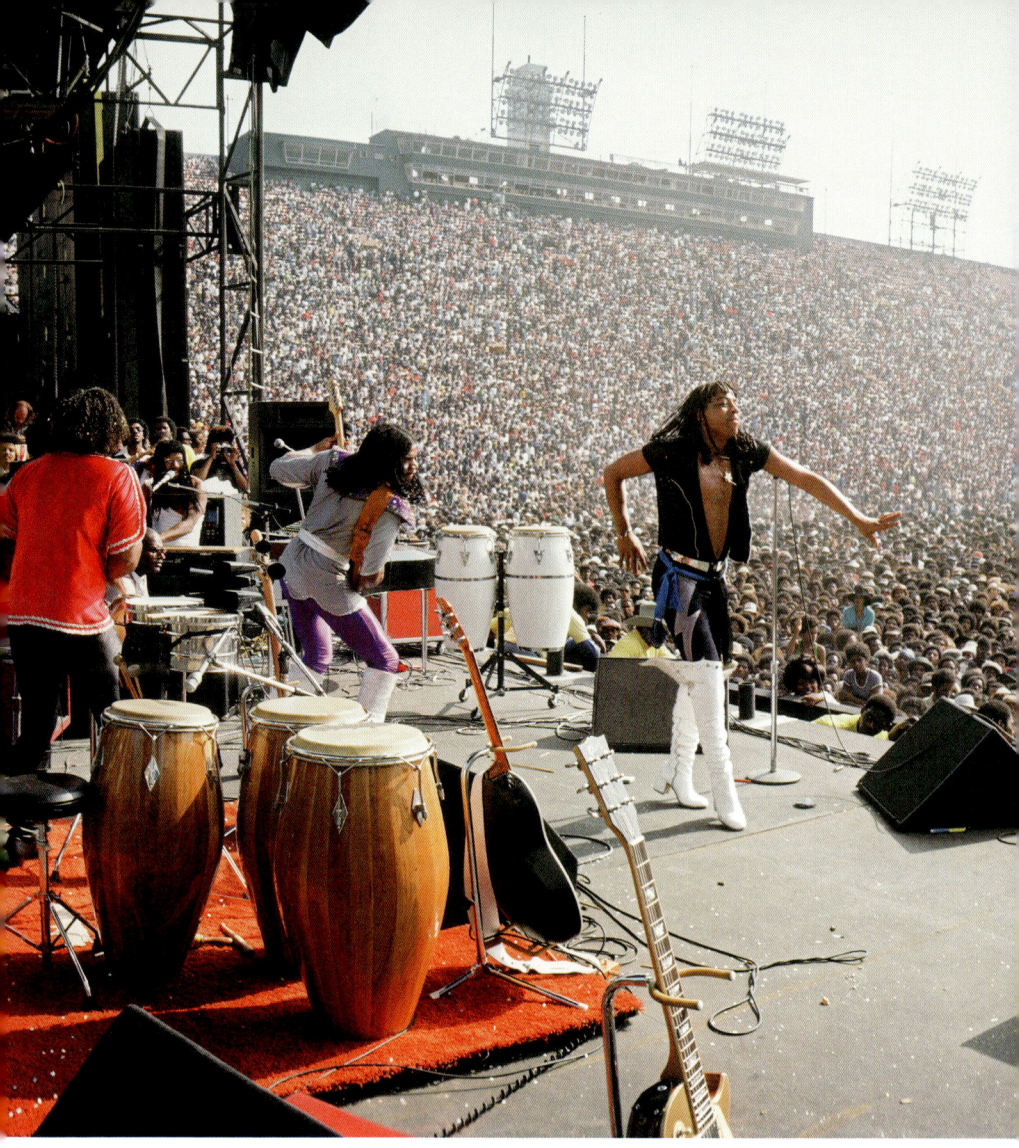

BOOTSY'S RUBBER BAND
P-Funk Earth Tour, Funk Fest, Los Angeles
Coliseum, 1977. (Pages 146–147)
Ever funkin' on!

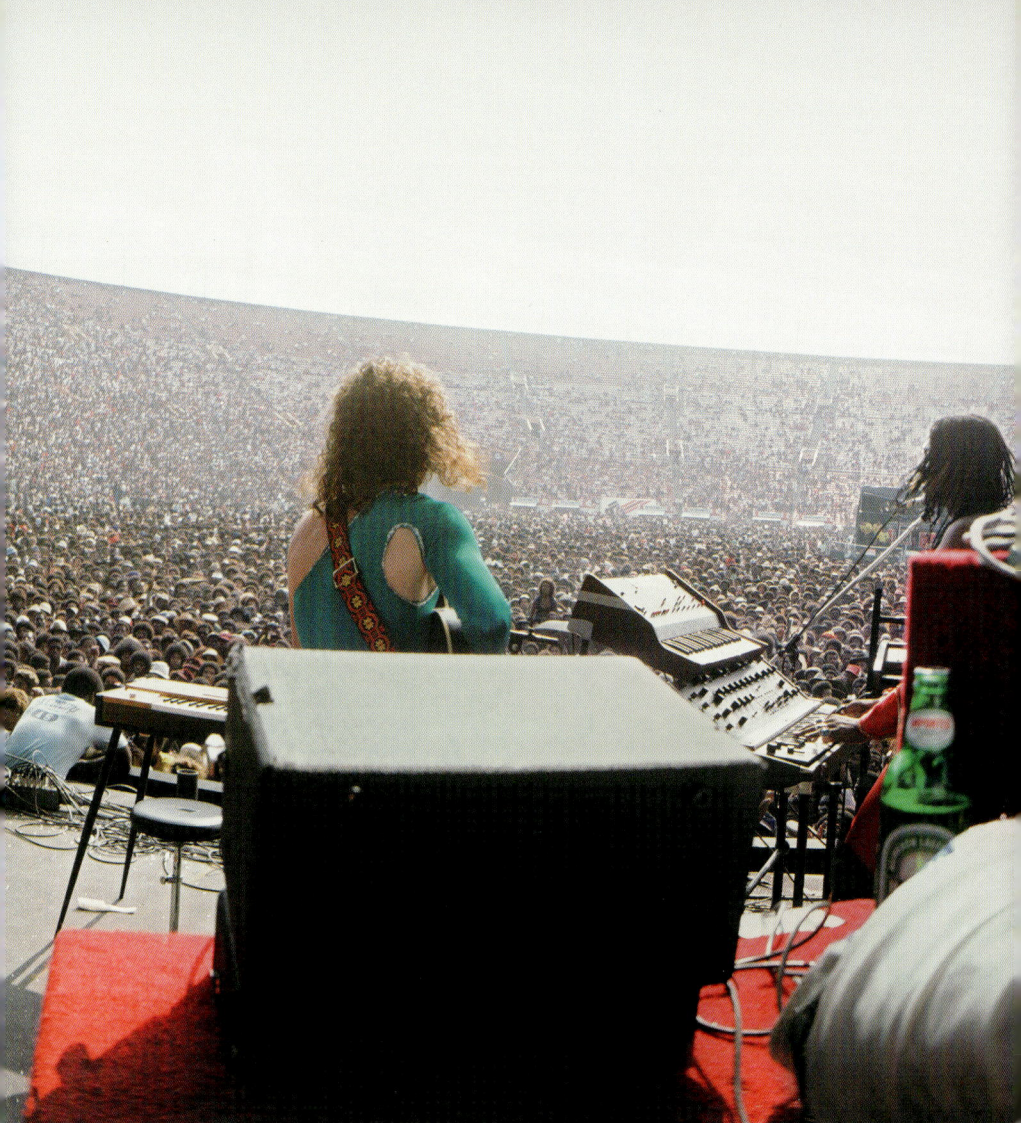

RICK JAMES
Funk Fest, Los Angeles Coliseum, 1977.
The creator of punk-funk, James solidified his rock-star style
and bad-boy image with songs like "Give It to Me Baby" and
"Super Freak." And he looked great in knee-high white boots.

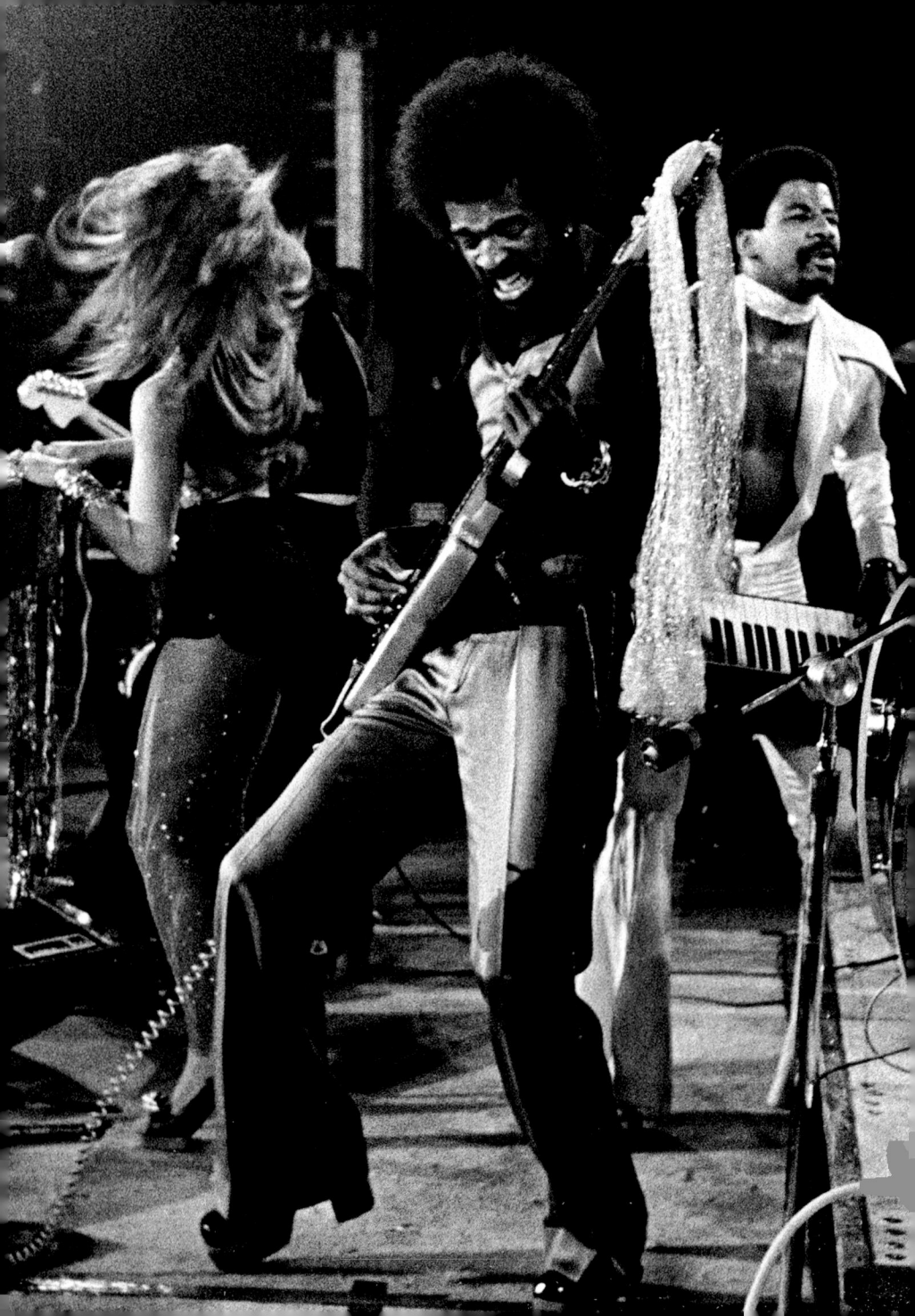

LARRY GRAHAM
The Forum, Inglewood, California, 1975. (Opposite)
With his band Graham Central Station, Graham — who was previously the
bass player for Sly & the Family Stone — would showcase his patented creation
of slap bass in the group's compositions. With idiosyncratic instruments
such as the Funk Box, the band would serve up funk- and gospel-infused jams.

SLY STONE
Hollywood Bowl, California, 1974. (Pages 152–153)

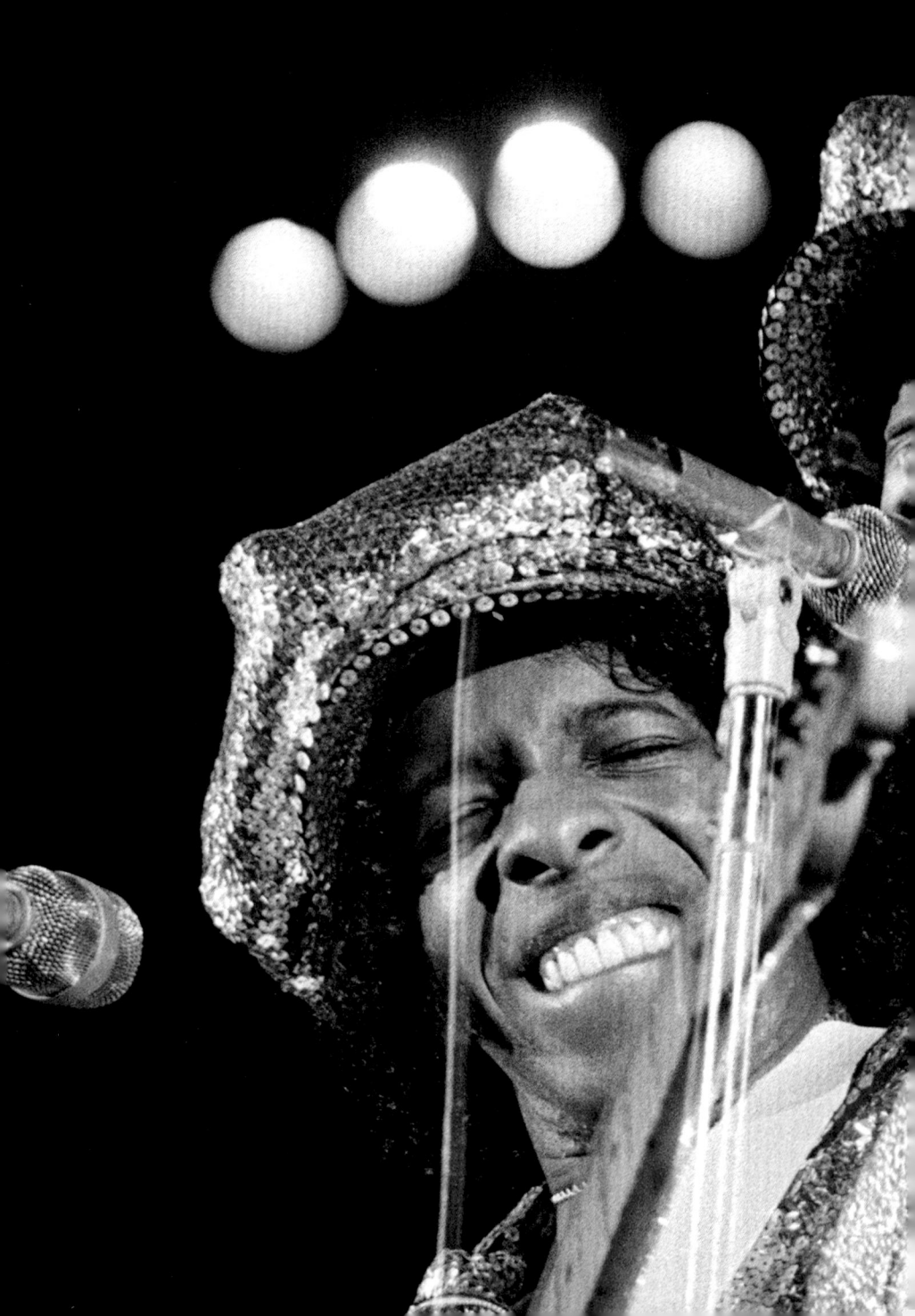

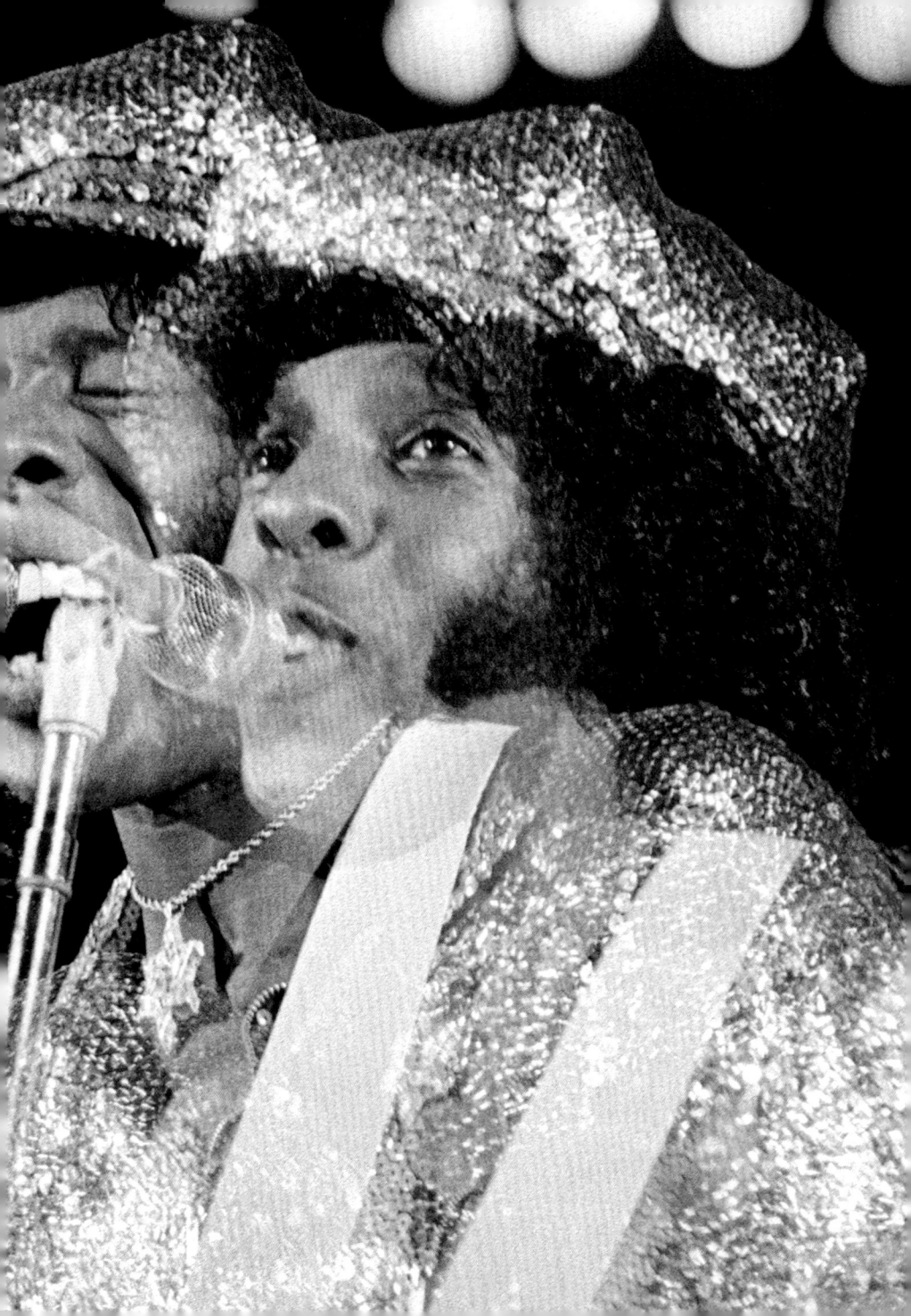

TOO HOT TA TROT

THE BAR-KAYS
COMMODORES
L.T.D.
OHIO PLAYERS
RUFUS FEATURING CHAKA KHAN

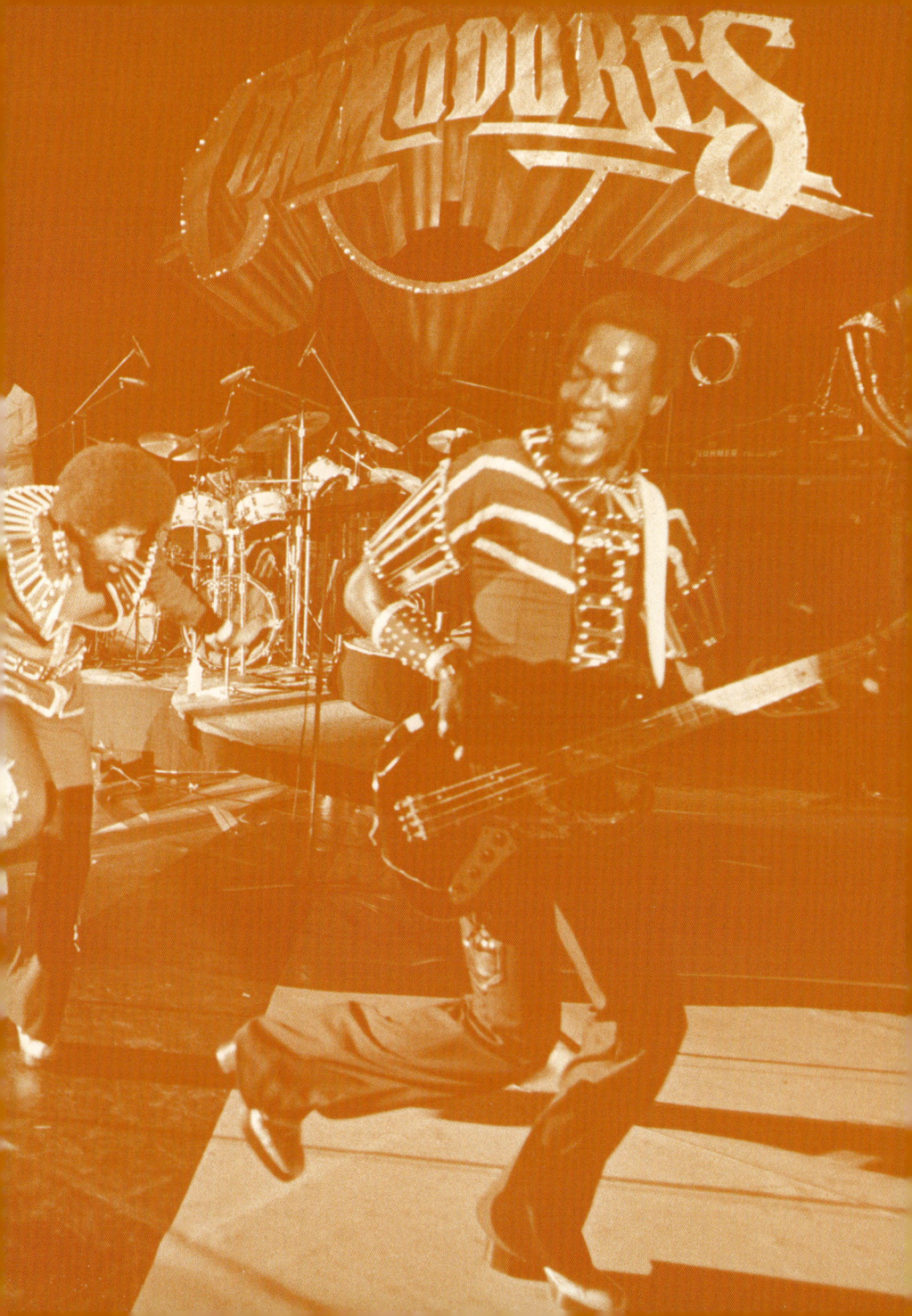

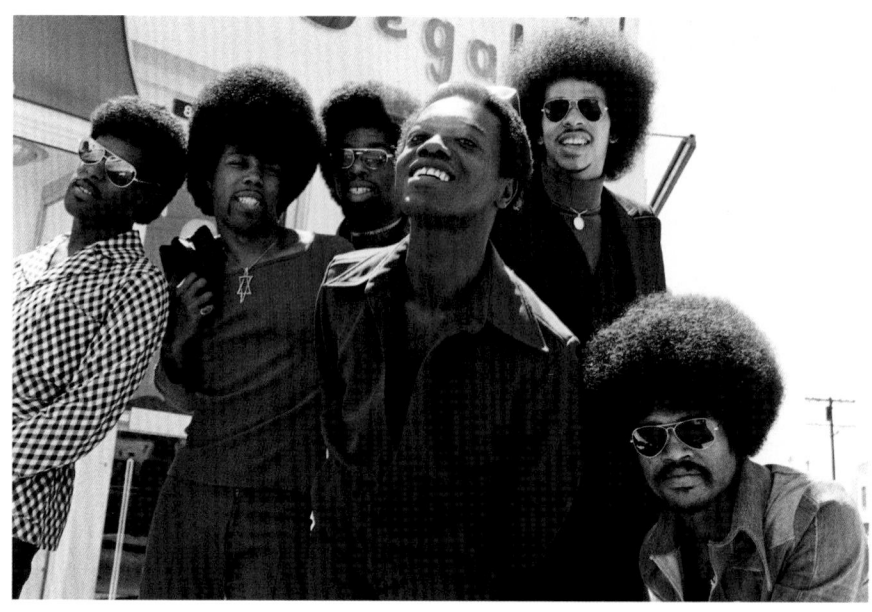

COMMODORES
The Forum, Inglewood, California, 1977. (Pages 154–155)

OHIO PLAYERS
Outside of Fred Segal clothing store, Los Angeles, 1974. (Above)
Formed in Dayton, Ohio, in the late 1960s, they were known for their
provocative album covers almost as much as for their hits. With a grittier funk
than most of their smoother contemporaries, their sexy anthem "Skin Tight"
was just taking off in 1974.

THE BAR-KAYS
Los Angeles, 1974. (Opposite)
Four of the band's original members perished in the same plane crash as
the great Otis Redding in 1967. Rebuilt by the remaining two members, the
group would soldier on for the next 20 years. The second incarnation of
the band is reflected in original member James "Knuck" Alexander's glasses.

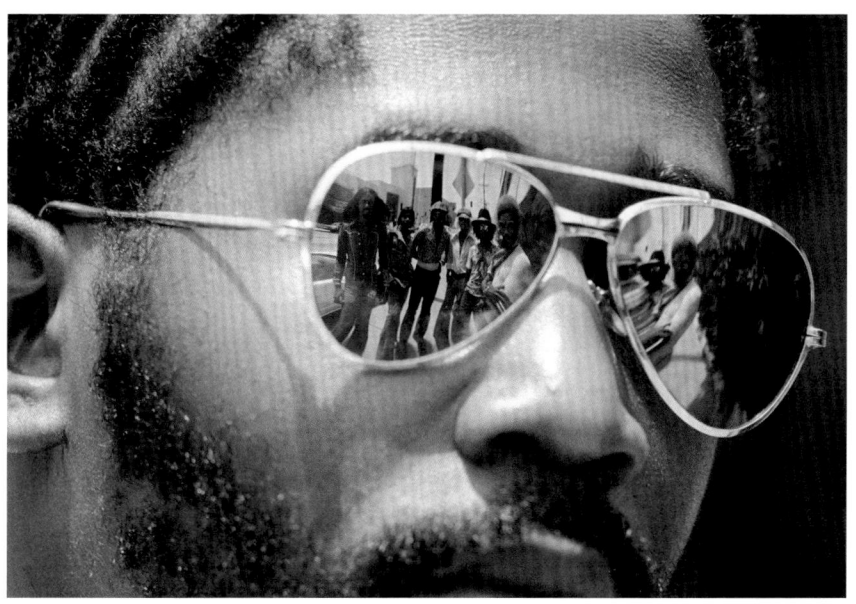

COMMODORES
Sunset Sound, Hollywood, California, 1978. (Page 158)
Formed at Tuskegee Institute in the late 1960s, the band would eventually become crossover mavens. Vocalist Lionel Richie left in 1982 and launched a massive solo career. Richie would also write hit songs for Kenny Rogers and Diana Ross, and co-wrote with Michael Jackson the charity-inspired "We Are the World."

L.T.D.
Los Angeles, 1974. (Page 159)
"They called it 'The Big House.' Four bedrooms, two baths, and $200 a month. Keyboardist Billy Osborne told me more: 'That house was our university. We lived there with our musical director. We rehearsed every day. Most of the band lived there. We could literally roll out of bed and practice. The main thing was… that house held us together.' I remember the missing ceiling tiles and the sign tacked in the rehearsal room. 'Miss ONE day (You'll Know It), Miss Two Days (Your Friends Know It), Miss Three Days (Everybody Knows It).'" — Bruce Talamon

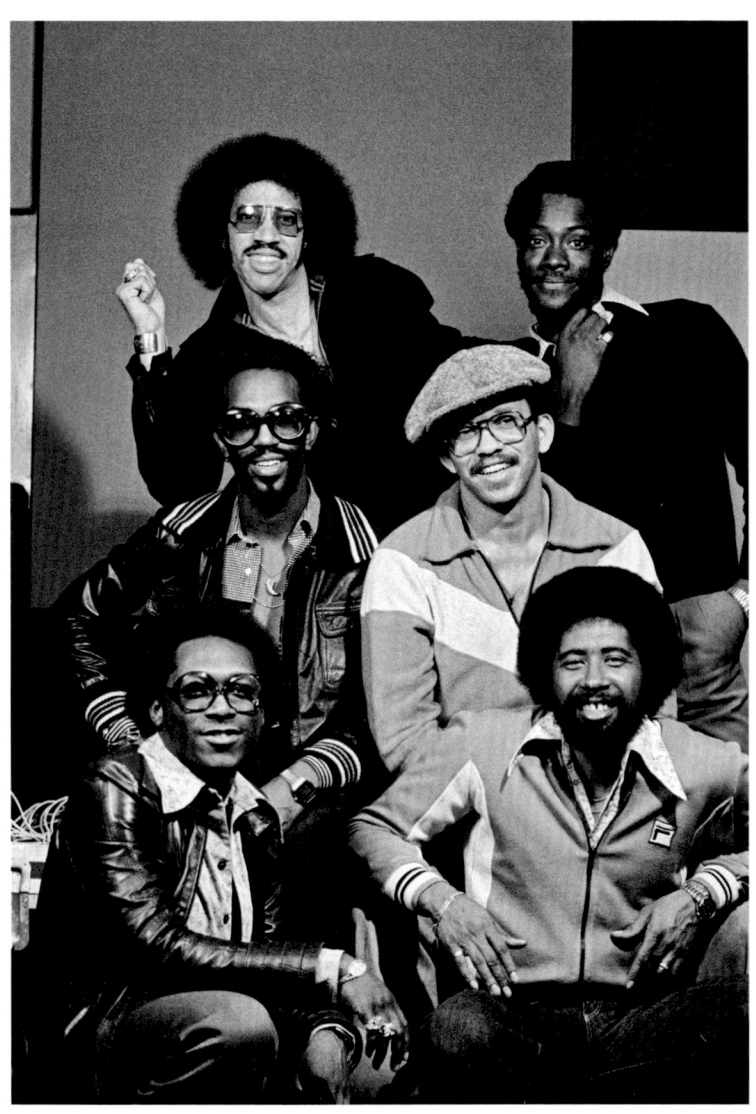

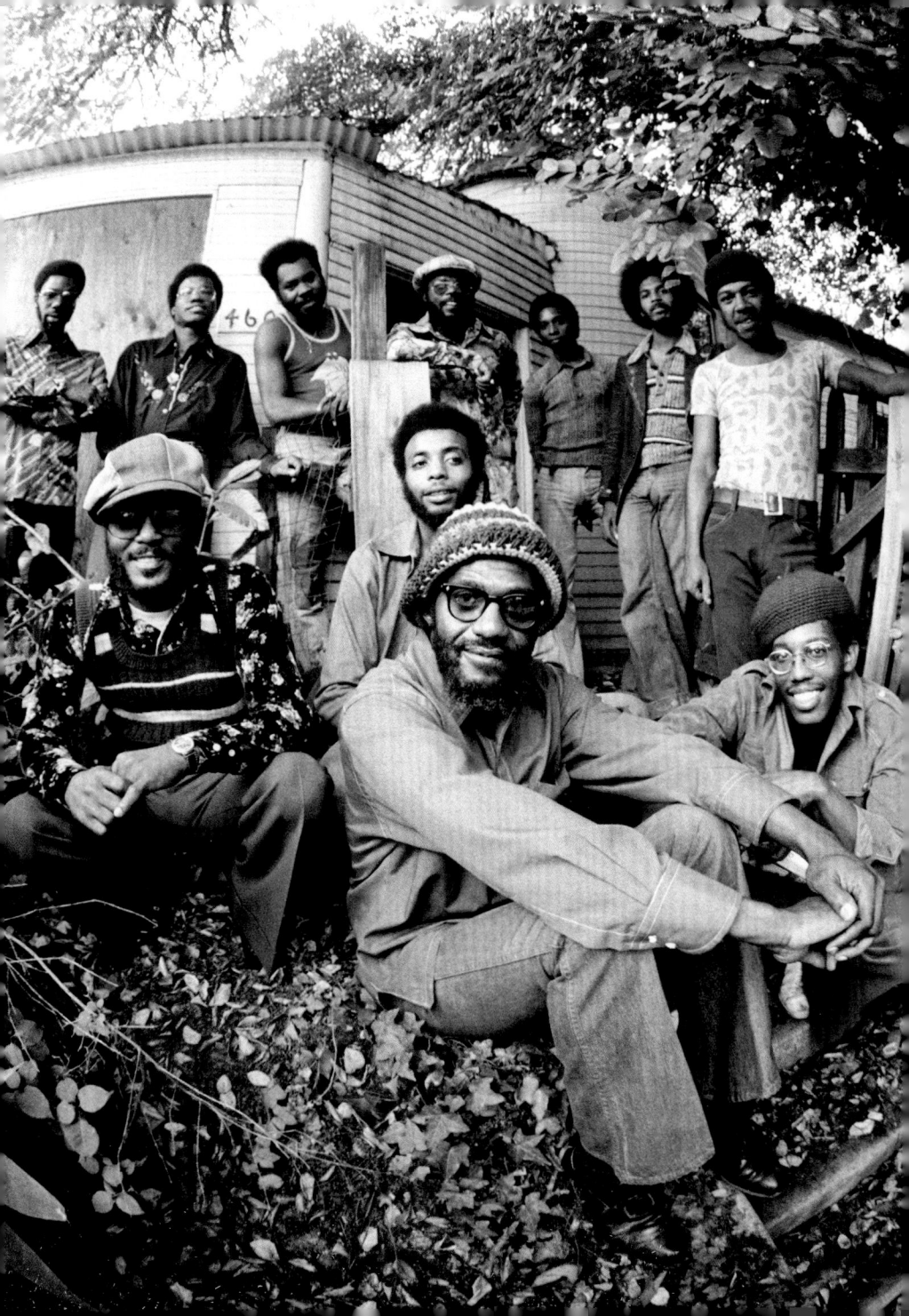

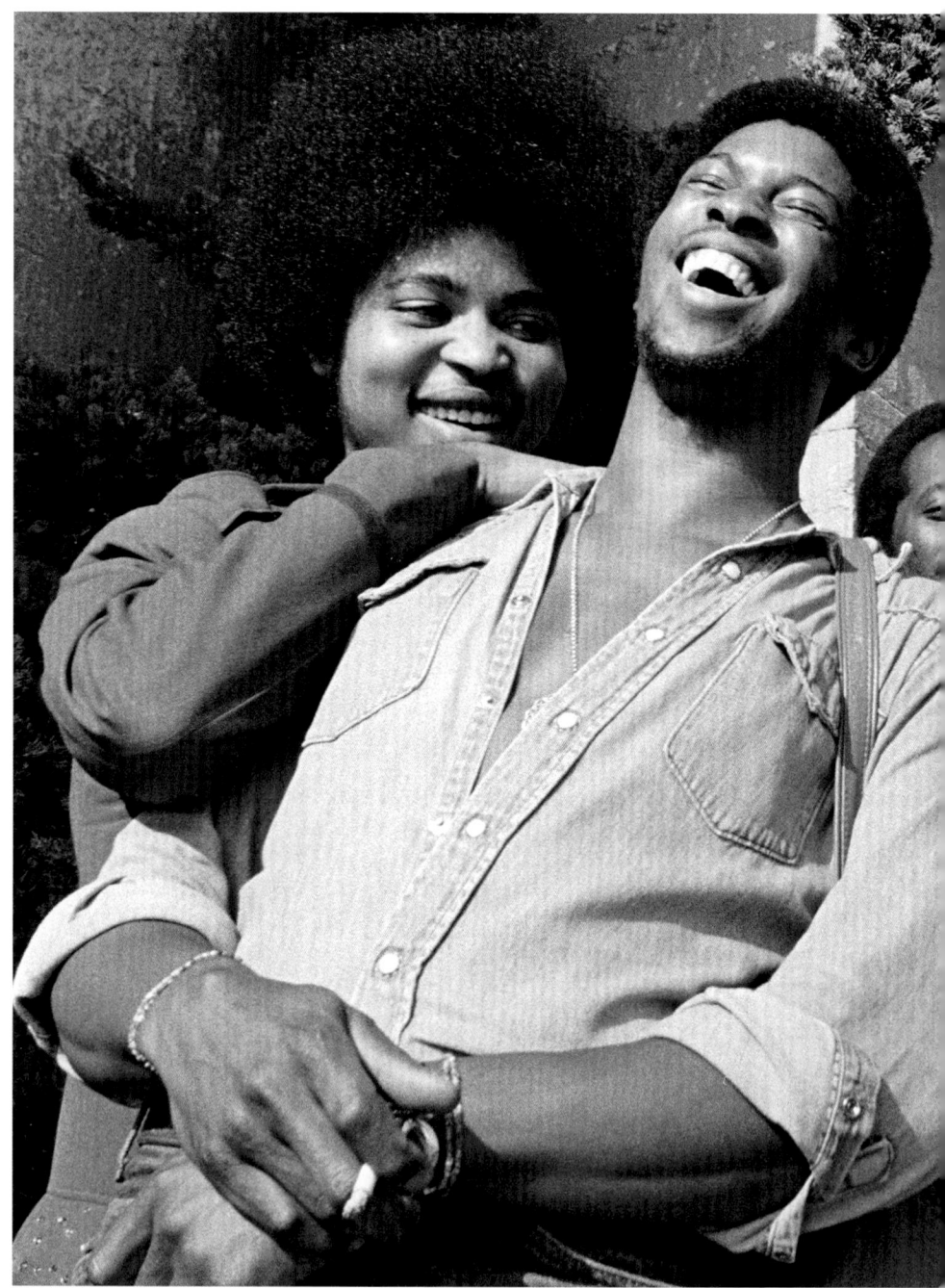

RUFUS FEATURING CHAKA KHAN
ABC, Dunhill Recording Studios, Los Angeles, 1974. (Pages 160–161)

Rehearsal, Los Angeles, 1975. (Opposite)

Funk Fest, Los Angeles Coliseum, 1977. (Pages 164–165)
Khan's solo career would only grow her reputation as an artist.
Through songs that covered R&B, jazz, and pop, the 10-time Grammy
winner is recognized as one of the greatest female singers of all time.

The Roxy, West Hollywood, California, 1977. (Pages 166–167)
Backstage. The Roxy is a venue of choice for the biggest stars and wannabe
stars. Seating only 500 people, it is intimate enough that you can feel the
audience, and yet the stage is large enough that you can bring your arena-sized
amplifiers. Additionally, Bob Marley & The Wailers, George Benson, and
Guns N' Roses were a few of the artists that recorded live albums there.

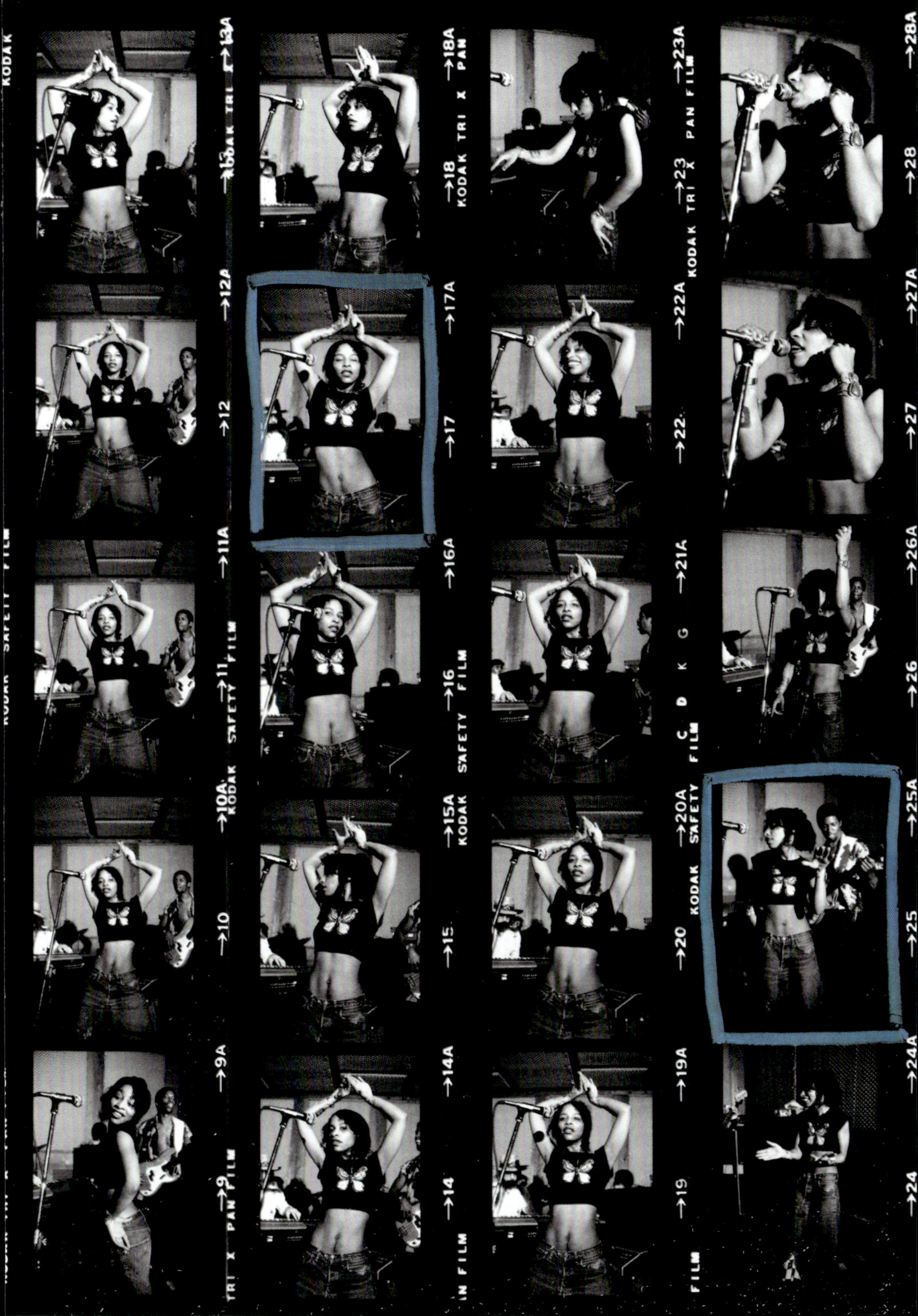

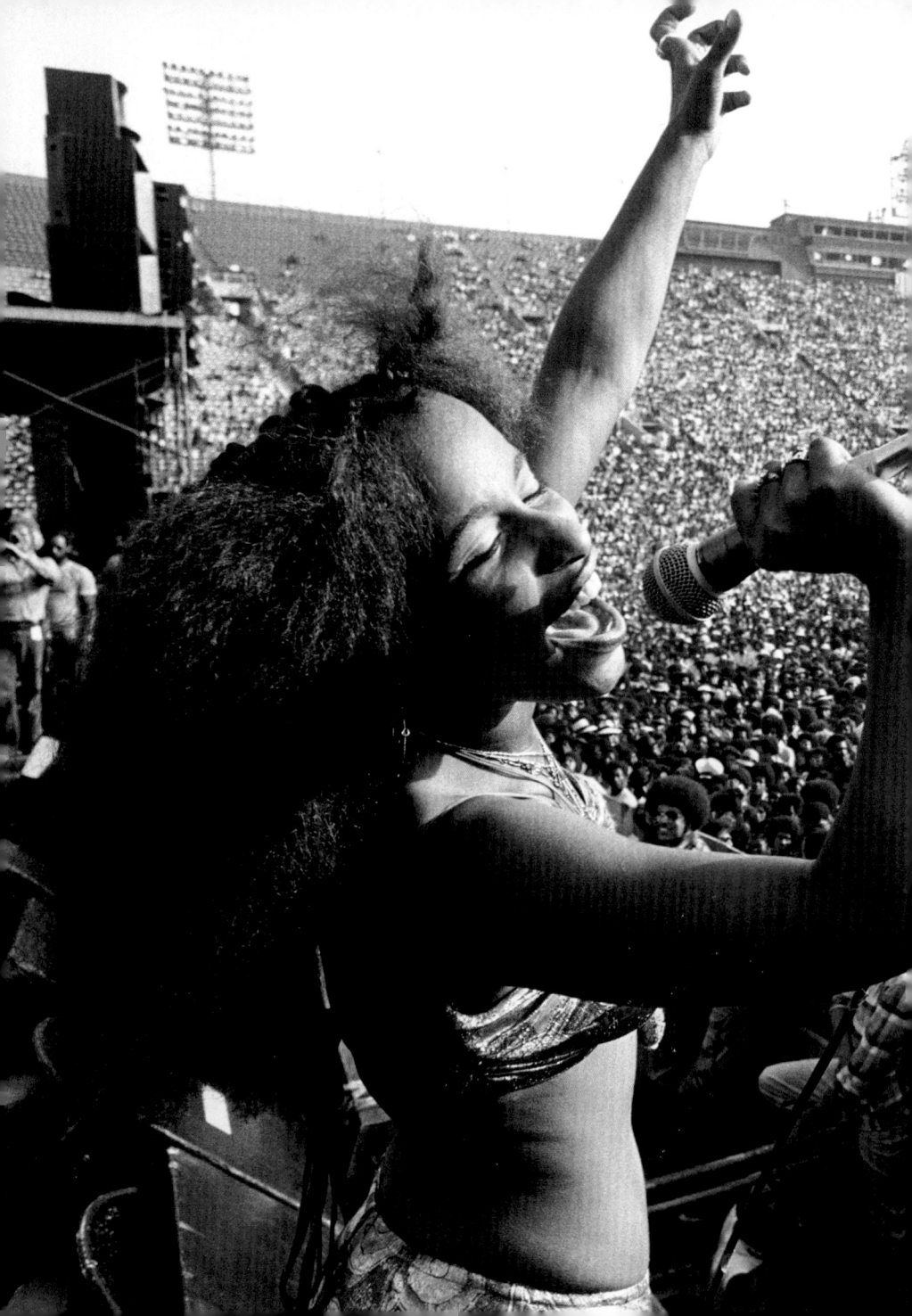

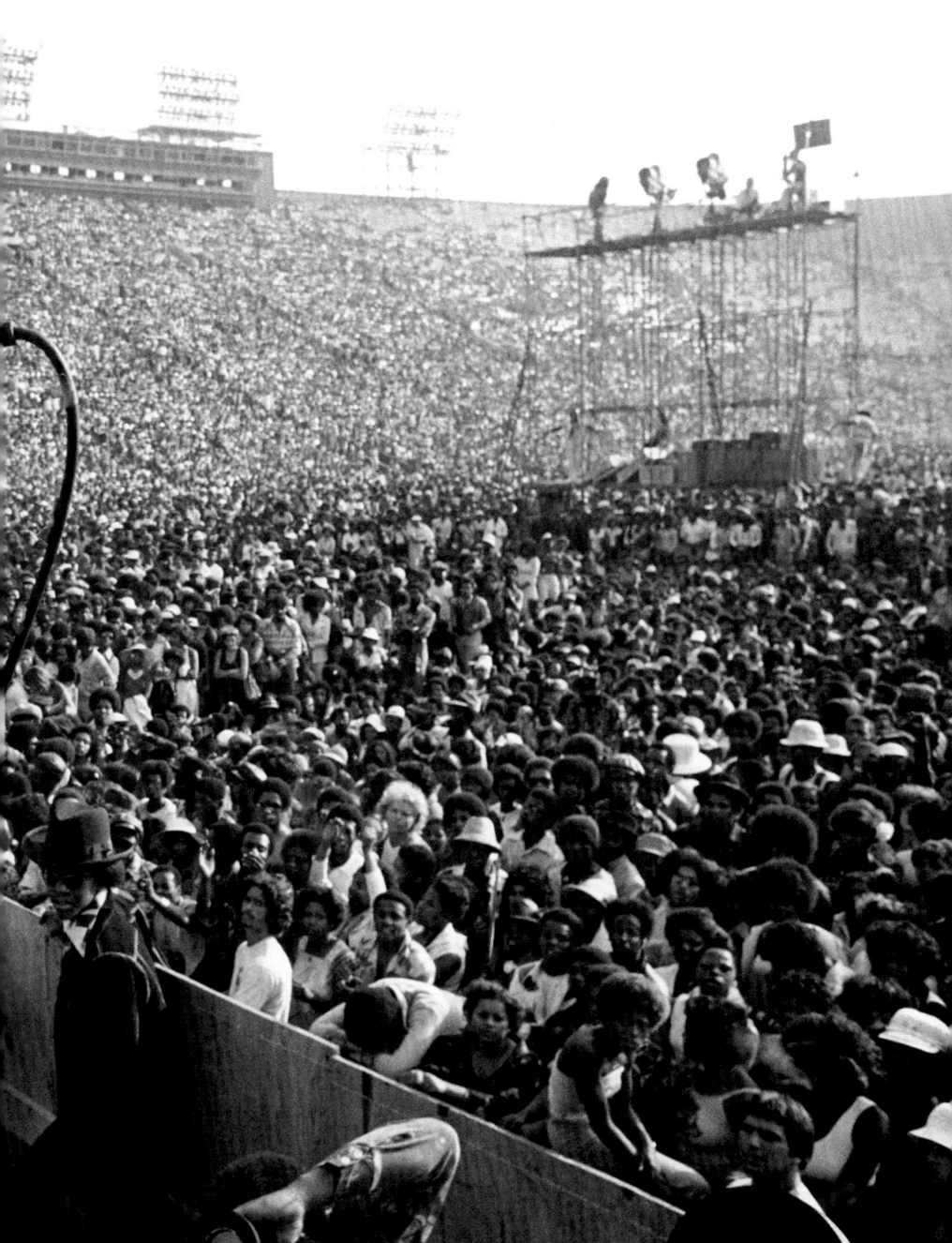

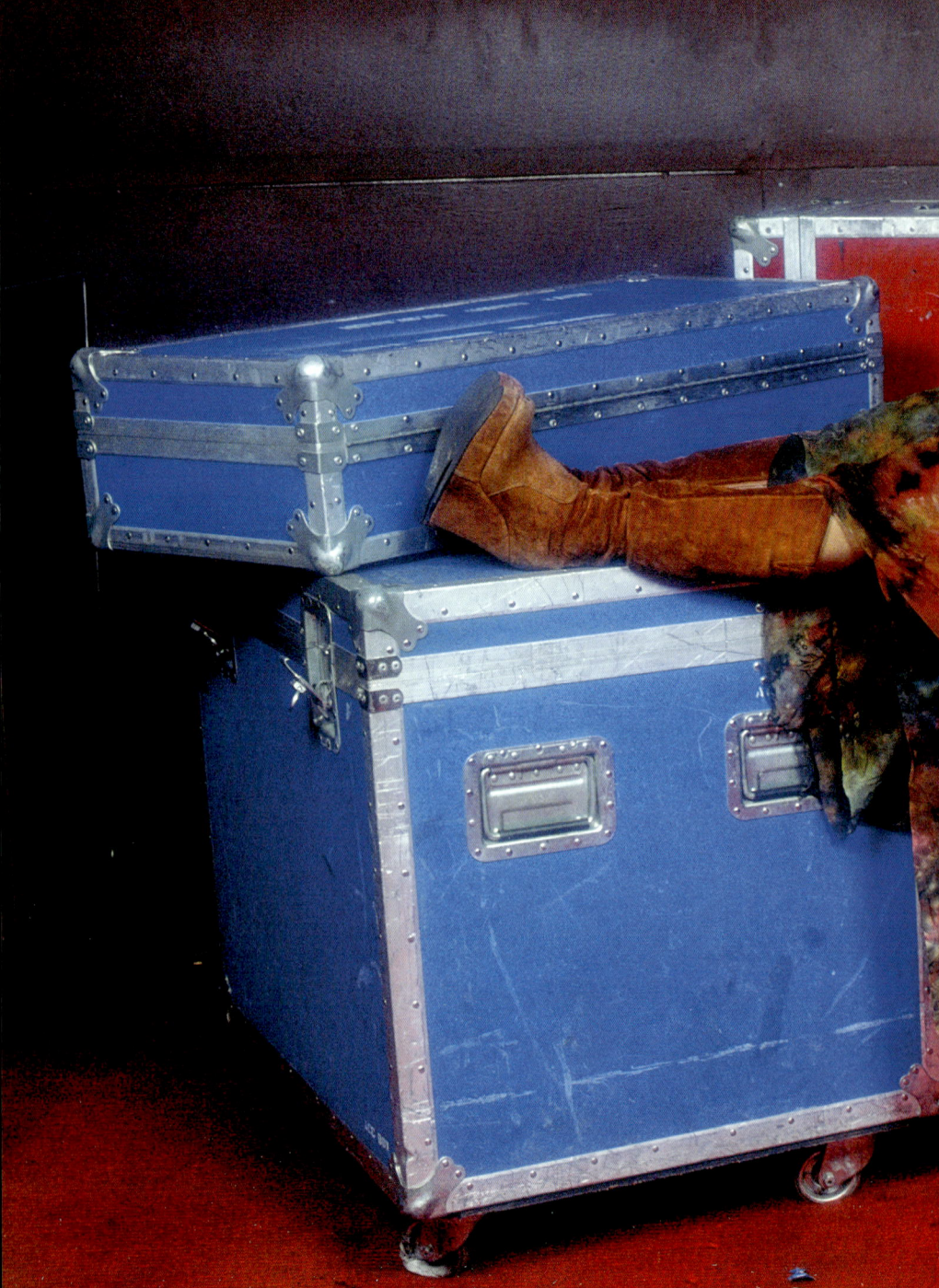

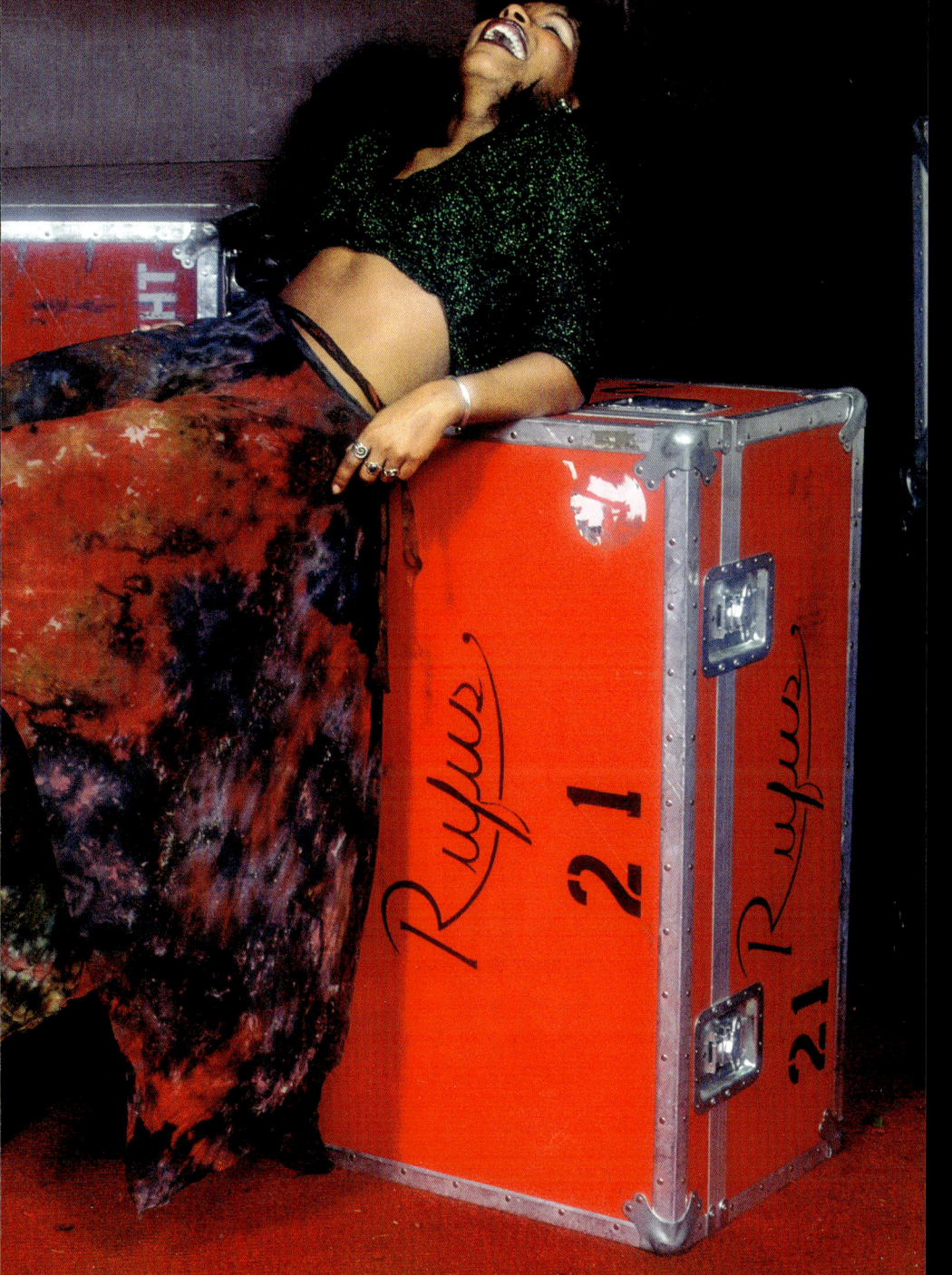

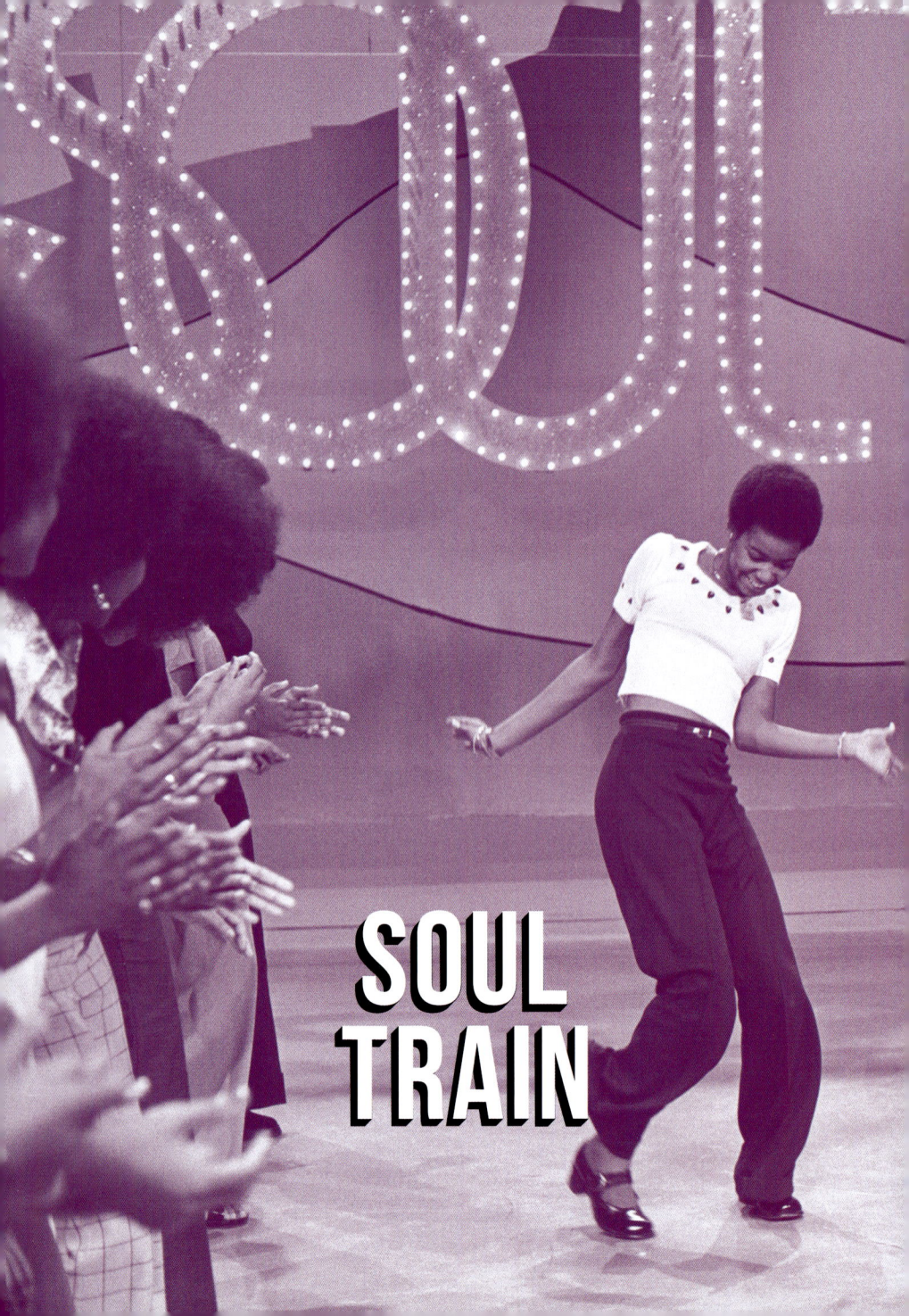

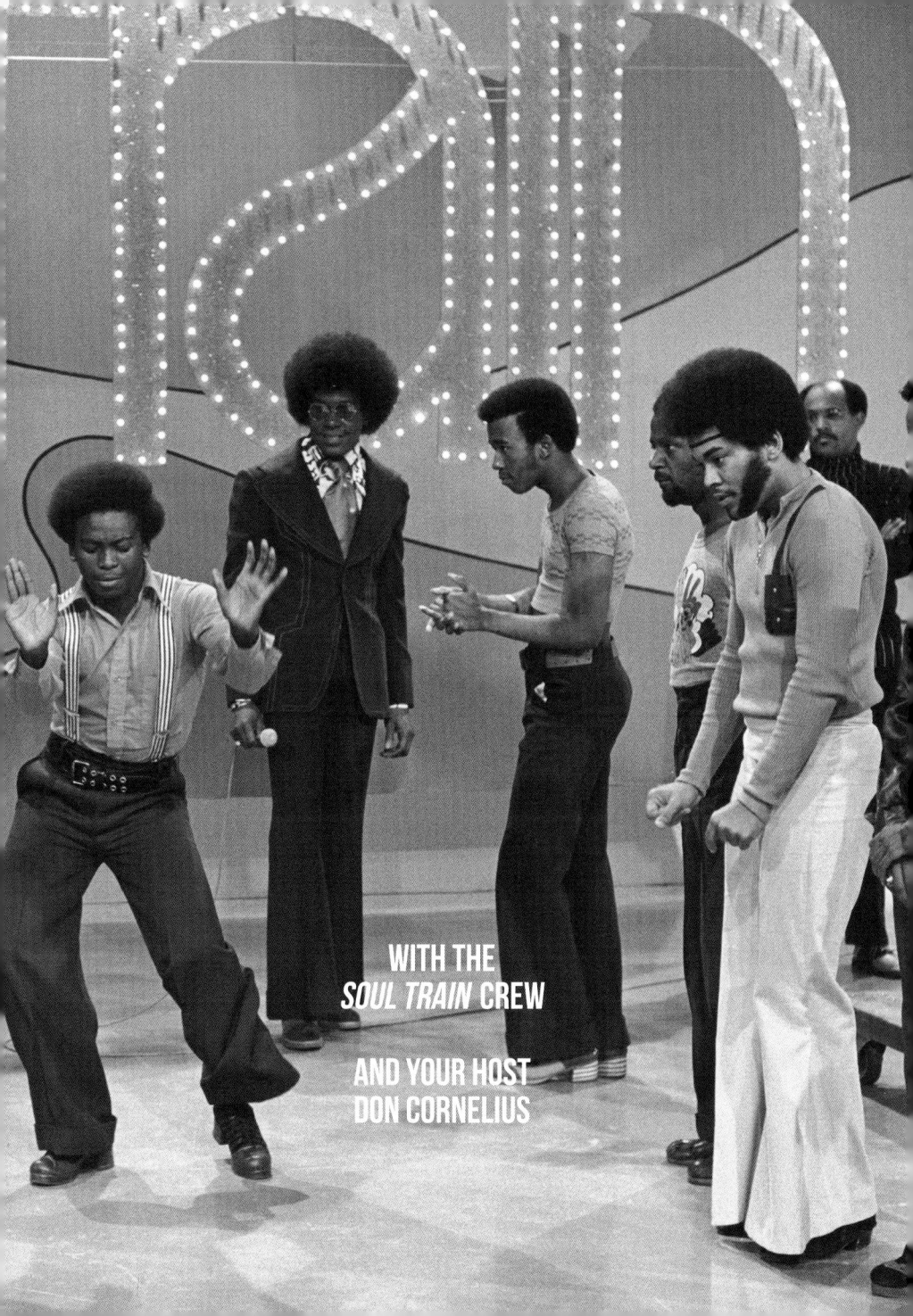

WITH THE
SOUL TRAIN CREW

AND YOUR HOST
DON CORNELIUS

If Elvis Presley/ is King
King
Who is James Brown, God?
– AMIRI BARAKA

SOUL TRAIN
Soul Train, Los Angeles, 1972. (Pages 168–169)
The legendary dance line.

JAMES BROWN AND DON CORNELIUS
Soul Train, Los Angeles, 1973 broadcast. (Opposite)
Cornelius tells a famous story about Brown's first visit to the
Soul Train soundstage. Impressed with what he saw, Brown asked,
"Brother, who's backing you on this?" Cornelius replied, "It's just me."
Throughout the day, Brown repeated the same question;
Cornelius gave the same answer. Brown could not believe the
African American Cornelius owned Soul Train's operation.

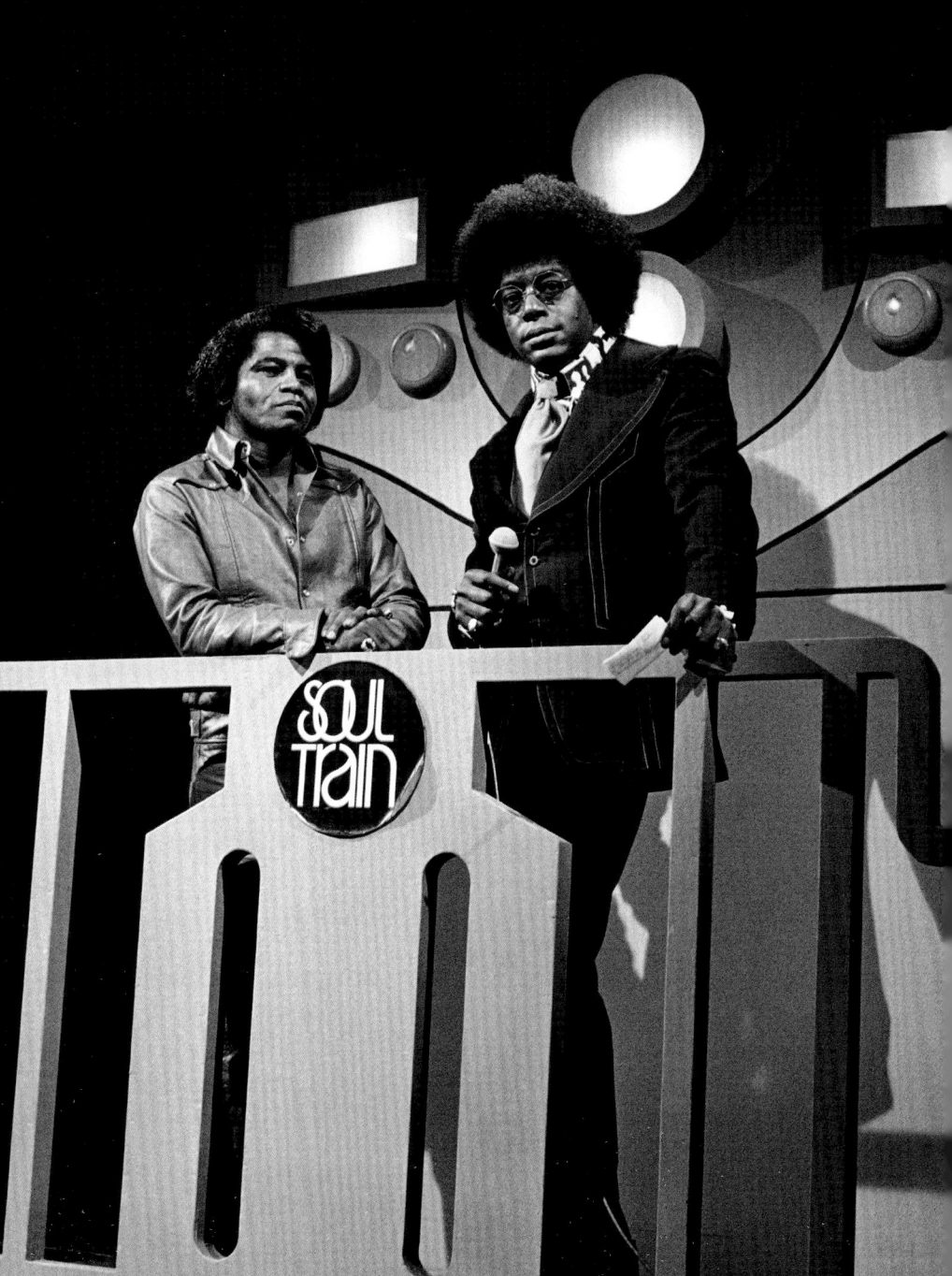

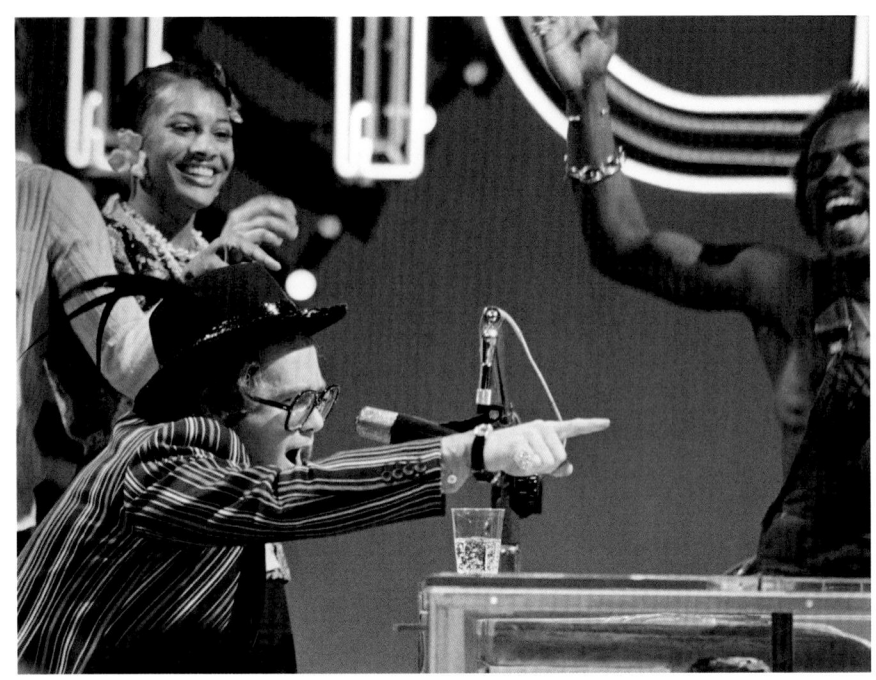

ELTON JOHN
Soul Train, Los Angeles, 1975. (Above)
Singing "Philadelphia Freedom" live with his plexiglass piano, John created one of his more memorable *Soul Train* appearances. Behind him are *Soul Train* dancers Lisa Jones and Little Joe Chism.

ASHFORD & SIMPSON
Soul Train, Los Angeles, 1976. (Opposite)
As songwriters, the duo wrote many well-known Motown classics such as "Ain't No Mountain High Enough," "Ain't Nothing Like the Real Thing," and "Reach Out and Touch (Somebody's Hand)." They would go on to write hit songs for others as well as enjoy a solid career as a duo.

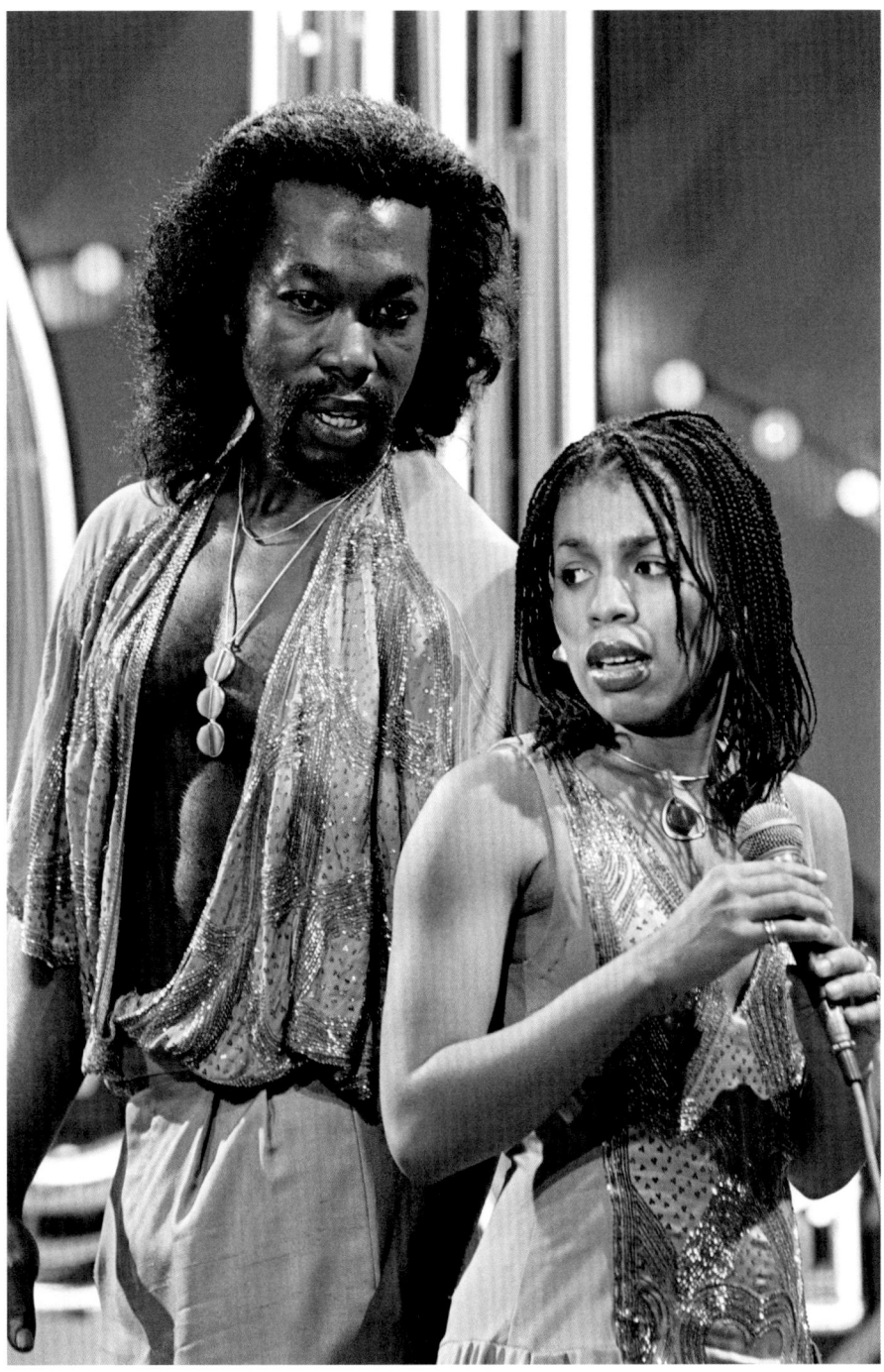

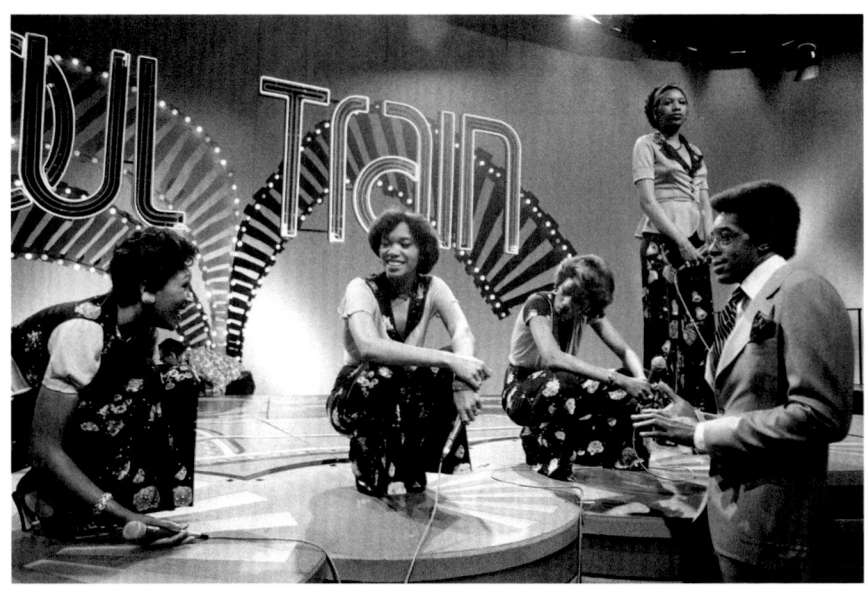

THE POINTER SISTERS
Soul Train, Los Angeles, 1975. (Above)
Starting out as a group of four, the Oakland-born sisters had a thrift-store-fashion look and almost a bebop-soulful sound. Eventually becoming a trio and moving into a more pop direction, they would rack up a string of the biggest hits of the early to mid-1980s.

SOUL TRAIN
Soul Train, Los Angeles, 1976. (Opposite)
The early dancers on the show were mostly from the local L.A. high schools Locke, Crenshaw, and Dorsey. They had to be at Denker Park in South Los Angeles at 7 P.M. to catch the bus to Metromedia Square in Hollywood. Their payment was a chicken dinner and a Coca-Cola. The *Soul Train* dancers were the unbroken artistic link from week to week and elemental to the show's success. They created moves that quickly swept across the country and became fashion trendsetters. The regulars became stars. At left, Damita Jo Freeman and Tyrone Swan show us how it's done.

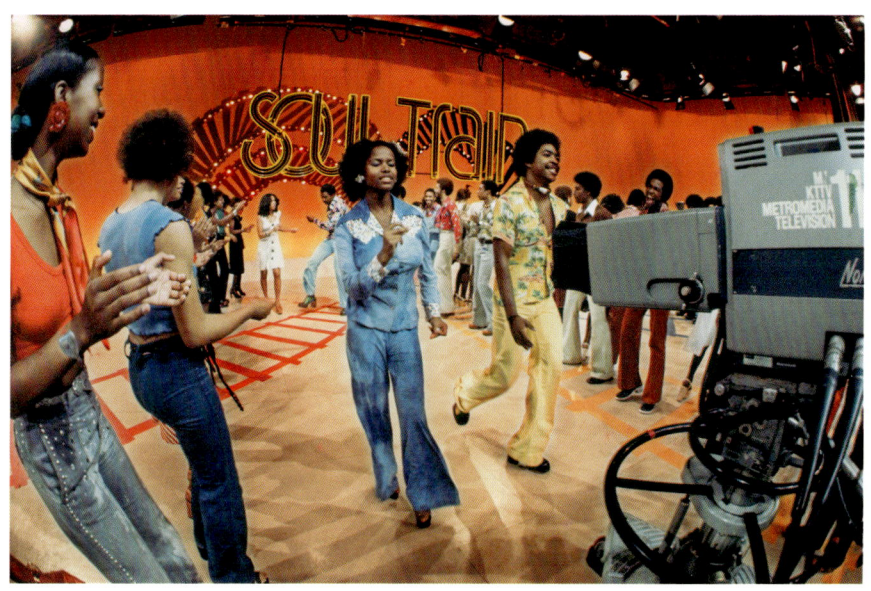

SOUL TRAIN
Soul Train, Los Angeles, 1972. (Pages 176, 177)
The *Soul Train* strut wasn't a dance. It was a performance feat of showcasing your best moves and walking forward. Since dancing is generally a stationary act, to do a righteous strut down the *Soul Train* line, you had to become a choreographer — as if you were on the Broadway stage.

EARTH, WIND & FIRE
Pavillon de Paris, France, 1979. (Pages 178–179)
Abracadabra! The removal of the band's helmets at the end of the show gives the ultimate reveal of Doug Henning's mesmerizing illusion for the group.

Pavillon de Paris, France, 1979. (Pages 180–181)
With the help of superstar magician Doug Henning, the band was the first to bring high-tech, spellbinding magic to rock—including this feat of levitation as band leader Maurice White reacts to his brother Verdine White's magical powers.

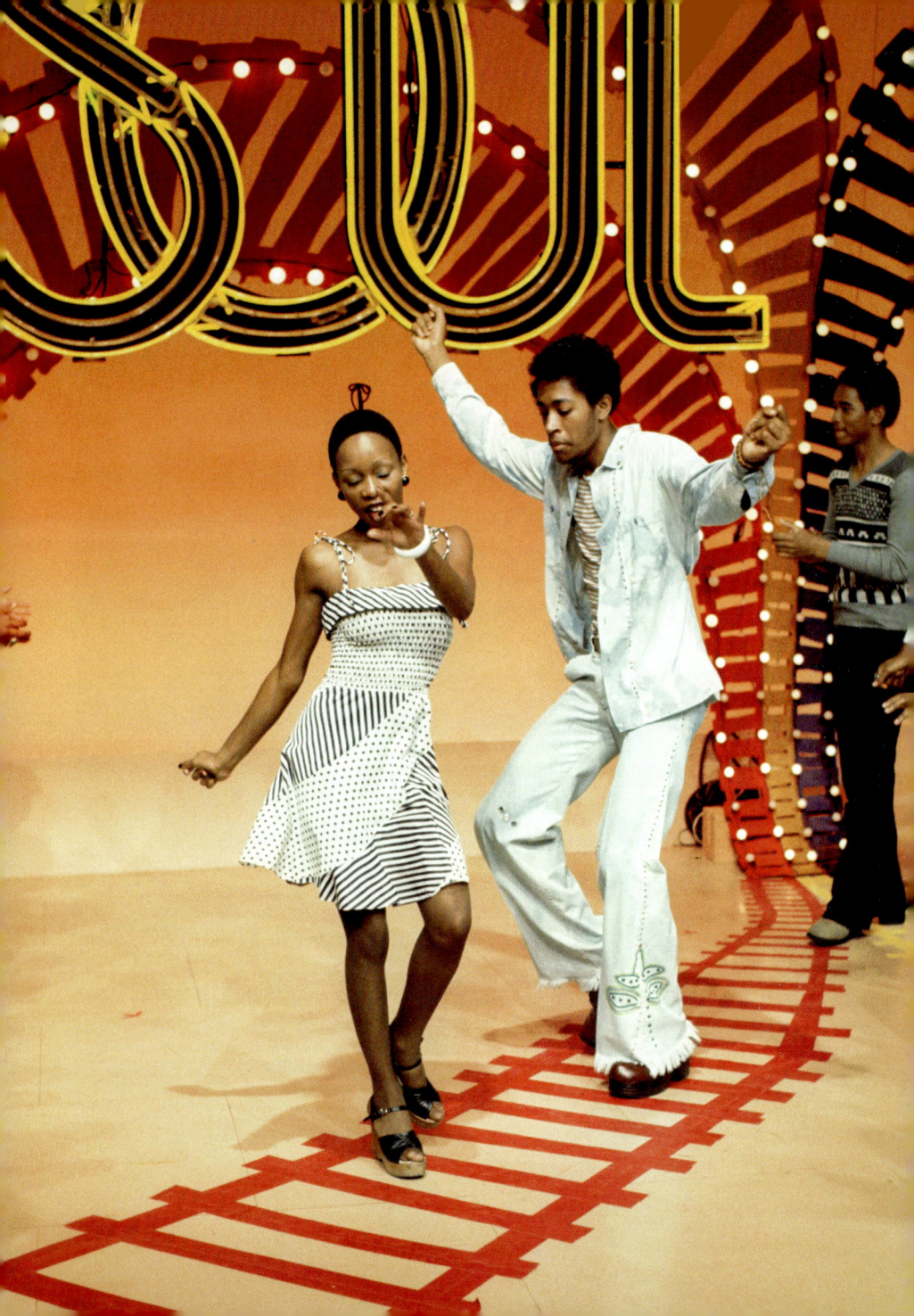

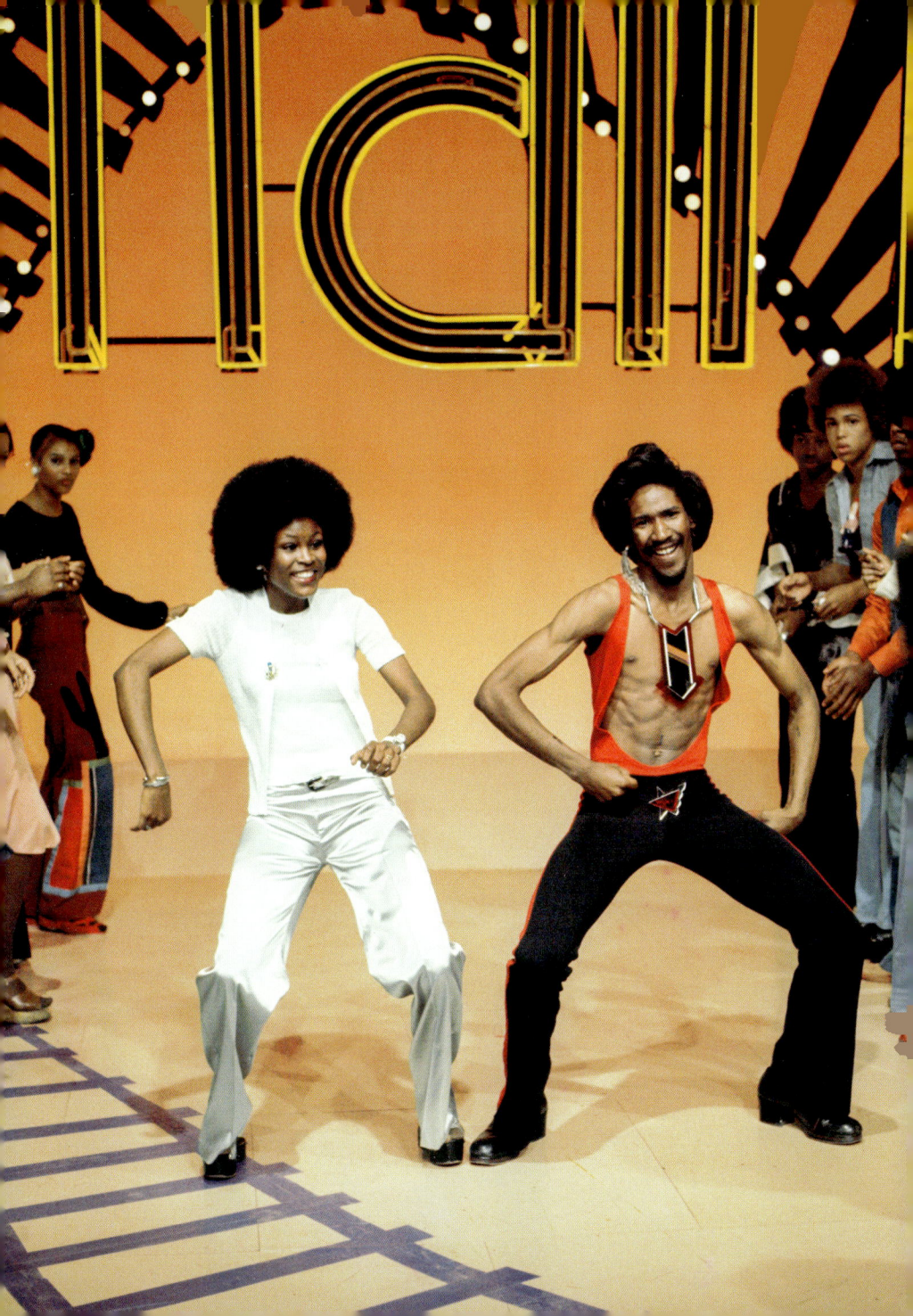

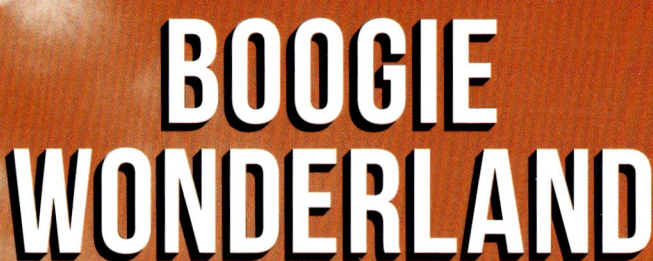

BOOGIE WONDERLAND

EARTH, WIND & FIRE

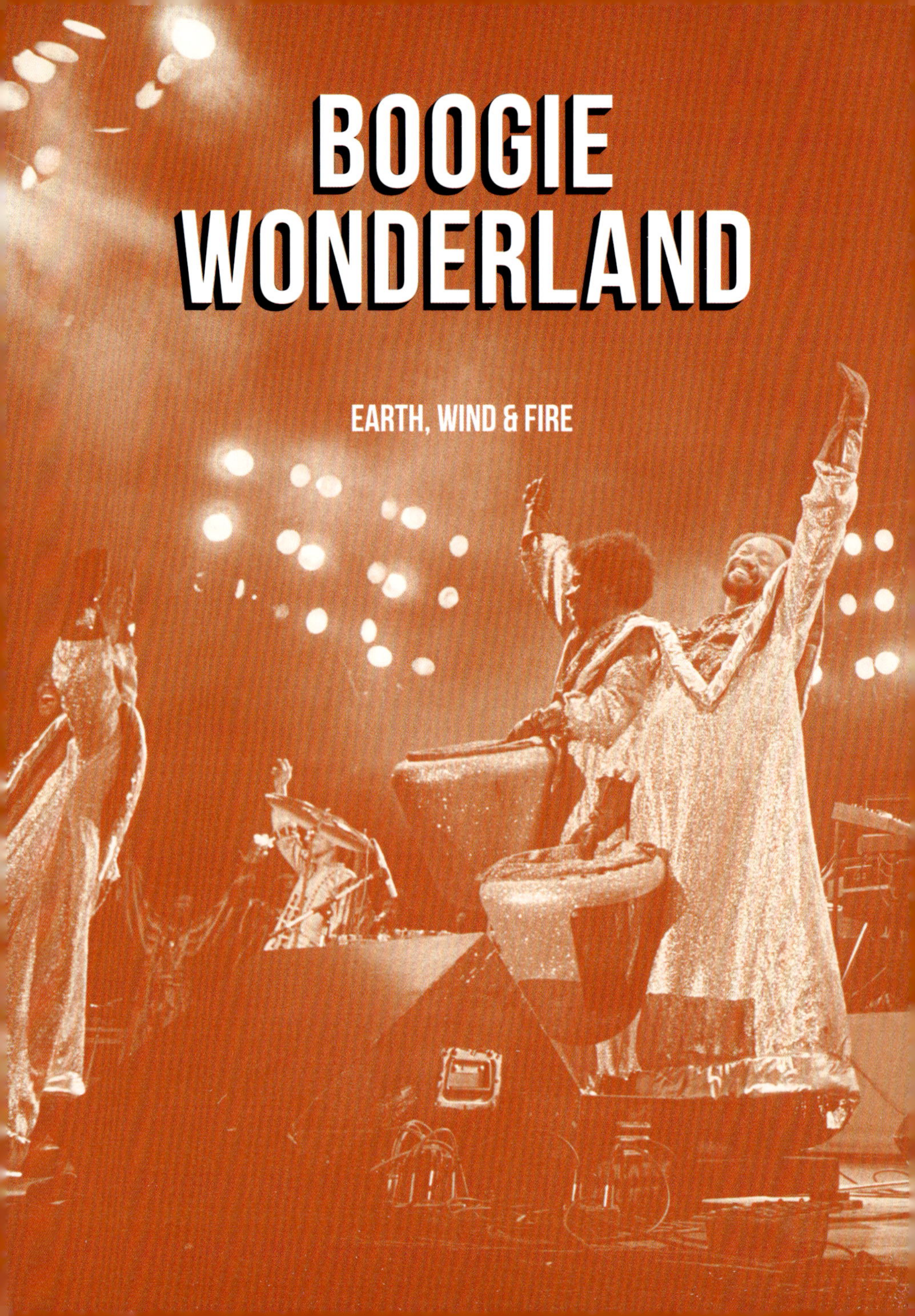

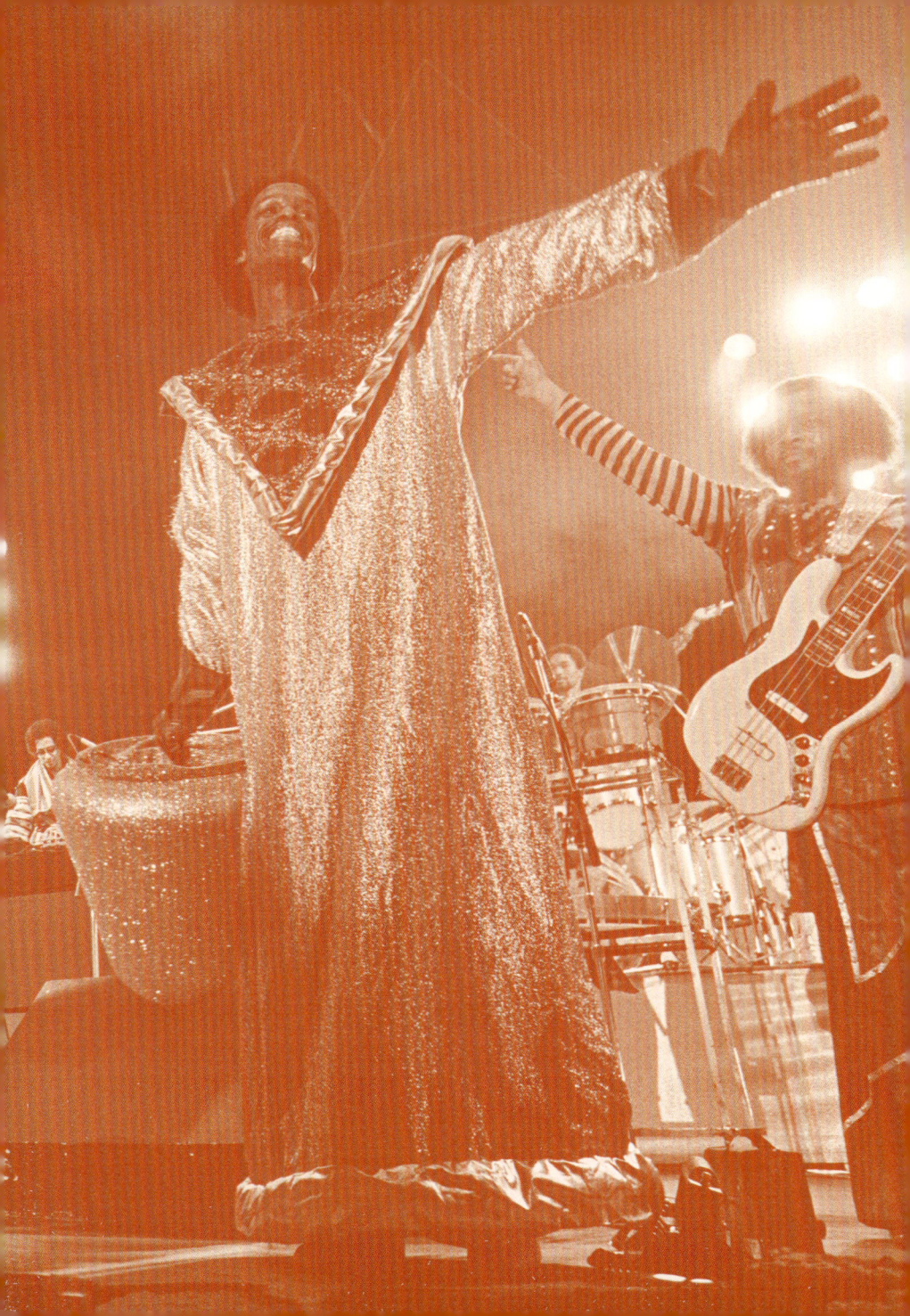

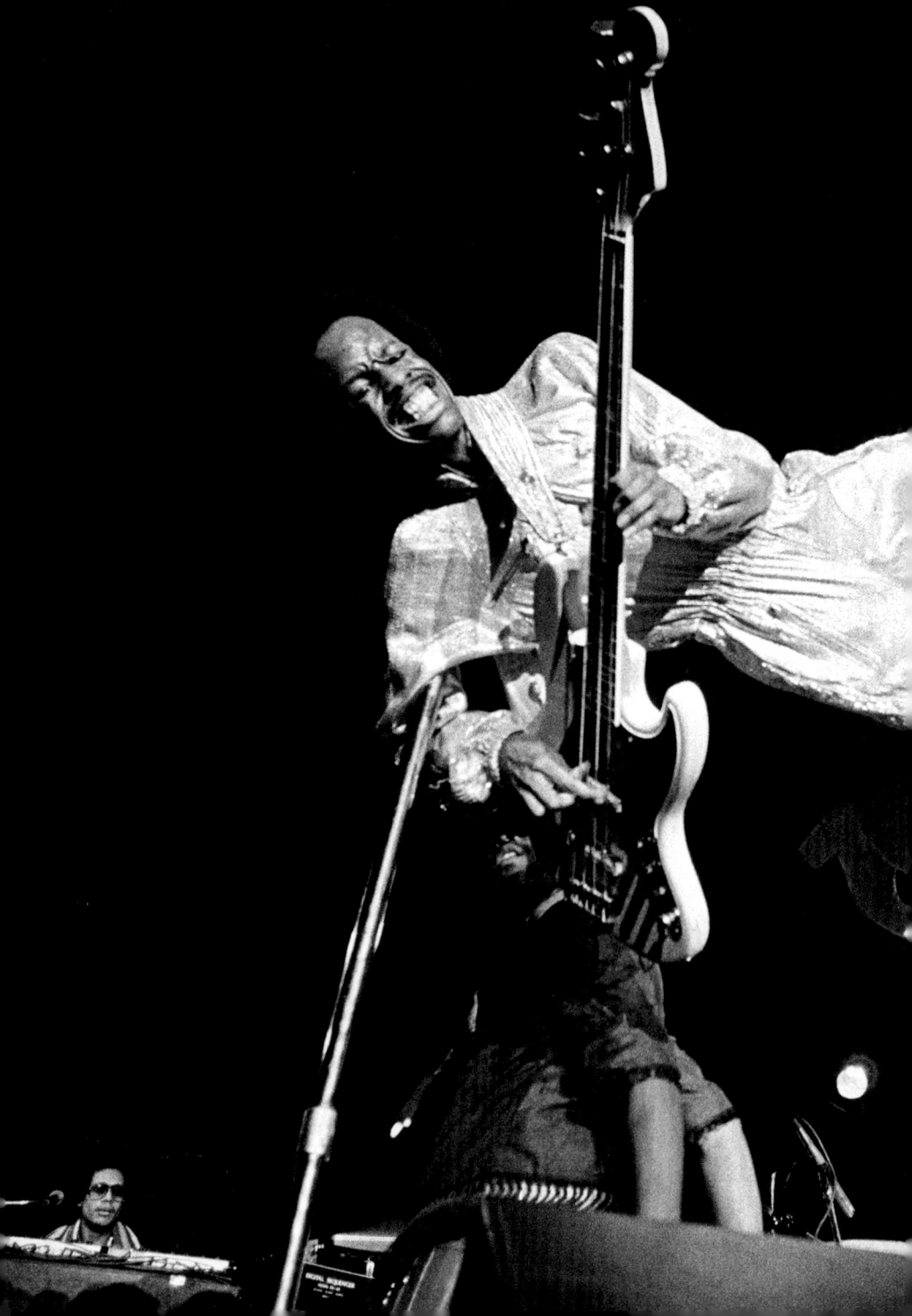

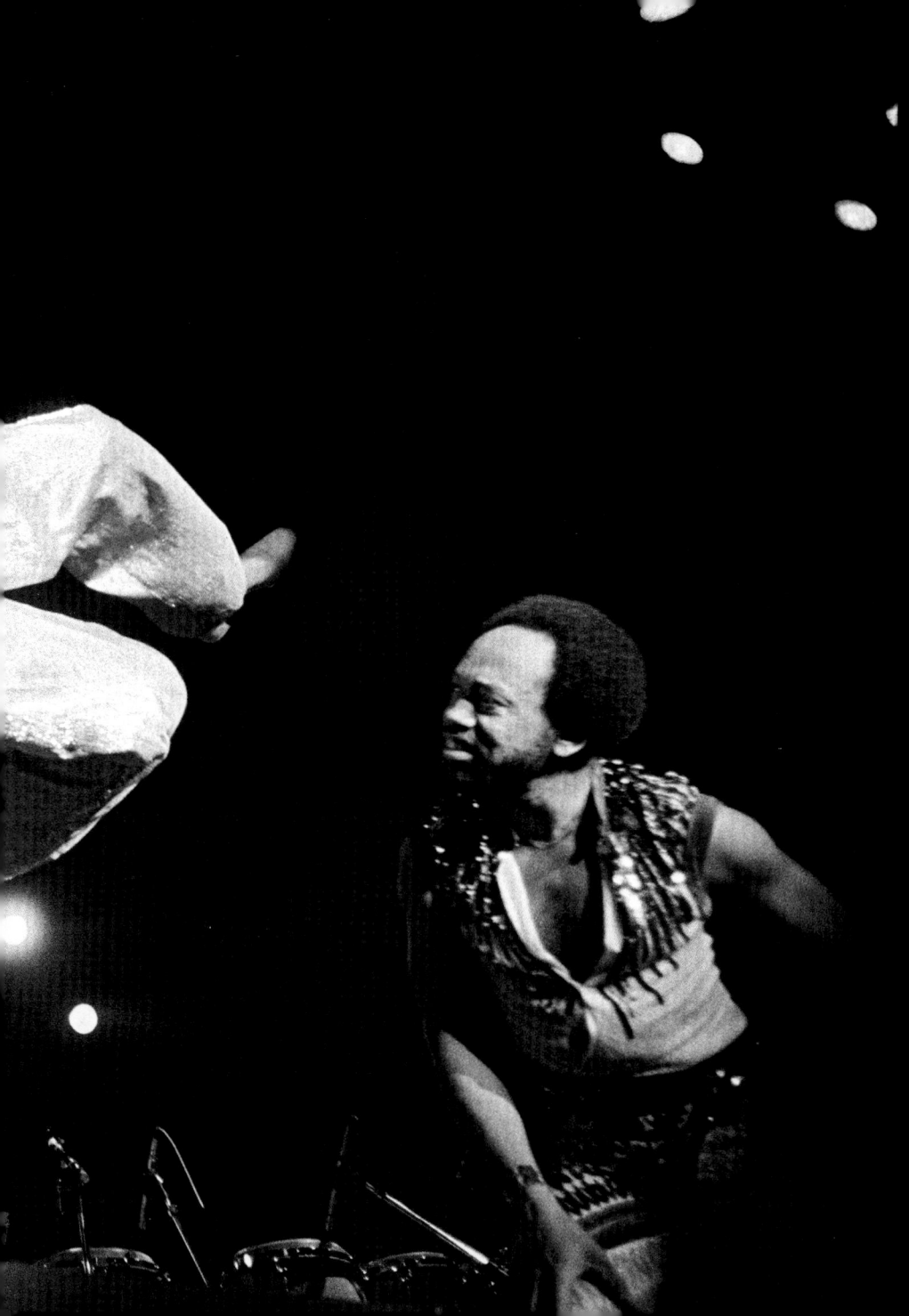

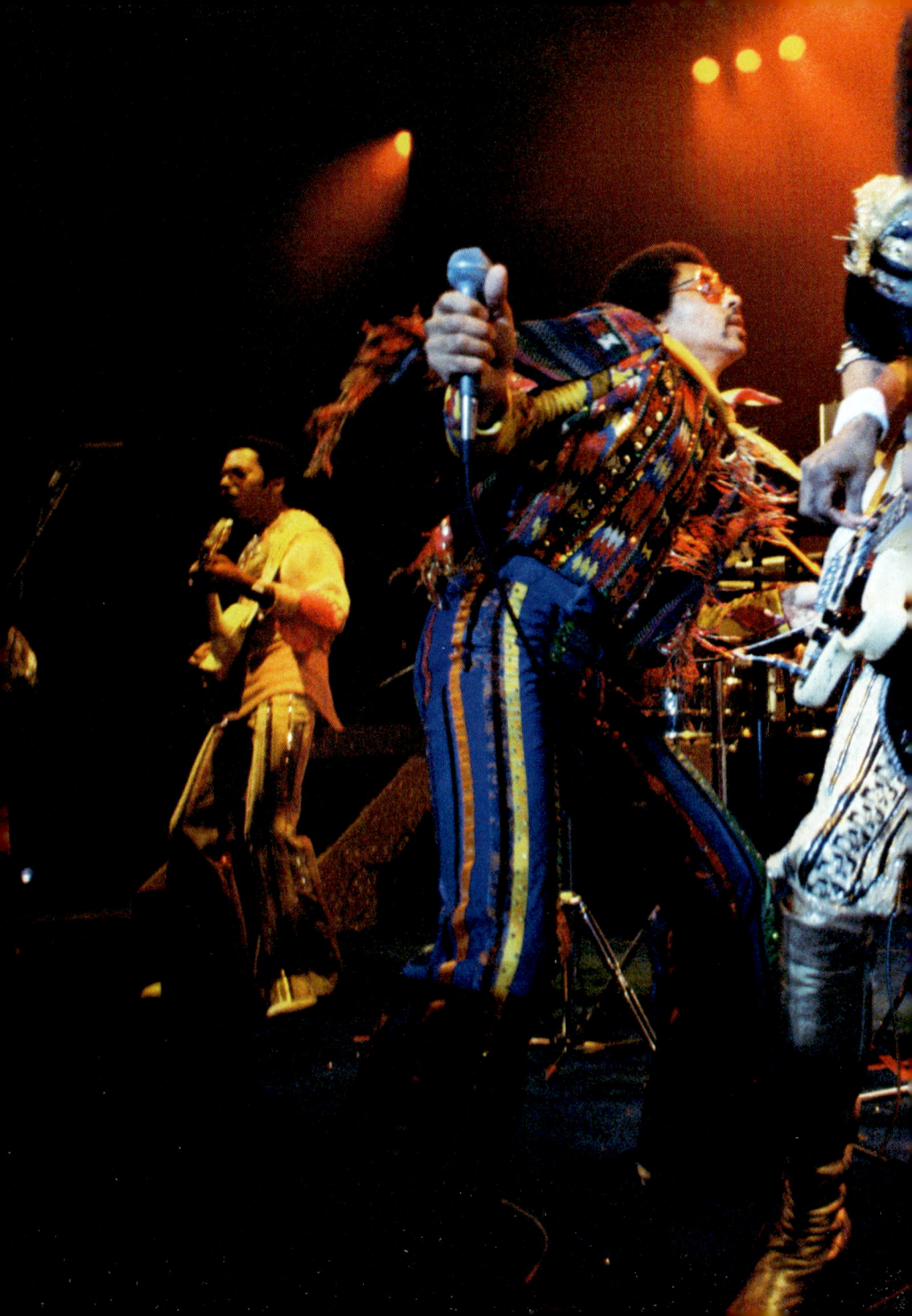

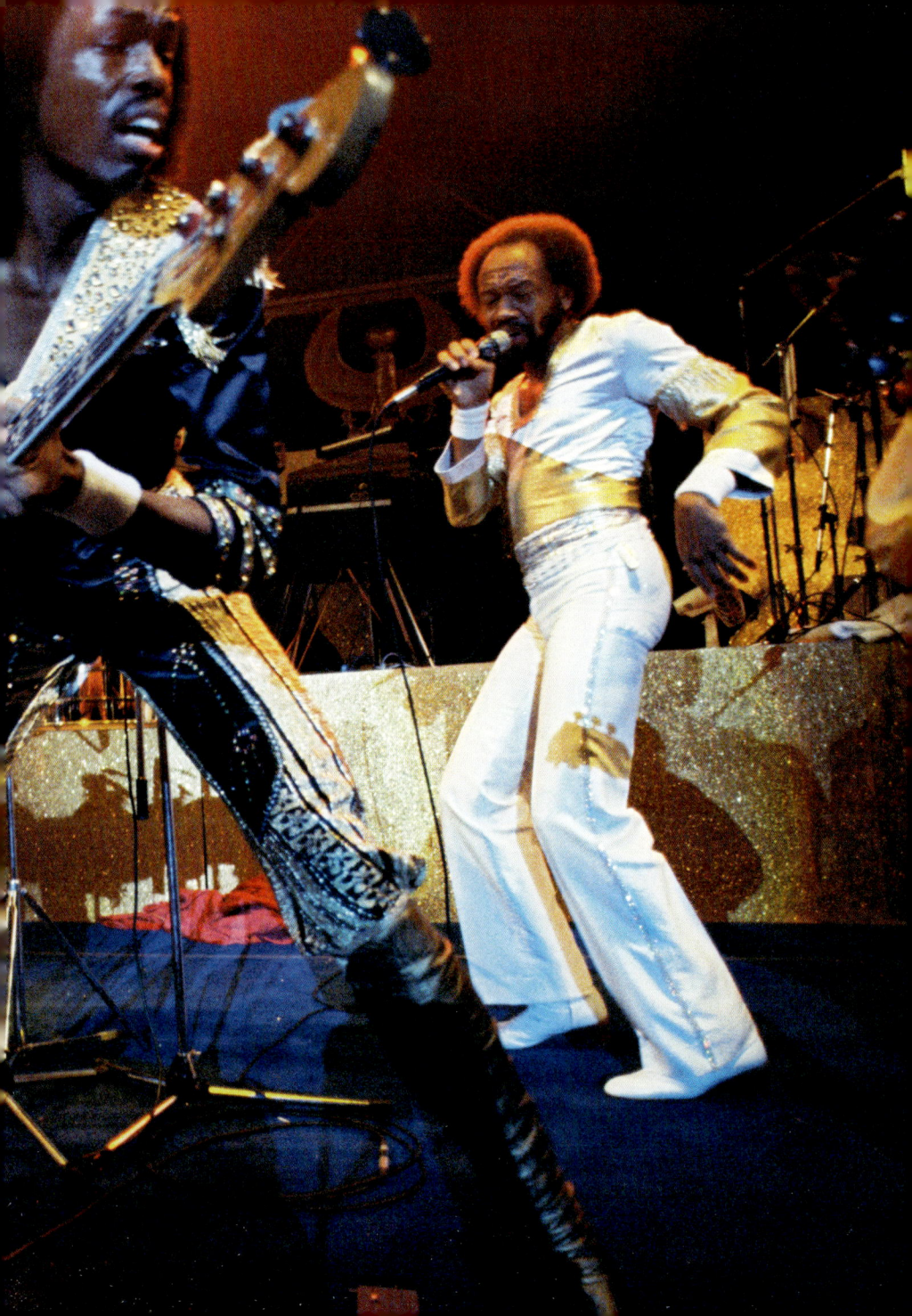

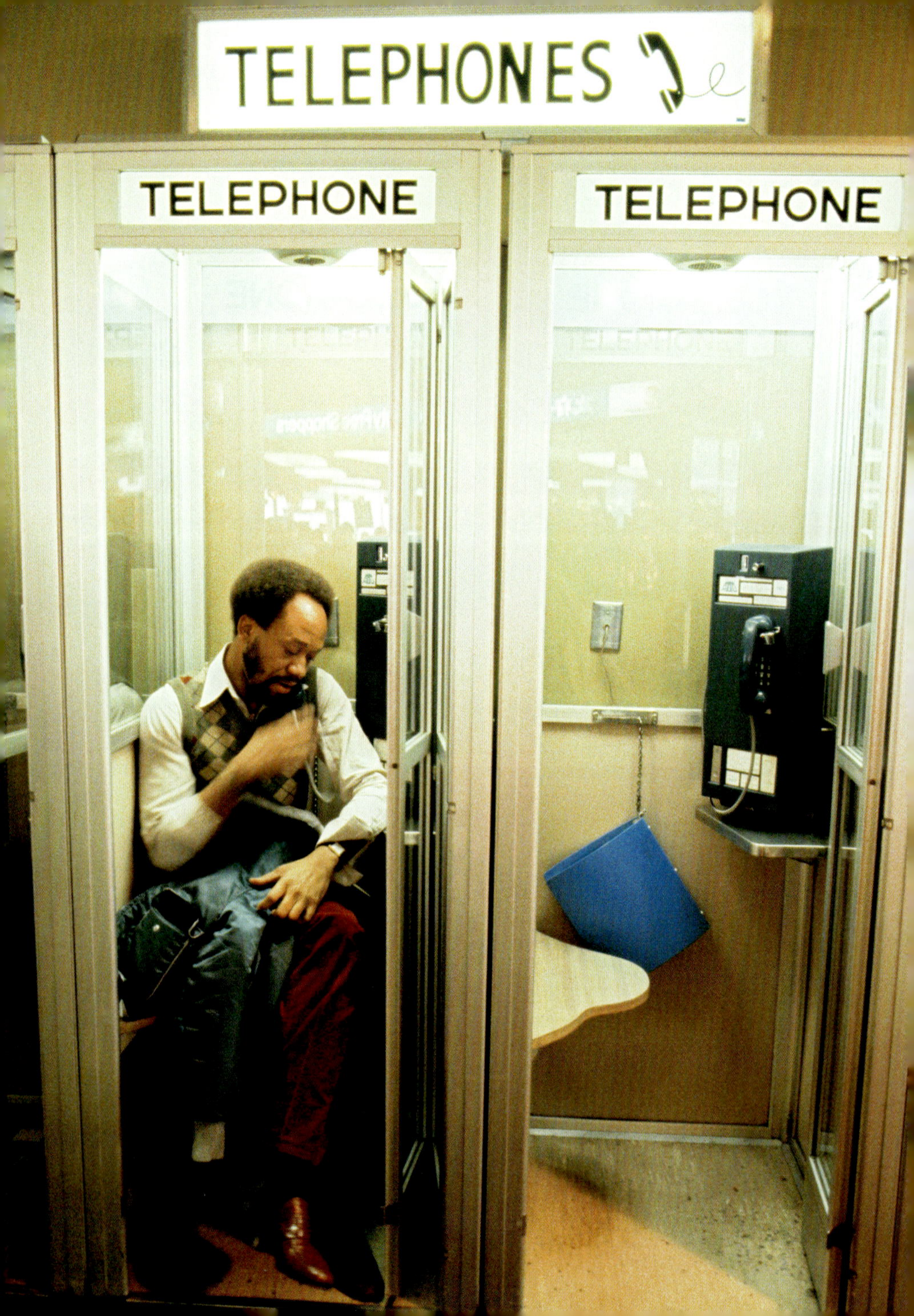

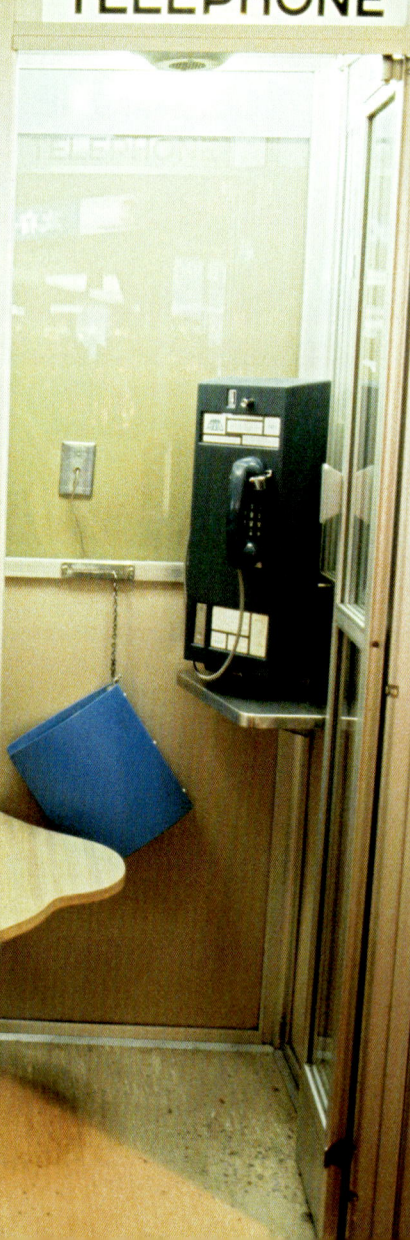

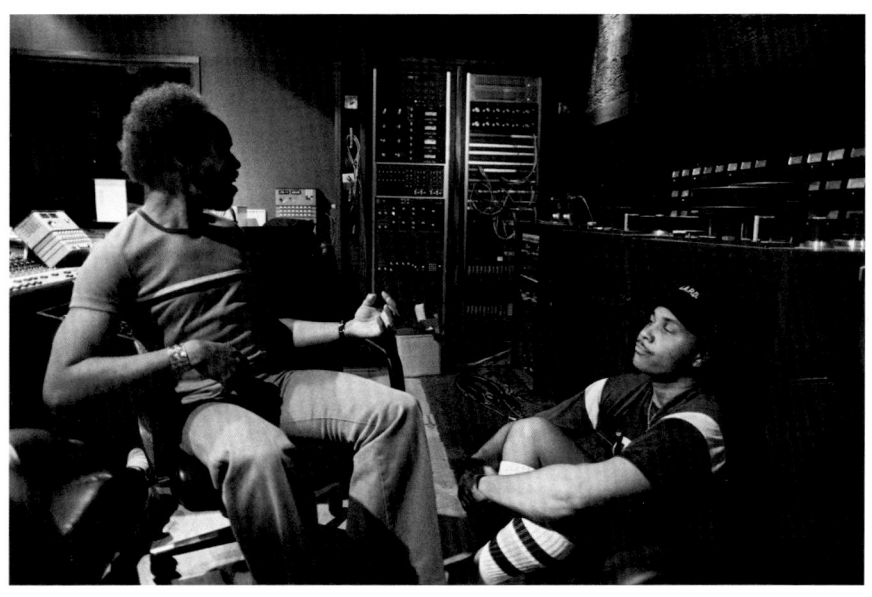

EARTH, WIND & FIRE
Luna Park Stadium, Buenos Aires, Argentina, 1980. (Pages 182–183)
The fire burning red hot.

Los Angeles, 1979. (Opposite)

AIR Studios, Montserrat Island, West Indies, 1980. (Above)
Maurice White and Al McKay teamed up to write the hits "Sing a Song" and
September" for the band. They would also collaborate on "The Best of My Love" for
the female trio The Emotions. The massive smash went number one on the pop,
R&B, and disco charts, ultimately becoming one of the biggest songs of the 1970s.

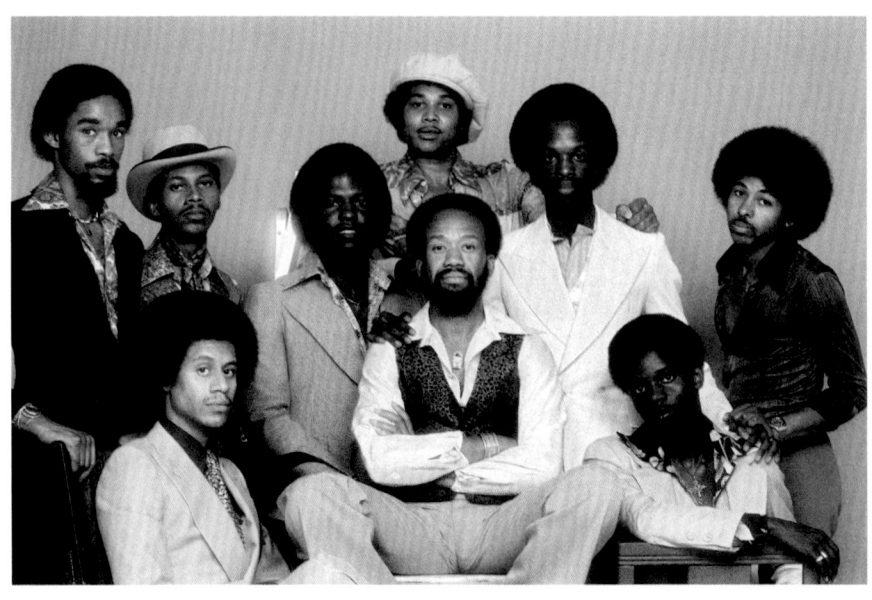

EARTH, WIND & FIRE
Los Angeles, 1977. (Above)
*"This was my first photo session with Earth, Wind & Fire. We had food,
a great studio, and the music blastin'. The brothers came in sharp. Nobody
wanted to go home, and we even brought lights out to the street and shot
there. It was a perfect day. A week later, I got a call from Maurice White's
brother Monte: "Bruce, Maurice likes the way you handled yourself at
the session. We're getting ready to start our 1979 tour of the world: Europe,
Egypt, and Japan. We would like you to come along."* — Bruce Talamon

Los Angeles, 1978. (Opposite)
*"In 1978 Maurice White asked me to create an image of Earth Wind & Fire
as Superheroes. Larger than life. This EWF Superhero portrait lives
on as a giant 30" x 40" print. In 2019 it was selected as one of six
photographs for the Portrait of a Nation Prize. The copy now hangs in
the National Portrait Gallery in Washington, DC."* — Bruce Talamon

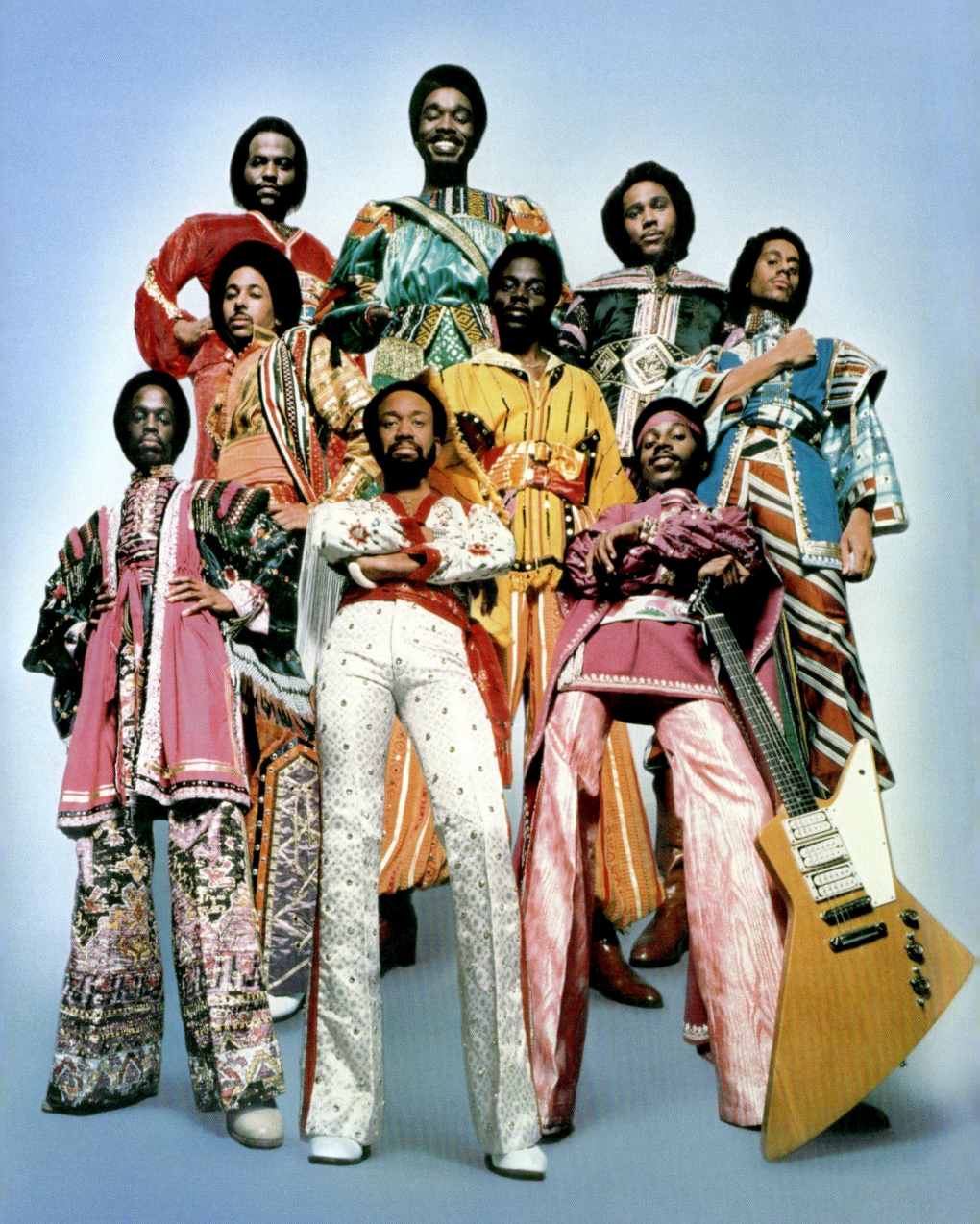

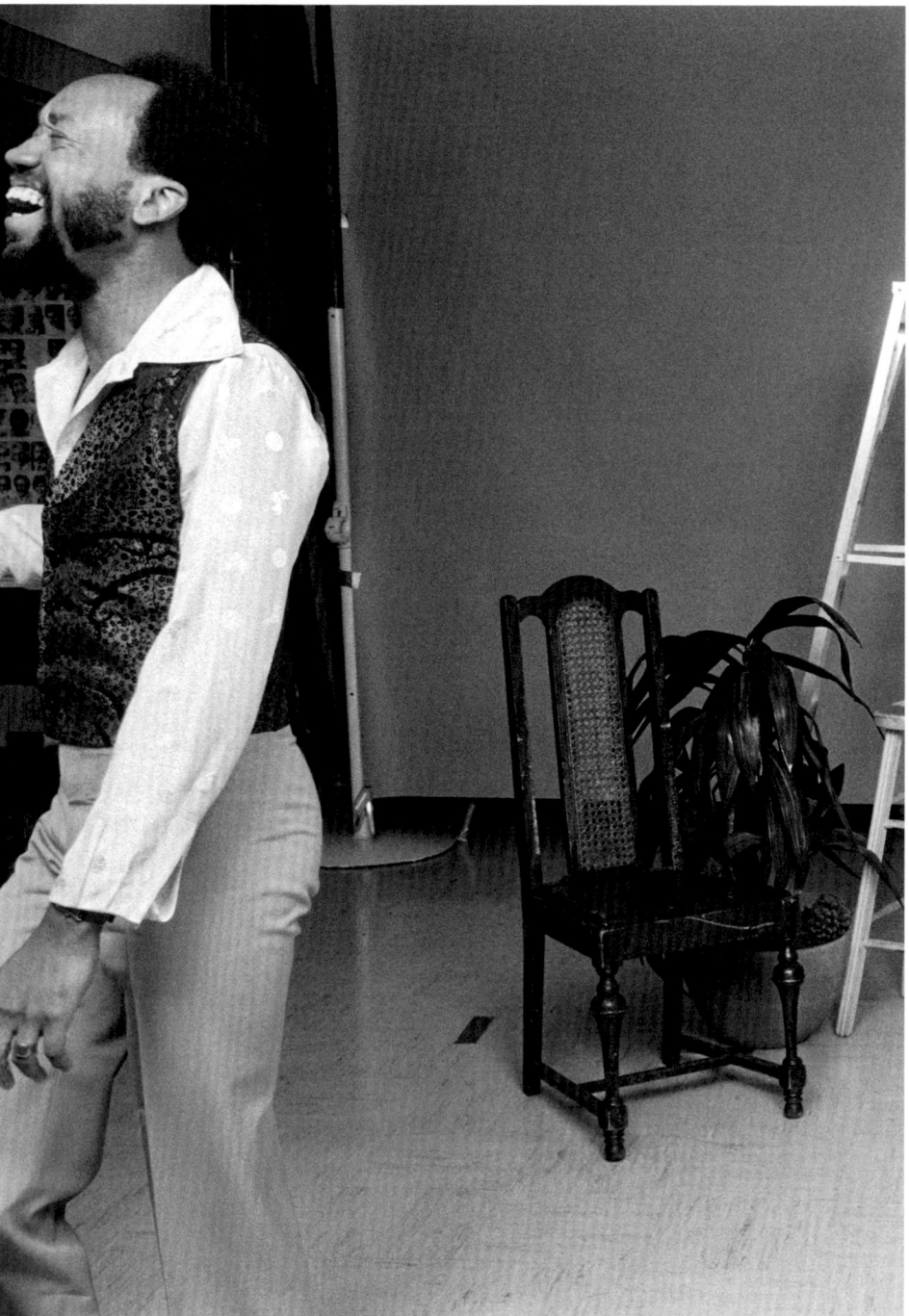

EARTH, WIND & FIRE
Los Angeles, 1978.
This was the first of a series of creative collaborations between
the band and Bruce Talamon that lasts to this day. The maestro
Barry White once said, "Earth, Wind & Fire is our Duke Ellington,"
meaning the absolute best of what America can produce.

ACKNOWLEDGMENTS

To Benedikt Taschen, thank you for believing in this project and for entrusting it to editor Reuel Golden and art director Josh Baker. Reuel and Josh…first round's on me.

Regina Jones, publisher of *SOUL Newspaper*. You introduced me to R&B royalty. You provided opportunity and extended your hand. I love you. Herb Powell, your spirit is on these pages. Natasha Calzatti, JoAnne Robinson: Your early designs inspired me. Pearl Cleage: I will slosh through snow and sleet for you. Eddy Emilien: Your photo assistance was the key!

Book scans and prints were made by Contact Photo L.A. under the direction of Chris McElrath. Thank you. Also: Evan Walsh, Jose Roberto Diaz, Peter Holzhauer, Gary and Joshua McElrath, Yunice Kang, and Sal Sanchez Jr. At TASCHEN I'd also like to thank Sarah Wrigley, Pim Phongsirivech, Brandy Colbert, Annie Marino, Jascha Kempe, Alexandra Hollis and Jörg Schwellnus.

SOUL Newspaper family: Bobby Holland, Steve Ivory, Leonard Pitts Jr., Dwight Russ, Steve Kopstein, Helen Chertow, Tsuyoko Sako, Naomi Rubine. Motown: Bob Jones and Jim Britt. CBS: Gerry Griffith and Von Thomas. Casablanca: Jheryl Busby and Nellie Prestwood. Monte's Camera: Chris, Mark, and Monte. Samy's Camera: Samy and Hedy Kamienowicz, George, Terry, and Karen. Gil Scott-Heron, George Clinton, Archie Ivy, and Tom Vickers. Montague The Magnificent, Ndugu Chancler, James Nash, Jovon Gillohm, Marco De Santiago, Cheryl Song, and Pam Brown. Photo Image Lab: Harold, Jim, Mario, and Iva. Pro Lab: Win Muldrow and Joe Flowers. Robin Gordon and Deidre Gordon. Cat Jimenez. Neil Leifer, Leor Levine, Mike Jones, Matt Schodorf, Jules Allen, Jim Marshall, Monte White, Eli Reed, and David Hammons. Jeffrey L. Otto, Larry Kuromiya, Ashley Walker, Billy Osborne, Hiroshi Okuhara, Michael Thomas, Lisa Guerriero, and Verdine White.

Maurice White, I'll never forget your trust.

Thanks to my book agent, Faith Childs. Also to Pat Bates, Brad Talamon, Amelia Davis, Bonita Passarelli, Terry Hayes, Brian R. Wolff, Jack and Margaret Brown, Stanley Gold, Dr. Robert J. Siegel, and my copyright attorneys, Doniger-Burroughs.

To James and Clelie Talamon: You taught me there were no limits.

In 2005, National Public Radio host Alex Chadwick stated that I was the fortunate husband of his colleague, Karen Grigsby Bates. Truer words were never spoken.

To our son, Jordan, thanks for being you. Karen, you can have your dining room table back. Again.

George Clinton said it best: "Free your mind and your ass will follow!"

—Bruce W. Talamon, Los Angeles

IMPRINT

© **All photos Bruce W. Talamon**
"Can I Get an Amen" © 2018 Pearl Cleage
Music consultation and captions by
Herb Powell
All photographic scans by Contact
Photo Lab www.contactla.com
"If Elvis Is King" © 1996, is used with the
permission of the Estate of Amiri Baraka
and the Chris Calhoun Agency.

© **2026 TASCHEN GmbH**
Hohenzollernring 53, D–50672 Köln
www.taschen.com

Original edition: © 2018 TASCHEN GmbH

Editor: Reuel Golden, New York
Art Director: Josh Baker, Oakland

Printed in Italy
ISBN 978–3–8365–9706–7

Page 1 Isaac Hayes, Wattstax, Los Angeles
Coliseum, 1972.
Pages 2–3 Rick James, Funk Festival, Los
Angeles Coliseum, 1977.
Pages 4–5 The O'Jays,The Forum, Inglewood,
California, June 1977.
Pages 6–7 Kool & The Gang, *Soul Train,*
Metromedia Square, Los Angeles, 1975.

Page 9 George Clinton, Los Angeles Sports
Arena, 1977.
Page 192 Taking a surreal break while on tour
with Earth, Wind & Fire. Photo by Maurice White.
El Giza, Egypt, 1979.
Front cover Stevie Wonder, 1980.
Back cover Rufus featuring Chaka Khan, 1977.

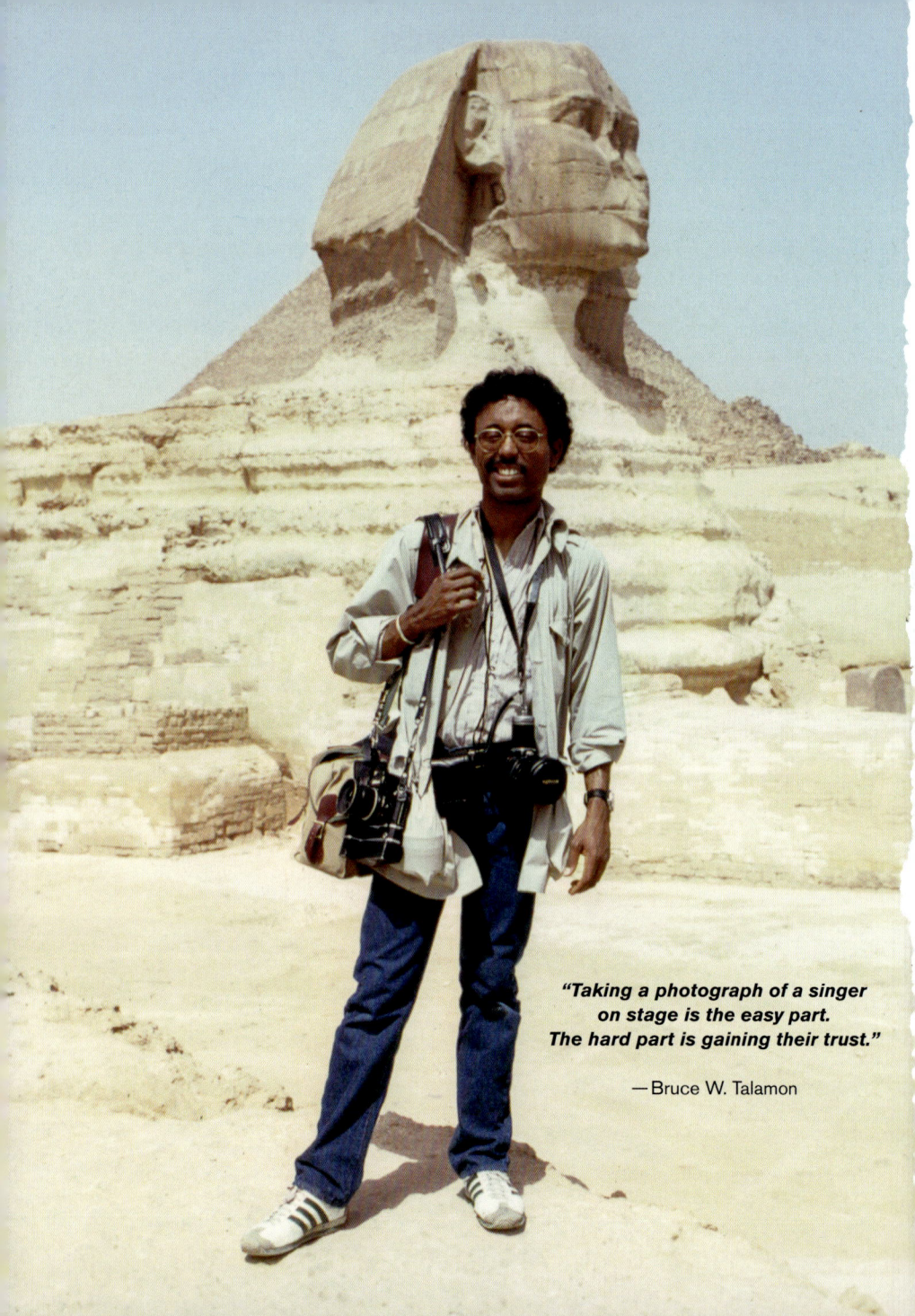

"Taking a photograph of a singer on stage is the easy part. The hard part is gaining their trust."

—Bruce W. Talamon